The New Local Government Series
No. 15

LOCAL GOVERNMENT
AND EDUCATION

The New Local Government Series
Series Editor: Professor Peter G. Richards

1. A HISTORY OF LOCAL GOVERNMENT
    by K. B. Smellie

5. THE REFORMED LOCAL GOVERNMENT SYSTEM
    by Peter G. Richards

6. THE FINANCE OF LOCAL GOVERNMENT
    by N. P. Hepworth

8. TOWN AND COUNTRY PLANNING IN BRITAIN
    by J. B. Cullingworth

10. HOUSING AND LOCAL GOVERNMENT
    In England and Wales
    by J. B. Cullingworth

11. THE GOVERNMENT OF GREATER LONDON
    by Gerald Rhodes and S. K. Ruck

12. DEMOCRATIC THEORY AND LOCAL GOVERNMENT
    by Dilys M. Hill

13. THE LOCAL GOVERNMENT ACT 1972: PROBLEMS OF IMPLEMENTATION
    by Peter G. Richards

14. THE PROCESS OF LOCAL GOVERNMENT REFORM 1966–1974
    by Bruce Wood

LOCAL GOVERNMENT AND EDUCATION

BY

D. E. REGAN

London School of Economics and Political Science

London

GEORGE ALLEN & UNWIN LTD

RUSKIN HOUSE   MUSEUM STREET

© George Allen & Unwin (Publishers) Ltd 1977

ISBN 0 04 352064 2 hardback
0 04 352065 0 paperback

Jacket and cover illustration: Courtesy of the Cavendish School, Hemel Hempstead

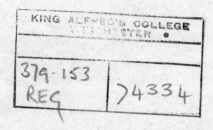
Printed in Great Britain
in 10 pt Times Roman Type
by Willmer Brothers Limited, Birkenhead

PREFACE

Most books on the education system in England and Wales are written by educationists. The object of this book is to describe and discuss the education service from the perspective of the academic discipline of public administration. The coverage is comprehensive but special attention is paid to topics of wide administrative interest like central–local relations and the impact of local government reform. On all issues care is taken to assess the role and contribution of local government. Education is one of the most demanding and important, and certainly the most costly, of local government responsibilities. Yet, as is argued in Chapter XIII, education benefits from being in the local government sphere, and local government benefits from its guardianship of this remarkable service

As is generally the case with a work of this kind many people contributed at various stages to its progress. I acknowledge first, with thanks, the financial assistance of the Nuffield Foundation under its Small Grants Scheme. This enabled me to employ two research assistants for a short period at the beginning of the project. The two involved (Mr David Adams, now at the Australian National University and Mr John Hyman, now at Tottenham Technical College) proved ideal researchers – thorough, scholarly and conscientious. I am grateful to them for helping to ensure that the book started off on a firm foundation. I have also received much help from many councillors, local government officers and civil servants. It would be impossible to list them all individually or to detail the huge variety of ways in which they were helpful – from granting full-scale interviews to me or my research assistants, to supplying a small piece of information by letter or telephone. I extend my profound thanks to them all. I am also grateful to Professor John Griffith, Professor Peter Self, Mr Alan Evans and, especially, Professor Peter Richards, editor of this series, for reading and commenting on drafts of the book. Of course I bear sole responsibility for all that appears. I offer my thanks too to Miss Ann Boucher, Mrs Paula Da Gama Pinto, and Mrs Pat Urwin for typing the manuscript so skilfully. Finally I am grateful to my wife Dorothy for acting as supernumerary secretary, research assistant and general encourager.

D. E. REGAN
January 1976

CONTENTS

Preface   *page* 7
  I   *Founding the System*   9
  II   *Naming the Partners*   13
  III *Classifying the Schools*   37
  IV   *Running the Schools*   54
  V   *Educating the Handicapped*   73
  VI   *Attending to the Health and Welfare of*
       Schoolchildren   95
  VII *Inspecting the Schools*   103
  VIII *Building the Schools*   121
  IX   *Providing the Teachers*   136
  X   *Educating the School Leaver*   165
  XI   *Financing the Education Service*   186
  XII *Reforming the Structure of* LEAs   212
  XIII *Summing Up*   231
Bibliography   244
Index   252

Chapter I

FOUNDING THE SYSTEM

At midday on Wednesday 19 January 1944, the Speaker, Colonel The Rt Hon. Douglas Clifton Brown, in a packed, sunlit House of Commons, called upon the Rt Hon. R. A. Butler, President of the Board of Education, to move the Second Reading of the Education Bill.[1] Seven months later the measure received the Royal Assent as the Education Act 1944. There is no doubt about Mr (later Lord) Butler's deep personal involvement in the Act; indeed its common appellation, the Butler Act, is a personalisation of legislation most unusual in Britain.[2] The Act was the most enduring landmark in a notable political career.

Butler badly wanted the job of President of the Board of Education. Indeed Churchill was rather surprised at Butler's enthusiasm for education and his willingness to leave the Foreign Office where he was serving as under-secretary of state. According to Butler's account (1971, p. 90) of the interview, 'I then said that I had always looked forward to going to the Board of Education if I were given the chance. He [Churchill] appeared ever so slightly surprised at this, showing that he felt that in wartime a central job, such as the one I was leaving, is the most important. But he looked genuinely pleased that I had shown so much satisfaction and seemed to think the appointment entirely suitable.'[3]

Moreover, when later Butler first floated the idea of a new Education Bill, Churchill reacted very adversely, fearing its potential to stir up religious controversy and party conflict in the middle of the war. He virtually forbad Butler to proceed with a Bill, but the veto was ignored and Churchill seems to have forgotten it. When the Act finally reached the Statute Book Churchill waxed quite enthusiastic about it.

The Education Act 1944 was a wide-ranging piece of legislation but seven of its provisions can be picked out as particularly important. It increased the role of the central government in education by creating a new Minister (and therefore Ministry) of Education with far greater powers than his predecessor. It made the county boroughs and the counties the sole local education authorities, and

thus deprived county districts of the substantial educational responsibilities they previously exercised. It introduced secondary
education for all, to the age of 15. It recast the system for educating
handicapped children, and improved health and welfare arrangements for all children. It made major changes in post-school education. Last but by no means least it made a new settlement of the
religious question in education – non-denominational Bible-teach-
ing in local authority schools, higher subsidies for schools controlled by voluntary bodies, and a new alternative for voluntary
schools whereby the trustees could surrender control (and financial
responsibility) to local authorities but retain certain rights and influence.

It is sometimes forgotten today how large the religious question
loomed at the time. Sir Frederick Mander, a former General Secretary of the National Union of Teachers, termed the problem of
denominational control of part of the education system before 1944
'a tank trap across the highway of educational advance' (quoted by
Gould, 1969, p. 10). Lord Butler has himself (1965) traced the
origin of the Act to a letter to *The Times* in December 1940 from
leaders of the Anglican, Roman Catholic and Free Churches calling
for a new education settlement. This rather unusual display of
ecclesiastical solidarity seems to have impressed the Board of Education, for when Butler was appointed to its presidency the following July he found its staff already heavily engaged upon a new
Education Bill. A Green Book containing draft proposals had already been produced and circulated to interested organisations. One
is tempted to speculate that but for the need for a new religious
settlement there might that have been no Education Act 1944; but
a Cleopatra's nose approach to history is rarely profitable.

If the religious question provided the stimulus it also provided
the most intractable problem. Significantly, Butler devoted to it
fully one fifth of his $1\frac{1}{4}$-hour speech on the Second Reading. And it
had proved the major headache long before the Bill's introduction;
in his own words (1965), 'The religious problem proved to be by
far the biggest obstacle in the negotiations leading to the Act'. There
were obvious irreconcilable standpoints; the Roman Catholics and
the Anglicans ideally would have liked to combine their own control with a 100 per cent state subsidy while at the other extreme a
considerable body of public opinion, including some of the smaller,
nonconformist churches, would have preferred no public funds to
go to church schools. The compromise settlement was probably
wholly satisfactory to few, as is demonstrated by many of the
speeches from all parties and in both Houses during the passage
of the Act.[4] Nevertheless it also contained elements pleasing to

most sectors of opinion and the bitter sectarian strife which had accompanied the passing of the Education Act 1902 ('Rome on the rates'), and the failure of the Liberal Government's 1906 Education Bill, was avoided. It has proved a most enduring settlement.

Apart from the religious settlement there was little in the Butler Act that was original or unexpected. In many ways it was a logical conclusion to trends which had been gaining increasing acceptance throughout the interwar period. For instance the concept of universal secondary education beginning at the age of about 11 had been powerfully advocated in the Hadow Report of 1926; the Hadow proposal in turn can be traced to even earlier antecedents.[5] Similarly the raising of the school-leaving age to 15 had been scheduled to come into effect on 1 September 1939, when the German Fuehrer set in train the invasion of Poland. Nevertheless the importance of consolidating legislation must not be under-rated and Butler's genius was to see such changes in the context of an entire, reformed educational system. His vision was holistic.

Moreover, the repercussions of the Butler Act have been far greater than the sum of its provisions. The social assumptions which it encapsulated have had even more profound consequences. The philosophy underlying the Act was that more and more people would want the kind of length and quality of education thitherto largely confined to an elite and that this should be provided free. From this has flowed the series of great post-war educational reports – Crowther, Newsom, Albemarle, Robbins, Plowden, James, Russell – all, in effect, concerned to increase provision and opportunity. From it too has flowed the enormous increase in resources devoted to education, described below in Chapter XI.

It is clear from a perusal of *Hansard* for 19 and 20 January 1944 that MPs on all sides fully appreciated the importance of the measure. They were conscious of legislating for a generation. Indeed the Butler Act has served for even longer if, as is usual, one takes a generation to represent twenty-five years. Although there have been a number of subsequent Education Acts, these have made relatively minor changes, and the 1944 system remains fundamentally unaltered.[6] A whole generation in England and Wales has been educated under its provisions.

In the Labour Government of 1965 to 1970, there was much talk of a new Education Act to replace the Butler Act. Indeed in 1968 it was reported that the Government had decided to proceed on a new Bill.[7] Subsequently there was much consultation of interested bodies for their views and ideas.[8] These plans were brought to an abrupt termination by the general election defeat of June 1970. The succeeding Conservative Government, though it produced plans for more expansion of education, did not consider that a new, major Act was necessary. Perhaps two generations will be educated under the Butler Act.

Of course the structure of an educational system does not entirely determine the content of the education provided. Since 1944 there have been profound changes in teaching methods, educational philosophy, school design, the role of head teachers, and much else. A child at school in 1945 would find much strange if he were to return in 1976. Nevertheless these changes have occurred within an enduring framework.

NOTES

1 The House of Commons met at this time in the Chamber of the House of Lords because of bomb damage to their own Chamber. Sittings commenced at 11.00 a.m., with an hour of questions on Wednesdays.

2 It is interesting, however, that legislation has been personalised in respect of two other landmarks in education: the Elementary Education Act 1870 (the Forster Act) and the Education Act 1918 (the Fisher Act).

3 A more apocryphal version has Churchill responding to Butler's enthusiastic acceptance by growling 'Just like you, Rab. I meant it as an insult'. See 'Politics and the Reform of Education' by Rodney Barker in *Municipal Review*, No. 541 (January 1975).

4 For the Commons Second Reading debate see *HC Deb*. 5s Vol. 396, cols 207–322, 405–508.

5 As far back as 1913, Mr J. A. Pease, then President of the Board of Education, proposed that special provision be made for all children over 11 in elementary schools.

6 There were Education Acts in 1946, 1959, 1962, 1964, 1967, 1968 (two) and 1973; Education (Miscellaneous Provisions) Acts in 1948 and 1953; Remuneration of Teachers Acts in 1963 and 1965; an Education (School Milk) Act in 1970; an Education (Milk) Act in 1971; an Education (Handicapped Children) Act 1970 and an Education (Work Experience) Act 1973.

7 See, for instance, 'New Education Act will eliminate 11 plus tests' by Richard Bourne in the *Guardian*, 16 October 1968.

8 See, for instance, 'Education as the NUT would like it' in the *Guardian*, 9 December 1969.

Chapter II

NAMING THE PARTNERS

The 1944 Act established, for England and Wales, a Ministry of Education in place of the old Board of Education. The latter body had existed since 1899 although curiously the board never once met; in practice its president had run the department alone, like an ordinary minister.[1]

The new Ministry of Education did not include universities within its orbit; the University Grants Committee (UGC) remained a semi-autonomous unit attached to the Treasury. In 1963, however, the Robbins Committee on Higher Education reported, recommending *inter alia* the appointment of a Minister for Arts and Science to be responsible for university affairs, scientific research and certain cultural activities. In a 'dissenting report' one member of the Committee, Mr H. C. Shearman, argued that such a minister should also be responsible for the lower levels of education. A large section of educational opinion supported Mr Shearman on the grounds that to continue the bifurcated central responsibility for education in a new form would not only retain problems of co-ordination but might lead to dangerous new rivalries. It was argued that, with the UGC in the Treasury, the universities' financial demands were somewhat restricted by the Treasury's concern for economy; if the UGC were transferred to a powerful new minister with no such inhibitions, there might be direct competition for funds between him and the Minister of Education. It was feared that the latter would usually be worsted and schools become the poor relations of the universities.

The Government seemed to vacillate between the views of the Robbins Committee majority and those of Mr Shearman and his supporters. In December 1963 the Lord President of the Council was made responsible for the UGC and for co-ordinating government activity on higher education; since the Lord President at the time, Mr Quintin Hogg (later Lord Hailsham), was also Minister for Science, his responsibilities were close to those proposed for the Minister for Arts and Science. In April 1964, however, the Department of Education and Science (DES) was created, incorporating the

Ministry of Education and the Ministry of Science and absorbing the Lord President's responsibilities for the UGC and higher education. Seven months later there was a further small adjustment when the Labour Government's new Ministry of Technology took over certain technological functions from the DES. The responsibilities of the DES then remained fundamentally unaltered until 1970. In the Conservative Government's reorganisation of central departments of that year, responsibility for primary and secondary education in Wales was transferred from the DES to the Welsh Office.

Today, therefore, the DES covers the whole range of educational responsibilities for England; it is the department for post-school education in Wales, and responsible for government relations with universities in England, Wales and Scotland. The department also promotes civil science and the arts, and is responsible for national library policy and for the administration of the Victoria and Albert and Science Museums.

The minister in charge, the Secretary of State for Education and Science,* is counted a senior member of the Government and always has a place in the Cabinet. He or she is, however, generally considered one rank lower than the holders of the very highest portfolios – Chancellor of the Exchequer, Home Secretary, Foreign Secretary. Thus the post tends to be thought suitable for politicians on the way up or for those not thought worthy of further promotion, but not as a fitting terminal post for the really able. Ministers of Education and Secretaries of State for Education and Science are set out in Table 2.1. The list includes some very notable names, with Mrs Margaret Thatcher perhaps the most notable of all. After three and a half years as secretary of state, but no further experience of high government office, in 1975 she displaced Mr Edward Heath as leader of the Conservative Party (one small step for a man, one giant leap for a lady). The secretary of state is assisted by two parliamentary under-secretaries. The Minister for the Arts is also usually a junior minister in the DES, often doubling the portfolio of Paymaster General.

The department is organised into nineteen branches or equivalent units – four for higher and further education, two for schools and one each for teachers, arts and libraries, civil science, architects and buildings, external relations, medical advisers, statistics, legal, finance, establishments and organisation, a planning unit (especially concerned with the programme analysis review, PAR, exercise), HM Inspectorate and the UGC. The department also has a Welsh Educational Office in Cardiff and a separate Welsh Inspectorate. There

---

* Henceforth the term 'secretary of state' will refer to this minister except where the context clearly indicates otherwise.

Table 2.1 *Ministers of Education and Secretaries of State for Education and Science 1944-75*

A Ministers of Education

August 1944	Mr Richard A. Butler (later Lord Butler)
May 1945	Mr Richard K. Law (later Lord Coleraine)
August 1945	Miss Ellen C. Wilkinson
February 1947	Mr George Tomlinson
November 1951	Miss Florence Horsbrugh (later Baroness Horsbrugh)
October 1954	Sir David Eccles (later Viscount Eccles)
January 1957	Viscount Hailsham (later Mr Quintin M. Hogg)*
September 1957	Mr Geoffrey W. Lloyd
October 1959	Sir David Eccles (later Viscount Eccles) again
July 1962	Sir Edward Boyle (later Lord Boyle)

B Secretaries of State for Education and Science

April 1964	Mr Quintin M. Hogg (later Lord Hailsham)*
October 1964	Mr Michael Stewart
January 1965	Mr C. Anthony Crosland
August 1967	Mr Patrick C. Gordon Walker
April 1968	Mr Edward W. Short
June 1970	Mrs Margaret H. Thatcher
February 1974	Mr Reg E. Prentice
June 1975	Mr Frederick W. Mulley

* Mr Quintin Hogg inherited his father's Viscountcy of Hailsham in 1950, disclaimed it and reverted to commoner in 1963 but in 1970 returned to the House of Lords with a life peerage as Lord Hailsham of Marylebone.

are, however, no regional offices in England except for HM Inspectorate.

In the 1970s the vogue is for giant, amalgamated departments (although the Department of Trade and Industry was unscrambled again); indeed the DES is a prototype of the model. In this context, however, the DES is a rather small department as may be seen from Table 2.2. It is a popular one to serve in; new entrants to the Civil Service place it high on their list of preferences. Perhaps this says something about our current political and social culture. In other countries education is not always such a popular public service posting; technical or industrial departments may, for instance, be rated higher. In public relations language, the DES has a rather good image both within the Civil Service and to a large extent outside – a go-ahead, lively kind of place.

Although the DES has always had offices in several parts of London, for many years its headquarters were in Curzon Street, Mayfair.

Table 2.2 *Numbers of Civil Servants in Post by Departments on 1 January 1975*

	'000
Agriculture, Fisheries and Food	15·2
Cabinet Office	0·6
Civil Service Department	5·3
Customs and Excise	27·1
Education and Science (including UGC, V&A and Science Museums)	4·0
Employment	15·6
Energy	1·2
Environment (including Property Services Agency)	69·7
Foreign and Commonwealth Office	10·3
Health and Social Security	86·7
HM Stationery Office	7·1
Home Office	30·3
Industry	10·2
Inland Revenue	73·5
Lord Chancellor's Department	9·6
National Savings Department	13·6
Northern Ireland Office	0·2
Overseas Development	2·3
Trade	7·3
Treasury	1·1
Welsh Office	1·3
Scottish Departments	12·2
Other Civil Departments	23·3
Defence	266·5
Total for All Departments	693·9

Note: Figures are rounded up to one decimal place and include all industrial and non-industrial staff.
Source: Civil Service Statistics 1975, Civil Service Department (HMSO, 1975).

The building must be one of the most bizarre ever occupied by a government department. Never an architectural gem, wartime damage and subsequent restoration with cement had produced the effect of a military bunker. This impression was heightened by the entrance – inconspicuous and opening into a long, narrow tunnel which had to be traversed before at last corridors and offices were reached. One felt that a trio of assistant secretaries armed with pikes could have held off a horde of angry teachers or parents indefinitely. In 1969, however, the department began to move staff from the grim charm of Curzon Street over the river to Elizabeth House, a typical modern, tombstone slab near Waterloo designed by architect John Poulson, who was subsequently jailed for corruption in public contracting. Most DES branches are now concentrated there.

Whether based in Mayfair or Waterloo, the DES headquarters have always been somewhat apart from the main block of departments in Whitehall.

Local Responsibility

The Education Act 1944 made the councils of counties and county boroughs the local education authorities (LEAs). Previously the position was more complex. Non-county borough councils and urban district councils which according to the 1901 census had a population exceeding 10,000 and 20,000 respectively were LEAs for 'elementary education'; they were commonly known as 'Part III authorities' after the relevant part of the Education Act 1902. The county councils were thus left with reponsibility only for 'higher' education in the Part III authorities, although for both 'elementary' and 'higher' education elsewhere. The county boroughs being single-tier units were, naturally, LEAs for both.

The 1944 Act swept away the Part III authorities' functions by making the counties and county boroughs the sole LEAs responsible for all three stages of education – primary, secondary and further (concepts which replaced those of 'elementary' and 'higher' education). This change had two particularly significant results: a reduction in the number of LEAs (from 315 to 146) and an increase in their average size. Subsequent local government reorganisation has accentuated both trends.

Delegation of Educational Functions

The Part III authorities bitterly resented their deprivation of educational responsibilities by the 1944 Act. To sweeten this pill the Government provided in the Act for a system of delegation of certain educational functions in the counties to enable the county districts to play some part in the service.

Two types of delegated authority were permitted – divisional executives and excepted districts. First, a number of county districts could be grouped together under schemes drawn up by the county, and delegated certain educational responsibilities as a group. Such groupings were known as divisions; each division was controlled by an executive containing representatives of all the constituent county districts plus some co-optees. In a few rare cases a divisional executive consisted of just one county district but was still distinct from the excepted districts described next.

Secondly, certain non-county boroughs and urban districts could

be given delegated educational responsibilities alone, not in combination with other county districts, under schemes which *they
themselves prepared*, not their counties. Such authorities were known
as 'excepted districts' because they were excepted from the county
schemes of divisional administration creating divisional executives.
Excepted districts were, therefore, a special kind of divisional executive always composed of a single county district rather than
several combined. As such they did not need a special executive;
the council of the borough or urban district was the controlling body.

To become an excepted district an urban district or borough had
to apply to the minister before 1 October 1944; if on 1939 figures
it had a population of 60,000 or more or an elementary school
population of 7,000 or more its application *had* to be granted; otherwise the minister had discretion. The Local Government Act 1958
allowed new applications for excepted district status at specified
intervals from boroughs and urban districts with populations of
60,000 or more or other special circumstances. The minister, later
secretary of state, had power to deprive a local authority of excepted district status if by any census its population was found to
be less than 60,000.

By no means all counties contained divisional executives or excepted districts. Under the 1944 Act all counties were obliged to
prepare schemes of divisional administration unless the minister
exempted them; in fact he did exempt a large number of the smaller
counties. In 1974 twenty-two counties in England and Wales contained neither divisional executive nor excepted district; a further ten
contained a single excepted district each but no divisional executive.
Twenty-six counties contained divisional executives. In the case
of ten of them, however, there was just one divisional executive,
and in eight others, while there were two or more, some areas of the
county were administered direct by the county council. In only eight
counties was there a complete network of divisional executives plus
perhaps one or more excepted districts.

Under the 1944 Act there were originally established 169 divisional executives and 44 excepted districts. Through amalgamations
and boundary changes both were reduced in number to 142 and 30
respectively in 1974.

The schemes of divisional administration drawn up by counties
for their county districts and excepted districts for themselves had
to be approved by the minister, after considering any objections and
making any modifications he thought necessary. Counties and excepted districts could vary, revoke or supplement existing schemes
with the minister's (later secretary of state's) consent; the latter also
had power to direct that a new scheme be prepared.

No scheme of divisional administration could authorise a divisional executive or excepted district to borrow money or raise a rate;
this was the only prohibition. Certain other county responsibilities
were not usually thought appropriate for delegation, such as the
form of secondary education which should harmonise over the whole
county. In general many functions in the field of day-to-day administration of primary and secondary schools were delegated to
divisional executives: appointment of teachers (other than head
teachers), caretakers and clerical assistants, maintenance of property, provision of school meals, milk and textbooks, and similar
matters. A few divisional executives also had some functions in the
field of further education. Divisional executives were also able to
advise their counties on matters which were not their delegated
responsibility.

Since excepted districts prepared their own schemes of divisional
administration it is not surprising that they tended to give themselves rather more functions than counties were prepared to con-
cede their divisional executives. Their schemes required ministerial
approval, however, and this, as Richards (1956, pp. 74, 75) shows,
prevented the arrogation of excessive powers. Besides day-to-day
control, excepted districts usually played a larger role in policy.
They were, for instance, usually delegated responsibility for determining the general educational character of most schools, and
could even thus be influential in determining their form of secondary
school organisation. They also played a major part in new school
building and maintenance of existing property. They had a considerable measure of financial discretion within 'main heads' of the
estimates (e.g. teachers' salaries) and perhaps even 'virement'. They
usually appointed their own head teachers.

While delegation was primarily inspired by a need to mollify the
Part III authorities it could be justified on more reasoned grounds,
namely, that it permitted decision making at a less remote scale
than county level and greater participation of individuals and interests. It had, however, massive drawbacks. A universal system
of delegation would have been difficult enough for the average
citizen to grasp. Since the arrangements varied both between and
among divisional executives and excepted districts, and since large
areas were subject to neither, the system was a mystery to all but
the most determined of laymen. Moreover it was not only complicated to understand but complicated to operate, with tensions
arising especially between excepted districts and their mother
counties. In any case one could argue that local involvement was
more appropriate at the level of the individual school than on the
basis of units as large as the divisional executives and excepted

districts; there was hardly scope for *both* strong and active governing bodies *and* powerful divisional administrations.

The Government decided that the drawbacks outweighed the benefits and took the opportunity of local government reorganisation to abolish the whole system of delegation. In 1974 all divisional executives and excepted districts ceased to exist. The only crumb of comfort left for the delegationists is a general power accorded the counties (under Section 102 of the Local Government Act 1972) to set up area committees to *advise* on the discharge of any service, including education. At the time of writing it is too early to tell whether much use will be made of area advisory committees in education. In any case they are pale shadows of the old delegated agencies with their *executive* functions.

Reducing the Numbers of LEAs

The first major post-war change came in London. By the London Government Act 1963, the Greater London Council (GLC) and 32 London boroughs replaced 3 county boroughs (West Ham, East Ham and Croydon), and two counties (London and Middlesex), besides parts of 4 others (Kent, Surrey, Essex and Hertfordshire), together with 28 metropolitan boroughs, 39 non-county boroughs and 15 urban districts. The City of London, like Old Father Thames, marched on unchanged. Thus 5 LEAs (the 2 counties and 3 county boroughs) disappeared completely and parts of 4 others were absorbed. The structure of educational administration which replaced them was 21 LEAs – 20 London boroughs in outer London and an Inner London Education Authority (ILEA), covering the 12 inner London boroughs and the City of London.

The London reorganisation, far from creating fewer and larger LEAs, did the exact opposite. At the same time, however, as the 21 new LEAs were set up the complicated delegated arrangements for education in Greater London were swept away. In the area now covered by the ILEA and 20 outer London boroughs, in other words the GLC, there had previously existed 25 excepted districts, 16 divisional executives and 1 district sub-committee. The 1963 Act thus effected a considerable rationalisation of educational administration in London. Moreover, the reorganisation of local government in London was the morning star to the reorganisation of local government in the rest of Britain a decade later, and this reduced the number of full LEAs by roughly a third.

Under the Local Government Act 1972, English and Welsh local government was substantially reformed. So far as education was concerned in England, outside Greater London 79 county boroughs and 45 counties were replaced by 39 counties and 36 metropolitan

Table 2.3   *Local Education Authorities in England and Wales*

	Population	Rateable value at 1 April 1974 £	Rateable value per capita £
A Counties			
Avon	914,180	107,435,962	117·52
Bedfordshire	418,050	69,221,607	143·90
Berkshire	651,100	102,333,273	157·17
Buckinghamshire	496,470	77,000,000	155·09
Cambridgeshire	533,480	62,893,079	117·89
Cheshire	895,770	114,400,059	127·71
Cleveland	566,740	67,965,117	119·92
Clwyd (W)	368,880	34,802,583	94·35
Cornwall	391,490	38,138,000	97·42
Cumbria	474,080	41,584,000	87·72
Derbyshire	888,340	136,927,560	154·14
Devon	920,550	98,674,451	107·19
Dorset	566,360	72,133,354	127·36
Durham	609,840	50,489,709	82·79
Dyfed (W)	316,960	26,758,670	84·42
East Sussex	657,720	87,381,469	132·86
Essex	1,397,840	203,500,000	145·58
Gloucestershire	481,700	56,234,969	116·74
Gwent (W)	441,090	41,972,669	95·16
Gwynedd (W)	222,090	19,227,311	86·57
Hampshire	1,422,060	178,000,000	125·17
Hereford and Worcester	577,140	72,000,000	124·75
Hertfordshire	939,520	149,129,300	158·73
Humberside	847,230	87,230,000	102·96
Isle of Wight	109,680	11,596,742	105·73
Kent	1,434,960	158,704,870	110·60
Lancashire	1,362,800	127,921,654	93·87
Leicestershire	824,360	95,242,730	115·54
Lincolnshire	512,880	49,033,980	95·61
Mid Glamorgan (W)	536,080	33,739,000	62·94
Norfolk	643,940	74,458,319	115·63
Northamptonshire	487,930	56,823,231	116·46
Northumberland	283,310	26,220,174	92·55
North Yorkshire	644,830	60,973,071	94·56
Nottinghamshire	984,190	107,179,292	108·90
Oxfordshire	529,640	67,952,900	128·30
Powys (W)	99,370	7,429,057	74·76
Salop	347,770	35,912,726	103·27
Somerset	398,900	41,706,177	104·55
South Glamorgan (W)	392,250	44,667,747	113·88
Staffordshire	984,620	106,005,860	107·66

Table 2.3   *Local Education Authorities in England and Wales*—Contd

	Population	Rateable value at 1 April 1974 £	Rateable value per capita £
Suffolk	561,540	64,051,502	114·06
Surrey	1,011,810	155,149,198	153·34
Warwickshire	468,270	57,338,979	122·45
West Glamorgan (W)	372,560	35,309,729	94·78
West Sussex	629,890	81,724,183	129·74
Wiltshire	501,200	49,999,733	99·76
B Metropolitan Districts			
Barnsley	225,140	16,165,163	71·80
Birmingham City	1,087,660	152,976,657	140·65
Bolton	261,250	25,298,123	96·83
Bradford City	462,990	38,269,032	82·66
Bury	181,290	17,678,682	97·52
Calderdale	192,650	n.a.	n.a.
Coventry City	336,040	41,146,300	122·44
Doncaster	282,550	25,105,525	88·85
Dudley	297,760	38,514,042	129·35
Gateshead	223,730	20,010,215	89·44
Kirklees	371,460	29,712,581	79·99
Knowsley	193,380	20,788,965	107·50
Leeds City	748,070	77,214,220	103·22
Liverpool City	574,560	70,634,632	122·94
Manchester City	530,810	70,424,791	132·67
Newcastle upon Tyne City	299,800	37,541,616	125·22
North Tyneside	206,710	18,421,716	89·12
Oldham	225,350	20,938,233	92·91
Rochdale	208,020	18,873,956	90·73
Rotherham	245,990	20,145,824	81·90
St Helens	192,140	20,494,513	106·66
Salford City	272,840	29,752,180	109·05
Sandwell	324,000	48,389,837	149·35
Sefton	308,420	34,052,428	110·41
Sheffield City	565,500	60,915,489	107·72
Solihull	198,670	25,133,947	126·51
South Tyneside	172,990	15,237,889	88·09
Stockport	294,730	34,759,596	117·94
Sunderland	295,160	23,648,957	80·12
Tameside	222,600	19,914,819	89·46
Trafford	229,540	35,298,572	153·78
Wakefield City	304,360	26,844,948	88·20
Walsall	271,800	35,779,753	131·64
Wigan	306,070	27,483,842	89·80
Wirral	352,280	38,565,000	109·47
Wolverhampton	269,530	37,810,260	140·28

Table 2.3   *Local Education Authorities in England and Wales—Contd*

	Population	Rateable value at 1 April 1974 £	Rateable value per capita £
C London			
ILEA	2,649,540	1,095,490,667	413·47
Barking	157,800	26,833,437	170·05
Barnet	302,140	56,103,438	185·69
Bexley	217,210	28,150,922	129·60
Brent	275,150	48,995,798	178·07
Bromley	305,530	45,170,000	147·84
Croydon	332,880	63,814,490	191·70
Ealing	292,510	53,930,000	184·37
Enfield	264,790	46,138,183	174·24
Haringey	234,690	33,764,880	143·87
Harrow	204,660	32,497,154	158·79
Havering	245,610	35,999,626	146·57
Hillingdon	235,030	51,543,892	219·31
Hounslow	207,380	45,862,353	221·15
Kingston upon Thames	138,620	27,662,037	199·55
Merton	176,640	29,623,133	167·70
Newham	231,300	35,259,060	152·44
Redbridge	237,180	35,333,650	148·97
Richmond upon Thames	170,940	28,834,066	168·68
Sutton	168,210	25,835,342	153·59
Waltham Forest	232,580	30,694,148	131·97

(W) = Wales
n.a. = not available
Source: *The Municipal Year Book 1975* (The Municipal Journal Ltd, 1975).

districts; in Wales 13 counties and 4 county boroughs were replaced by 8 counties; Greater London was left unchanged. The new counties and metropolitan districts commenced operations on 1 April 1974. Today, therefore, there are 96 LEAS in England (39 counties, 36 metropolitan districts, 20 London boroughs and ILEA) and 8 in Wales (all counties). Basic data on these authorities is set out in Table 2.3.

Education Committees
The Butler Act required all LEAS to establish in accordance with arrangements approved by the secretary of state '. . . such education committees as they think it expedient to establish for the efficient discharge of their functions with respect to education'. This requirement was continued when local government in England and

Wales was reorganised in 1972. In effect every LEA must have an education committee and the rules for its compostion (size, number of co-optees) must be satisfactory to the secretary of state. LEAS are not required to seek his approval of the number and composition of *subcommittees*. Nor does he have to sanction details of the delegation of functions to the education committee. In practice most educational responsibilities are invariably delegated to the education committee, though technically the full council remains the LEA.

Two or more LEAS were permitted under the Education Act 1944 to establish joint committees to consider questions of common interest. This special provision was replaced in 1972 by a general empowerment of local authorities to set up joint *advisory* committees in respect of any function (including education). A further provision of the 1944 Act whereby the secretary of state could establish by order a joint committee of LEAS with some *executive* responsibilities remains in force. In the past such executive joint committees were sometimes used where a small LEA wished to co-operate with a larger neighbour. Thus Kent and Canterbury set up, with government sanction, a joint committee to administer education within the City of Canterbury and the St Augustine division of Kent. Of course this arrangement became redundant when Canterbury was amalgamated with Kent in the 1972 reorganisation. Executive joint committees have also been used, and still are, to administer *institutions* in which several LEAS are involved, principally colleges of education and polytechnics. The most distinctive of these joint committees is undoubtedly, however, the Welsh Joint Education Committee first set up in 1948. Today it contains representatives of all Welsh LEAS plus some co-opted members representing special interests. It co-ordinates activity in fields like special education, further education, teachers' refresher courses and the like; it is also an examining body for several examinations including the Certificate of Secondary Education.

Every education committee and joint education committee must under the Butler Act 'include persons of experience in education and persons acquainted with the educational conditions prevailing in the area for which the committee acts'. Contrary to popular belief this does not mean that *co-option* is obligatory. Where the elected members of the committee represent a sufficient range of experience, co-option may be unnecessary. In the overwhelming majority of cases, however, education committees fulfil their statutory obligation by co-opting representatives of teachers, religious denominations, industry, commerce, agriculture and perhaps others with special interests or experience. Indeed DES Circular 8/73 makes it clear that co-option is today considered essential and that new education committee proposals are unlikely to be approved by the secretary of state unless they contain provision for co-option. By law two thirds of the committee must be elected members, and the department urges that full use of co-option up to this limit be made; between one quarter and one third should be co-optees. Few education committees have such a high proportion. Fewer still, however, have none. Only Croydon and Hillingdon London boroughs at the time of writing are still standing out against co-option. One doubts that their resistance will be indefinitely prolonged. Not only is there the pressure from the department but absence or sparsity of co-optees can cause unfavourable local comment. In 1967 for instance the Leeds Association for the Advancement of State Education publicly criticised the education committee of Leeds City Council for containing only three co-opted members plus three non-voting teachers' representatives.[2] Indeed teachers themselves constitute another pressure. Their unions today urge the appointment of substantial numbers of representative teachers to education committees as full co-optees. Teachers are disqualified from being elected to the LEA which employs them, but are eligible for appointment to its education committee.

This widespread support for co-option is rather curious since it is a practice that could well be challenged. If its main purpose is to recruit educational *experts* it would appear unnecessary. The usual principle of British public administration is that the political controllers of a service, central or local, need not be experts themselves. In a local education authority the permanent educational staff provide the expertise; it would be a novel argument that there must be duplicate or even counter experts at the level of the controlling committee. True, co-optees sometimes have knowledge or experience not possessed by the education staff, but the benefits of this could be obtained as the need arose on an *ad hoc* consultative basis without making such people members of the education committee. At central government level the Ministry of Agriculture, say, would not think it necessary to have a Welsh hill farmer as a junior minister because no civil servant possessed his knowledge and experience. Even at local government level highways committees do not usually co-opt representatives of haulage contractors, civil engineering firms, lorry manufacturers and the like, although no doubt the engineering staff sometimes need to consult such specialists. Co-option is not indeed widely practised in local government. All committees except finance committees have the power to co-opt but except for education committees, social service committees and allotment committees it is a rare phenomenon.

If, on the other hand, co-option is primarily intended as a means of representing special *interests*, it might be undesirable as well as unnecessary. Through such privileged treatment they could obtain political influence disproportionate to their support in the community. Even if this danger is avoided, why should it be thought impossible for the ordinary councillors to speak on their behalf? Members of Parliament are considered able to represent all their constituents. The commonest co-optees are representatives of religious denominations but under the normally accepted theory of representation in Britain the elected councillors represent *all* citizens; a Methodist is not deprived of representation if his local councillor is Jewish. In any case education committees rarely co-opt representatives of the smaller denominations. Teachers' representatives are also today increasingly co-opted. Again, the value of this is dubious; invariably most of the education staff have teaching experience and in any case teachers can be consulted directly. Moreover it can lead to problems. Teachers are employees of their LEA; in employer–employee disputes teachers' representatives on the education committee are in an embarrassing position. During, for instance, the 1968 disputes about teachers' supervision of school meals many awkward situations of this kind arose; in some cases education committees went into special committee excluding the teachers' representatives to discuss the dispute. Finally, some co-options seem even less justifiable. Brent education committee, for instance, co-opted some members of the Brent Parents' Association – to represent *parents*! If councillors cannot even represent parents, one wonders what role they are left with.

Possibly, in a crude and confused way, advocates of co-option are really feeling their way to a participatory theory of democracy in local government rather than a representative theory – a distinction made, for instance, by Pateman (1970).

Perhaps the most serious objection to co-option is, however, its abuse. In many cases it is used, not to recruit neutral experts, but as a minor form of political patronage. Party faithful, especially unsuccessful council candidates, are often rewarded with co-opted membership of the education committee.

All this is not to deny that co-opted members sometimes make a useful contribution to the work of education committees. Nevertheless the theoretical justification for co-option is obscure and the practice sometimes problematical. Moreover, it is strange, if co-option is valuable, that it is not used more widely elsewhere in local government.

The education committee is invariably one of the largest committees in a local authority. Moreover its size does not necessarily reflect the population of the LEA. Thus Clwyd (population 368,880) has an education committee 76 strong, including 10 co-optees, while Kent (population 1,434,960) has an education committee with 60 members, including 15 co-optees. The education committee may well contain one third or even two fifths of the council membership.

Partly because of its size and partly because of its range of responsibilities, the education committee invariably has a number of subcommittees. The particular breakdown of functions among them is at the discretion of the LEA but usually some subcommittees cover sectors of the education service like further education, the youth service, and so on, while others cover horizontal topics such as finance and school building.

The chairman of the education committee is usually a very senior member of the council. In some cases he serves for many years; this is naturally less likely in the politically divided councils where his tenure is likely to be interrupted by swings of the political pendulum; the majority party almost always want to appoint one of their leading members to the post. A particularly interesting situation arose in April 1967 when the Conservatives, obviously to their own astonishment, won control of the ILEA. None of their Greater London councillors for the inner London area was thought experienced enough to take over the chairmanship of this, the biggest LEA in the country; they hurriedly made Mr Christopher Chataway, a former junior education minister, an alderman so that he could be chairman.[3] Theoretically, of course, chairmen are elected by the education committee but in practice even in the councils composed entirely of independents there is normally a candidate agreed well beforehand. The DES now insists that the chairman should be an elected member of the council.

By law any local government elector may have access to the minutes of proceedings of an education committee upon payment of a small fee. The Public Bodies (Access to Meetings) Act 1960 compelled education committees and divisional executives to open their meetings to the public except where this would be prejudicial to the public interest. In fact neither right is as important as it seems. Most debate and decision making takes place in the subcommittees; the full education committee has a primarily confirmatory role. Except where some contentious issue provokes an impassioned debate, the proceedings of the committee may not be fully revealing. Indeed sometimes meetings of the full education committee only last a few minutes.

The Education Staff

The education committee, like all local authority committees, is served by a body of professional administrators (assisted by clerical and other ancillary staff). Unlike traditional higher civil servants, they are specialist not generalist administrators (in this respect they accord with Fulton Committee ideas). A high proportion of education officers are recruited initially from the teaching profession. Indeed those recruited otherwise are definitely hindered in their advance in educational administration; rightly or wrongly, most education committees are reluctant to appoint people without teaching experience to the higher ranks. Most education officers thereafter serve for the whole of their careers in educational administration; they move between local authorities seeking promotion but normally keep to education departments.

The head of the education staff in each LEA is the chief education officer (some local authorities give him the title 'director of education'). By law LEAs must appoint a 'fit person' to be chief education officer. Nowhere are his necessary qualifications defined, but most LEAs expect a prospective chief education officer to have, besides an honours degree, considerable experience of educational administration as well as teaching.

When a new chief education officer was appointed, the LEA used to be obliged to send its shortlist of candidates to the secretary of state who could forbid the appointment of any considered unsuitable. This obligation was removed in 1972. The veto had in any case been exercised very infrequently. LEAs can today therefore appoint virtually whom they like; the only mandatory provision remaining is that they *must* appoint someone.

Local Authority Associations

Central–local relations in Britain are not confined to interactions between government departments and *individual* local authorities. Most local authorities are members of one or more of the local authority associations, *groupings* of local authorities, which negotiate with, exert pressure on, and are consulted by, government departments. Since 1945 the local authority associations have been increasingly involved in government decisions: most government bills and statutory regulations affecting local government are discussed with them before being laid before Parliament; most circulars are seen by them in draft; they are consulted about most significant policy changes; they participate in committees and advisory bodies; they have an important, statutory role in the determining of the Rate Support Grant.

Until 1973 there were six local authority associations covering English and Welsh local authorities. Five were associations of types of local authority: the Association of Municipal Corporations

(AMC) for boroughs, the County Councils Association (CCA) for counties, the Urban District Councils Association (UDCA) for urban districts, the Rural District Councils Association (RDCA) for rural districts, and the National Association of Parish Councils (NAPC) for parish councils. The AMC was the oldest, founded in 1873, followed by the CCA (1889), the UDCA and the RDCA (both 1895) and the NAPC (1947).

The sixth local authority association, the Association of Education Committees (AEC), was, and is, quite different. It is concerned with just one service, education, instead of all local government responsibilities, and is an association not of local *authorities* but of local authority *committees*. The AEC was formed in 1904, after the Education Act 1902 had transferred all educational responsibilities to the local authorities and dissolved the school boards. There was some fear that education might suffer with the change of control and a desire to retain a body to promote the service; there had been a School Boards Association until 1902. At first the education committees joining the AEC were all from county boroughs and Part III authorities; no county joined until 1919. After 1944, however, the Part III authorities departed (when deprived of educational responsibilities) and education committees from all English and Welsh county boroughs and counties became members of the AEC, together with those from Northern Ireland, the Isle of Man and the Channel Islands.

Since 1944 the General Secretary of the AEC has been Sir William Alexander (created Lord Alexander of Potterhill in 1974), a former chief education officer for Sheffield. For three decades Lord Alexander has been probably the most powerful single voice in the education world. His very continuity has contributed to his authority. He has remained in office while ministers and governments have come and gone, and there has been considerable movement of personnel in other educational organisations – secretaries of teachers' unions, chairmen of education committees, chief education officers, and so on. Moreover his formidable personality and intellect have dominated the AEC; its views and policies have been largely his. Thus his personal influence on national education policy has been considerable, his most apparent concern always being to secure major (and if possible increased) allocation of resources to the education service. For the general public Lord Alexander has to some extent been 'Mr Education'; the press invariably print his comments whenever some educational crisis occurs or some major new policy is mooted.

The AEC has always been regarded as somewhat anachronistic by the other local authority associations, and as rather unfortunate by

those who consider education no different from any other local
government service. Lord Alexander's alleged personal authori-
tarianism also makes him, and the AEC, unpopular in some quarters.
The hostile individuals and groups seized the opportunity presented
by the reorganisation of local government effected by the Local
Government Act 1972 to try to undermine the position of the AEC.
The reorganisation (discussed below in Chapter XII) swept away
certain types of local government unit, created new ones and (outside London) changed the functions of those it left. Naturally this
had a profound impact on the five local authority associations representing the old types of local authority. All five were dissolved or
substantially reformed. In place of the AMC, CCA, UDCA, RDCA and
NAPC there were set up in 1973: first an Association of Metropolitan Authorities (AMA) covering metropolitan counties, metropolitan
districts, the GLC, the London boroughs and the City of London;
secondly an Association of District Councils (ADC) covering non-
metropolitan district councils; thirdly an Association of County
Councils (ACC) covering non-metropolitan counties and, fourthly, a
National Association of Local Councils covering parish and community councils.

What of the AEC? Unlike the other local authority associations
it was able to continue little changed since education committees
were a mandatory feature of the new local education authorities.
However there were many determined that the AEC should not carry
on as before. Instead it was argued that any organisation speaking
for local government educational interests should represent local
education *authorities*, not local education *committees*. Such opinions
gained much support in the AMA and the ACC. New LEAs were asked
not to allow their education committees to join the AEC. An attempt
was made to reach a compromise between the AEC and the AMA and
ACC but the talks broke down. Undoubtedly personality conflicts
played a part but fundamentally there was no way of reconciling
Lord Alexander's view of education, as a unique service to be given
special privileges and a separate voice, with the view of the in-
tegrationists in the AMA and the ACC of education as merely one of
many important local government responsibilities.[4]

In January 1974 the AMA and the ACC set up their own joint
educational organisation, the Central Council of Local Education
Authorities. Nevertheless, Lord Alexander and his supporters decided that the AEC should continue and so it has. Today, however,
its membership embraces only one third of the English and Welsh
local education committees. Moreover as a result of pressure from
the AMA and the ACC the Government cancelled the AEC's membership of the Burnham Committee.[5] Whether in such ways Lord

Alexander will eventually be frozen out of the public educational scene one must wait to see.

The controversy over the AEC highlights the argument about the place of education in local government. It is a theme which recurs periodically throughout the rest of the book and one examined in detail in Chapter XIII.

The Partnership

The change from a Board to a Ministry of Education was more than titular. The new minister's duty was no longer mere 'superintendence' but, in the terms of the Butler Act, 'to promote the education of the people of England and Wales and the progressive development of institutions devoted to that purpose, and to secure the effective execution by local authorities *under his control and direction** of the national policy for providing a varied and comprehensive educational service in every area'. As Professor Griffith (1966, p. 98) has pointed out, such words to a foreign lawyer might seem an unambiguous statement of a highly centralised system. In fact they are not.

To begin with, the generality of these provisions, in particular the words in italics, are limited to the *specific* powers given to the secretary of state in subsequent sections. Secondly, his position is less dominant than the outline of his responsibilities would imply, because a large number of powers and duties are statutorily assigned to LEAs direct. It is true that in the exercise and performance of some of them LEAs have to obtain the approval of the secretary of state or work within regulations made by him. Nevertheless, their statutory possession of powers and duties allows LEAs much initiative and indeed discretion in the education service. The sharing of statutory responsibilities between local and central authorities means that the latter cannot be dictator. In some matters LEAs are able to defy the secretary of state.

An alternative scenario is conceivable. The minister, or secretary of state, could have been given complete executive responsibility for the education service, but with power to delegate certain functions to local authorities. In this case they would have been entirely his agents. The system would indeed have been highly centralised. Local authority discretion would have been strictly circumscribed and its potential for defiance slim or nonexistent. It is difficult for an agent to defy his prinicipal's authority.

The significance of the present system is that the secretary of state is *not* the source of the LEAs' authority. Parliament is. This is

* My italics.

not a mere legalistic quibble. In the short term the secretary of state
and his department have to work within the powers assigned by
Parliament, just as LEAs do. Both the DES and the LEAs can be
stopped by the courts if they act *ultra vires*. Indeed the constitutional
status of the DES and the LEAs is rather similar. Both owe their
creation and their powers and duties to the Queen in Parliament.
Thus the one cannot compel the other without specific power so to
do, received from that same Queen in Parliament.

Though the DES and the LEAs may be considered constitutional
equals, politically, of course, they are not. The DES is by far the
stronger. Not only does it already possess significant, specific
powers of control but in the long term it can add to them. The
secretary of state is almost always a member of a Government supported by a majority in the House of Commons. If he feels in need of
additional powers of control he will usually be able to persuade
his government colleagues to agree to a government Bill being
presented to Parliament and, given party discipline, he can expect
it to be enacted. Nevertheless this is by no means a simple process.
The Parliamentary timetable is today under heavy pressure and new
legislative commitments are not to be undertaken lightly. The secretary of state must feel the need of more power very keenly before
he will seek to add to Parliament's groaning burden. Moreover, in
the last decade, the apparent increasing volatility of the British
electorate has produced three changes of government in five elections, two paper-thin majorities and one stalemate. Thus it is by no
means certain that government bills will go through. The outstanding example is comprehensive education. A Labour Government
took a policy decision in 1965 that all LEAs should go comprehensive. After some years of struggle the Government decided that intransigent LEAs would have to be compelled by a change of law. A
Bill introduced to that effect lapsed, however, when Labour lost
the 1970 election. Thus ten years later the secretary of state *still* did
not have power to compel LEAs to introduce comprehensive reorganisation of their secondary schools. Another Bill was promised for
1976.

Education is, therefore, far from a totally centralised service. Substantial power and authority reside with the LEAs. Nevertheless the
central department wields enormous sway. Only perhaps in the
police and fire services has the central department a comparably
powerful role. The secretary of state's specific powers constitute a
formidable list. For instance he has to approve the establishment of
new schools and the closing of existing ones; he makes local education orders specifying the primary and secondary schools to be
maintained; he also makes regulations on special education, medi-

cal examinations and the standards of school buildings; he determines disputes between LEAS, and between LEAS and school managers or governors; he also arbitrates between LEAS and parents in school attendance controversies; he may authorise the compulsory purchase of land for educational purposes; he has default powers where LEA or school managers or governors fail to discharge their statutory duties.

He has too an extraordinary power to give directions where he is satisfied that any LEA or school managers or governors have acted or are proposing to act 'unreasonably' in respect of any of their powers or duties. Again this would appear to give him almost unlimited opportunity for intervention. In fact because there is a well-established legal doctrine of 'reasonableness' which interprets the term rather narrowly, this power is not of enormous significance and has been little used. While this power is less than it seems, the others compose a considerable armoury of controls.

To describe central controls is, however, to paint a very incomplete picture of central-local relations in the education service: first, because much of what flows from the centre is not a control or directive, and secondly because there is a considerable flow in the reverse direction.

Professor Griffith's conceptual framework (1966, pp. 515–28) for central departmental attitudes to local authorities has never been seriously challenged. He pointed out that the government departments are not an entirely homogeneous group. They have different buildings, often quite widely separated (remember the comparative physical remoteness of the DES); their staffs do not interchange much except at the highest levels; thus practices and attitudes develop which are peculiar to each department. Amongst these is a differing philosophy of local government.

Professor Griffith distinguished between broadly 'laissez-faire', 'regulatory' and 'promotional' philosophies. The first, typified by the old Ministry of Health, was a philosophy of as little intervention as possible in local government beyond the necessary fulfilment of departmental duties. The Ministry of Health did not itself carry out much research into the health and welfare services, did not often collect and disseminate the experience of local authorities, and imposed few controls over them. The second philosophy, regulatory, was characteristic of the Home Office and involved powerful departmental intervention *up to a point*. Minimum standards of performance by local authorities were strictly enforced but thereafter they were allowed wide discretion. The regulatory approach was characterised too by a considerable reliance upon inspection and the maintenance of a certain distance between the central department and the local authorities. In effect the regulatory philosophy was something of a middle way between laissez-faire and the last to be described, promotional. The DES was the clearest exponent of this philosophy. It involved on the part of the department a deep and unlimited interest in the whole service and a considerable involvement in much of it. The attitude was not to interfere as little as possible (laissez-faire) nor even just to uphold certain minimum standards (regulatory) but to promote every and any part of the service. This promotional orientation tended to be associated with substantial central control but it had other aspects too. The DES itself conducted or sponsored considerable research and experiment, even to the extent of building new schools or colleges itself to try out new ideas. Promotionalism also meant very close working relationships between the central department and the local authorities; the Inspectorate was not used as a buffer between central department and local authorities (as with the regulatory departments) but rather as an additional channel of communication.

While these differing attitudes arose partly, as was stressed, from the administrative individualism of government departments, other factors were also important such as the characteristics of the service. It was reasonable for a central department to be cautious in supervising a service at a fairly early stage of development like welfare; a department could be bolder with a longer established service like education. Similarly a service like the police by its very nature required a rather disciplinary approach from the centre. The degree of public interest could also be a factor. Education, attracting more intense and continuous interest than, say, the fire service or old people's homes, perhaps pushed the central department into a particularly activist stance.

This model of departmental attitudes seems eminently plausible and casts much light on central–local relations in the education service. Perhaps, though, it requires more elaboration than Professor Griffith was able to give it. It needs to be stressed that his three categories are not sharply distinct but rather a continuous spectrum. It would be useful too to build a dynamic element into the model; departments are not necessarily fixed in their attitudes to local government for all time; it seems for instance that the DES has dropped some of the more extreme manifestations of promotionalism. Perhaps one would want to emphasise more than Professor Griffith did that different parts of the same department can vary significantly in their philosophy. The DES is not as promotional in the youth service as in primary education.

The promotionalist analysis helps to explain why, despite the number of central controls, relations in the education service are not between a bullying, ogre-like DES and cringing, sullen LEAS. Naturally friction occurs, but on the whole the working relationships are close and mutually respectful.

Even promotionalism, however, does not tell the whole story of central–local relations in education. To it must be added a further vital ingredient – the flow of ideas from the LEAS to the DES. In technical fields, for instance, there were the famous developments in school building in the immediate post-war period associated particularly with Hertfordshire and Nottinghamshire. These were cheap and effective, suitable for areas with risk of subsidence and adaptable to industrialised building systems. Subsequently they were very widely adopted and strongly promoted by the department. In policy fields the best-known innovation was comprehensive education pioneered by a number of LEAS – the West Riding of Yorkshire, Leicestershire, Croydon and the LCC, to name only the most prominent. For decades certain local authorities were keen to develop comprehensive schools but were restrained by a reluctant department – a total reversal of current roles. Many other less well-known new developments emanating from the LEAS could be cited, from specially designed furniture for handicapped children to developments in educational television, from middle schools to the unification of sixth-form work and further education. As has been stressed, the department undertakes much research and development itself; by no means all the new ideas have been LEA-inspired. Nevertheless a very great deal has come from below. Indeed, the department has been particularly effective at picking up some promising development by an LEA and propagating it among others.

To sum up, therefore, the DES has much more power than the old, pre-war Board of Education, and more than most government departments today over their respective services. The DES is, however, characterised more by promotionalism, deep involvement in the service, than by a hierarchial, dictatorial determination to enforce its will – more like the chairman of a research group than a military commander. In any case there are substantial areas of education where no DES control exists, and it is no simple matter for the DES to increase its powers statutorily.

Partnership is a hackneyed term and does not fully convey the flavour of central–local relationships in education. Nevertheless no other term would do as well. The partners may not be equal; the DES is certainly far stronger politically, although the LEAS are not negligible political entities. The contribution of both is, however, equally indispensable and both sides know it. Though disputes may arise there is generally a consciousness of working together for the good of the service.

NOTES

1 The Board, set up under the Board of Education Act 1899, was composed of a President, the Lord President of the Council, HM Principal Secretaries of State, the First Lord of the Treasury and the Chancellor of the Exchequer.
2 See *Education*, Vol. 129, No. 3358 (2 June 1967), p. 1066.
3 The office of alderman was abolished by the Local Government Act 1972. Previously borough and county councils consisted three-quarters of councillors and one-quarter of aldermen. The latter were elected by the councillors from among their own number or from those eligible to be councillors. Aldermen had a six-year term of office as opposed to the three years of councillors. The GLC had aldermen too – hence Mr Chataway – but in a smaller proportion; six-sevenths of its members were councillors and one-seventh aldermen.
4 For an account of the political manœuvrings in 1973 when the new local authority associations attempted to demote the AEC see *The Times Educational Supplement*, No. 3066 (1 March 1974).
5 The Burnham Committees are concerned with the negotiation of national salary scales for teachers. (The name arises from Lord Burnham, 1862–1933, chairman of the first committee of LEA and teachers' representatives concerned with the subject.) Until the Second World War the machinery had no statutory force but the Butler Act required the Minister of Education to set up such committees and to appoint their chairman. Also the salary scales became mandatory on LEAs once approved by the minister. Remuneration of Teachers Acts in 1963 and 1965 extended the minister's (secretary of state's) powers. He now appoints, besides the chairman, other members to represent him; he determines which associations of teachers and local authorities shall be represented on the committees; and he arranges arbitration when the negotiations fail to reach agreement.

Chapter III

CLASSIFYING THE SCHOOLS

Schools may be classified in several different ways: on the basis of the ages of the children attending them, on the way in which they are controlled and financed, on whether they are single sex or co-educational, on whether they are open to all children in a particular area or selective in their admissions.

Before the 1944 Act the most important distinction was between elementary schools (providing basically instruction in the 'three Rs') and secondary schools (providing 'higher education', a wider range of subjects and at a more advanced level). All children had to attend elementary school from the age of 5 to the age of 14 unless they were transferred to a secondary school at about the age of 11, usually on the basis of a competitive examination. If transferred they had to remain in the secondary school to at least the age of 16 but could stay to 18.

All this was radically changed by the Butler Act. It provided that education should be organised in three separate, successive stages – primary, secondary and further. All children had to receive both primary education from the age of 5 to about 11 and secondary education from 11 to at least 15 and if desired to 18 or even 19. Further education, entirely optional, was full- or part-time education of persons over the compulsory school age (i.e. 15) of a vocational or recreational nature, other than in secondary schools. Nursery education, again not compulsory, was for children between the ages of 3 and 5. These provisions still fundamentally apply, except for the school-leaving age.

The Butler Act added one year to the period of compulsory schooling – 5 to 14 years under the old dispensation, 5 to 15 under the new. The Act included provision for the secretary of state to raise the upper limit to *16* years by Order in Council when satisfied that this was practicable. Sir Edward Boyle made such an Order in 1964 to come into effect in 1970/1; in 1967, however, the Labour Government deferred this as an economy measure until 1971/2. Mr Heath's Conservative Government imposed no further delay and the limit was then raised. There has been an acrimonious public debate on whether the net effect is beneficial or harmful to the children concerned, and whether the resources involved would have been better devoted to some other sector of the education service, say nursery education.

The basic distinction has thus become that between primary and secondary schools. Primary schools include infant schools for children from 5 to 7 years, and junior schools for those from 7 to 11 years. This is not, however, a statutory division and many primary schools take the whole range of children from 5 to 11 years.

The introduction of compulsory secondary education for all was one of the most important changes effected by the Butler Act. LEAs were, moreover, enjoined to provide this in separate secondary schools. The old elementary schools containing both junior and senior pupils were renamed 'all-age schools' and it became a top departmental priority to have these replaced as quickly as possible by separate primary and secondary schools. The latter are not all today straight 11 to 16 or 18 schools. A number of LEAs have divided their secondary schools to cover a smaller age range each. A growing favourite is the sixth-form college, a school for the 16- to 18-year-olds.

Until 1964 the statutory age of transfer from primary to secondary schools was between $10\frac{1}{2}$ and 12 years. In that year the secretary of state was empowered to approve the establishment of new schools with ages of transfer outside these limits. This was to allow experiments in new kinds of school, especially so-called 'middle' schools taking children from 8 to 12 or 9 to 13. Indeed, in 1966 the Plowden Committee recommended a new educational structure – 'first' schools taking children from 5 to 8, 'middle' schools 8 to 12, and 'secondary' schools over 12. The Government decided, however, to allow a period of experimentation before laying down a new structure.

Experimentation certainly occurred within a few years. Benn and Simon (1972) could list schools with twenty-one different age ranges: 5–11, 5–7, 8–11, 11–18, 11–15, 11–16, 5–12, 12–18, 12–16, 8–12, 9–12, 9–13, 10–13, 11–13, 12–14, 11–14, 13–15, 13–16, 13–18, 14–18 and 16–18. With the raising of the school-leaving age the 11–15 and 13–15 age ranges should have gone. Nevertheless even nineteen different age ranges is fair variety.

Today, therefore, while the basic difference between primary and secondary schools still obtains, a growing number of middle schools, straddling the two, have been established. Also, partly in consequence and partly independently, the age ranges of schools, especially secondary schools, are becoming increasingly heterogeneous.

The categorisation of schools on the basis of the way they are controlled and financed is more complex still.

Independent Schools

First there are the independent schools, wholly owned and financed privately, although subject to government inspection. A school wishing to be 'recognised as efficient' must provide certain minimum standards of accommodation, staffing and instruction. The vast majority of their pupils pay fees, although there are also some scholarships. They exist in all stages of education – nursery, primary and secondary – but the best-known are the preparatory schools and the perversely titled public schools. The former take children between the ages of 9 and 13 or 14, and 'prepare' them for entry to the public schools. The term 'public schools' is not only misleading, since of course they are privately controlled, but also vague since there is no universally agreed definition. It is applied by some to any independent, privately financed, secondary school. More often it is restricted to the independent boarding schools taking pupils from 14 to 18 or 19. An even narrower definition is to pick from the latter category only the most prominent – Eton and Harrow, Marlborough and Winchester, Roedean and Cheltenham Ladies College and the like. Three organisations of such schools restrict membership to those with the highest reputations – the Headmasters' Conference, the Association of Governing Bodies of Public Schools and the Association of Governing Bodies of Girls' Public Schools. The term 'public school' is sometimes restricted to their members. This was the definition adopted by the Public Schools Commission in 1968. In that year there were 273 such schools in England and Wales but over 1,000 other independent secondary schools and over 1,800 preparatory and pre-preparatory schools.

The possible integration of the independent schools with the publicly maintained schools, or at least the closer association of the two sectors, has been a preoccupation of educationalists for decades. Butler set up the Fleming Committee in July 1942 'To consider means whereby the association between the Public Schools . . . and the general educational system of the country could be developed and extended . . .'. The Committee produced unanimous proposals for both day and boarding schools. (The former are discussed in the next section on direct grant schools). For the latter the Committee recommended a scheme whereby schools would take at least 25 per cent of their pupils from grant-aided primary schools, some financed by government bursaries, some by LEAs. While many public schools were willing to try the scheme, the response of LEAs was unenthusiastic, partly because of the absence of criteria for determining which children should be sent and partly because of the cost of the fees. Subsequently many LEAS decided to help finance the attendance of *some* children at independent schools, usually in cases where boarding education was thought particularly suitable; the numbers of such subsidised children never approached, however, a quarter of those attending independent schools. Out of 138,000 boarding places in independent schools in 1968 20,000 (less than one seventh) were occupied by pupils wholly or partially subsidised by central or local government. A more sweeping scheme of integration was proposed by the Newsom Commission in 1968; all independent schools who wished to participate would have had to take eventually at least half their pupils from the state sector; these would have been chosen by LEAS entirely on the basis of 'boarding need' determined by social or academic criteria – adverse home conditions, peripatetic parents, no suitable school within daily reach and so on. A number of independent schools were prepared to accept the Newsom proposals but they also attracted much opposition. Many regarded them as effectively a way of subsidising independent schools at a time when other educational sectors were more deserving; the wisdom of sending children from abnormal home backgrounds to the peculiar atmosphere of the public schools was also questioned. 'To send children like this to Fettes, Rugby or Roedean is not just a bad solution to the children's problems; it is about the worst possible solution.'[1] The Government neither accepted nor rejected the Newsom scheme, but in practice it was quietly pigeonholed. Present economic circumstances appear to preclude its resurrection. Indeed a Labour Government today seems more likely to abolish than integrate the independent schools.

Direct Grant Schools

The direct grant schools occupy an intermediate position between the independent and local authority schools. LEAS play no part in their administration but unlike the independent schools they benefit from substantial government grants, received direct (hence their name). They first appeared in 1926 when all grant-aided schools were given the option of becoming wholly maintained or assisted by their LEA or of receiving government grant direct. A number chose the latter course. Provision for direct grant status was retained in the 1944 Act, although the number of such schools were reduced. In 1975 there were 331 direct grant schools: 7 technical schools, 20 nursery schools, 127 schools for handicapped children and 176 secondary schools (174 of them grammar schools). The direct grant grammar schools are the most significant, accounting for 90 per cent of the pupils in direct grant schools. Many of the direct grant grammar schools are denominational foundations; most of them have a very high academic reputation.

The basic feature of the direct grant schools is that, in return for the government grant, they have to offer a certain proportion of their places to LEA pupils. The Fleming Committee in 1944 proposed that a proportion of places at such schools be reserved and paid for by LEAs and that the remainder be paid for by parents on a sliding scale according to income with the government making up the difference between parental contributions and approved fees. A modification of the Fleming scheme was introduced in 1945. Each year direct grant schools must offer free places, numbering at least 25 per cent of their previous year's admissions, to children who have attended for at least two years a maintained or grant-aided primary school; the fees for the free place children are paid either by the LEA or by the governors or by an endowed foundation. In addition, they must offer a further 25 per cent 'reserved' places to the LEA which may fill them with any pupils irrespective of their previous education but in this case the LEA always pays the fees. The remaining places are known as 'residuary' and may be filled at the discretion of the governors.

Residuary pupils normally pay fees but about one third obtain partial or total remission on the basis of a scale of parental income approved by the secretary of state. The DES makes up the difference. In addition, the DES pays an annual capitation grant for every pupil aged between 11 and 19, plus a sixth-form grant for every pupil over 17 or who intends to take two subjects at advanced level in the General Certificate of Education. Allsopp and Grugeon (1966) estimated that about 75 per cent of the expenditure of the direct grant grammar schools came from local or central public funds; yet about 40 per cent of their pupils were in residuary places (i.e. private).

Despite their high academic standing, the direct grant grammar schools can be attacked as an unnecessarily complicating factor in the educational system. Since most of their pupils are day rather than boarding, in effect they form part of a local authority's educational system, but a part over which the LEA has little influence. This makes for particular problems where comprehensive reorganisation of secondary schools is planned. The direct grant grammar schools are also alleged to cream off a high proportion of the most able school children, to the intellectual impoverishment of the LEA's schools.

Absurd situations can also arise because of the dependence of direct grant schools upon LEA pupils. If, for instance, an LEA takes up fewer than the 25 per cent free places then the governors of the school have to fill *and pay for* the remaining free places themselves; this involves a loss of income which may well have to be met by raising the fees of other pupils. To avoid such financial repercussions LEAS are subject to considerable pressure from the schools, the parents and sometimes indeed the department, to take up at least the 25 per cent free places – even if they are not all needed! Saran (1967) describes how the Ministry of Education strongly urged Middlesex to lessen the severity of the reductions which the county proposed to make in the number of places they took up in direct grant schools. In consequence Middlesex retained more than they needed, and found themselves with empty places in their own grammar schools.

In 1970 the Donnison Commission recommended that direct grant status be phased out. It was divided about what should replace it. Eight commissioners wanted the schools to choose one of the existing varieties of locally maintained status. Seven commissioners wanted a new 'full grant' status whereby schools willing to be fully integrated with their LEA system would receive up to 100 per cent subsidy to cover approved debts and future capital expenditure. Four commissioners were happy with either approach. All agreed that direct grant schools should have the option of full independence. The Donnison Report was published during the last months of a Labour Government, and the succeeding Conservative Government buried it. The return of a Labour Government in 1974 sounded, however, the death knell of the direct grant schools. The Labour Secretary of State, Mr Reg Prentice, announced his intention of abolishing direct grant status.[2] His successor, Mr Frederick Mulley, laid regulations before Parliament in July 1975 under which government grants were halted for pupils admitted after September 1976. Despite a storm of protest from the schools themselves, supported by the Conservative Opposition, the Labour Government held to this policy. The direct grant schools were compelled to choose between complete independence and integration in the publicly maintained sector. Most of the fifty-five Roman Catholic direct grant grammar schools decided on the latter, switching to voluntary aided status (see the next section). This was, however, a minority reaction. More than 100 direct grant grammar schools opted for complete independence.

County and Voluntary Schools

Primary and secondary schools which are wholly owned and maintained by an LEA (other than nursery or special schools) are known as 'county' schools. The term is not altogether a happy one since, as has been explained, the counties are not the only LEAS; there are also the metropolitan districts and, in London, the outer London boroughs and the ILEA. Yet in every case their schools are technically 'county' schools. In view of its ambiguity the term will be avoided hereafter and such schools described instead as 'LEA schools'.

LEAs also help to finance and to run schools which they do not own. Such schools are known as voluntary schools and are in most cases the property of a religious denomination. The LEA schools and the voluntary schools are together called the 'maintained' schools since LEAs are responsible for the maintenance of both. There are three kinds of voluntary school: voluntary controlled, voluntary aided and voluntary special agreement. These categories reflect varying degrees of LEA control in return for varying amounts of financial assistance.

Where a voluntary school is granted controlled status the LEA assumes complete financial responsibility for its maintenance although ownership remains with the original foundation. The LEA appoints two thirds of the governors or managers and the original foundation only one third. All teachers are appointed by the LEA and none may be dismissed without its consent, but the governors or managers must be given an opportunity to make representations about the proposed appointee to the post of head teacher. The appointment and dismissal of caretakers and cleaners are also the responsibility of the LEA. The *foundation* managers or governors may determine how the school premises, including the playing fields, are used on Sundays; *all* the governors or managers have the same discretion in respect of Saturdays except where the premises are required by the school itself or by the LEA for some educational or child welfare purpose. On other days the LEA controls the occupation and use of the premises.

The parents of any pupils attending a controlled school may request that their children receive religious instruction in accordance with the persuasion to which the school adhered before it became controlled. If there is no such parental request religious instruction is in accordance with the 'agreed syllabus' (explained in Chapter IV). Where the teaching staff exceeds two it must include persons (called reserved teachers) competent to give denominational religious instruction; they are appointed by the LEA in consultation with the foundation managers or governors, who have a veto power over such appointments; they may also request the dismissal of reserved teachers. Not more than one fifth of the teaching staff may be reserved teachers; the head teacher must never be one.

Voluntary controlled schools are thus, as their name suggests, effectively controlled by their LEAs. Indeed, with the exception of religious instruction, they are almost indistinguishable from LEA schools. Controlled school status was an invention of the Butler Act and was undoubtedly a good one. Many voluntary bodies were quite unable to meet even a proportion of the cost of upkeep of their schools. The new status offered complete relief from the financial burden and yet allowed the voluntary bodies to retain a certain influence in the government of the school, especially as regards religious instruction. Nevertheless, since controlled status involves a transfer of effective control it has never been acceptable to Roman Catholic authorities. There are no Roman Catholic controlled schools, although there are Anglican, Methodist and others.

Roman Catholic authorities have, however, been able to accept voluntary *aided* status, because no substantial loss of effective control is involved. Two thirds of the managers or governors of an aided school must be foundation members. The governors or managers appoint the head teacher and assistant teachers although the LEA normally has to be satisfied as to their educational suitability; the LEA can also require the dismissal of a teacher, or can prohibit such a dismissal except in the case of religious instruction teachers; the LEA fixes the total number of teaching staff. The managers or governors similarly appoint all non-teaching staff (except those involved in school meals provision) but the LEA determines their number and conditions of service. The managers or governors have complete control of the occupation and use of the school, except that the LEA may direct them to provide free accommodation on a weekday for some education or children's welfare purpose, as long as it is not needed for a school purpose.

Secular instruction is under the control of the LEA in an aided *primary* school but of the governors in an aided *secondary* school. Religious instruction in both is in the charge of the managers or governors and must be in accordance with the provisions of the trust deed or the school's practice before it acquired voluntary aided status. Parents may, however, request some provision of instruction on the basis of the 'agreed syllabus'; if no other school in the reasonable vicinity could provide it their request must be met.

The financial arrangements for aided schools are particularly interesting. The LEA pays for the maintenance and repair of the *interior* of the school buildings and for all other educational expenditure, e.g. teachers' salaries; the managers or governors must pay for the upkeep of the *exterior* of the school buildings, and for any improvements inside or out. The managers or governors receive, however, a substantial grant direct from the government in respect of their expenses. The Butler Act fixed this at 50 per cent but it was increased to 75 per cent in 1959 and to 80 per cent in 1967 – not without protest from some quarters.[3]

What was already a generous settlement under the Butler Act has therefore been made exceedingly so. Short of completely subsidising voluntary schools (in which case every denomination and group could legitimately claim the provision of schools) it is hard to see how much farther the government could go. For only marginal loss of control, the voluntary body has only to find 20 per cent of the cost of external maintenance and of improvements. Most aided schools are denominational but there are a handful of no particular persuasion.

The final category of voluntary school is the special agreement school; this dates back to 1936. Although from 1902 the LEAs had been responsible for financing the maintenance of voluntary schools, the *capital* cost of improvements in many cases was beyond the capacity of voluntary school managers or governors. To provide some relief for these difficulties the Education Act 1936 allowed LEAs to contribute between 50 and 70 per cent of the cost of building new voluntary schools or making major improvements to existing ones. In return LEAs obtained some control over the government of the school, especially the appointment of teachers. The details of these arrangements were contained in agreements between the LEAs and the voluntary bodies – hence the title 'special agreement schools' – which had to be made within a specified period and approved by the Board of Education.

The Butler Act allowed LEAs to resuscitate existing agreements or enter into new ones, again within a limited period and subject to ministerial approval. New special agreement schools are rarely established today.

Special agreement schools are, in effect, an intermediate category between controlled and aided schools. As with aided schools, the managers or governors have to pay for exterior maintenance and for any improvements, in respect of which they now received a direct 80 per cent government grant; as provided in the agreement they also receive a grant from their LEA towards the erection of the school or substantial improvements (although they cannot receive money from both LEA and government in respect of the same improvement); in addition the LEA pays for the upkeep of the interior of the premises and for other education expenses.

Again as with aided schools, two thirds of the managers or governors are foundation members. The managers or governors control religious instruction which must be in accordance with the trust deed or denominational tradition of the school although parents can ask for the 'agreed syllabus' to be taught.

Special agreement schools also, however, resemble controlled schools in certain respects. The teachers are appointed by the LEA; reserved teachers competent to give denominational religious instruction must be appointed in consultation with the managers or governors; the number of reserved teachers is, however, laid down in the agreements, rather than restricted to one fifth of the teaching staff.

Special agreement status is another illustration of the British genius for complexity. There would seem no overwhelming reason for its perpetuation. The distinction between aided and controlled schools is comprehensible; but provision could be made for aided schools to qualify in certain circumstances for capital grants without the creation of a separate category of school.

The Comprehensive Controversy

Government aid to denominationally controlled schools has not proved a major issue in post-war Britain – partly at least because of the skill of Butler's 1944 settlement. Instead education has been dominated by a debate which few foresaw to be a matter of major contention in 1944, the organisation of secondary education. The issue in brief is whether the secondary schools should be divided into categories and pupils assigned between them on the basis of ability, or whether there should be a common type of secondary school (the comprehensive school) attended by all.

At first the former principle was almost universally applied. On government advice most LEAs adopted a tripartite division of their secondary schools: grammar, technical and modern. The grammar schools, inheriting a long-established tradition, concentrated on providing the highest level academic education designed primarily to fit children for university or the professions. Some grammar schools were ancient foundations but local authorities had greatly expanded their number in the twentieth century. The technical schools were fewer in number and more recent in educational tradition. The growth of institutions providing technical training for teenagers or adults in the second half of the nineteenth century led to a demand for schools to equip young people to enter these institutions. Local authorities were first specifically empowered to provide technical education by the Technical Instruction Act 1889 but most technical schools were not founded until the twentieth century. They were often attached to some higher level institution and were consequently termed junior technical colleges or junior commercial colleges; there were also various trade schools, including nautical training schools, and junior art departments attached to colleges of art. Most were transformed into technical schools after 1944. The technical schools thus were traditionally educating young people for the crafts or for skilled manual work especially in the engineering and construction industries. The third type of school, the modern school, was newer still. The growing desire to give special instruction to older children in elementary schools led occasionally to the establishment of separate schools for them. This movement received some impetus from the emphasis on advanced instruction in the Education Act 1921 and even more from the recommendations of the Hadow Committee. Most of those existing in 1944 had been founded in the late 1920s and 1930s; they were often termed 'senior' or 'central' as well as 'modern' schools but after 1944 the latter became the accepted appellation. Their purpose was to provide a general education embracing both academic and practical subjects. (In 1944 there were still many elementary schools with senior pupils and it became a top government priority to replace these 'all age' schools by separate primary and secondary schools.)

It was always emphasised that the grammar, technical and modern schools were not designed as a hierarchy of excellence; they were to be regarded as of equal status but serving differing ends. *The Nation's Schools*, a government pamphlet issued in 1945, explained: 'These three broad types, now at very different stages of development, are intended to meet the differing needs of differing pupils.' Nevertheless it was just as a hierarchy of excellence that the three kinds of school came to be regarded. Entry to the grammar schools was usually on the basis of a competitive examination for primary school leavers (the 11-plus examination) and to technical schools by a similar examination, usually at the age of 13; those who passed neither naturally tended to think of themselves, and to be thought of, as also-rans. Since grammar school places were available for only about 20 per cent, and technical school places about 5 per cent, of those completing primary education, this left roughly three-quarters of the school population to feel themselves to be failures. Moreover, since many LEAs contained no technical schools, for much of the country the system was effectively bipartite; this made even sharper the segregation between grammar school sheep and modern school goats.

This situation provoked growing opposition in the 1950s and 1960s. Parental anxiety became widespread. Educationists atttacked the system for containing too many barriers and for being insufficiently adaptable to the needs of the modern world. Doubts were thrown on the accuracy of the 11-plus examination (based usually on intelligence tests) as a means of selecting children with higher academic potential. Egalitarians attacked the system as elitist. The demand grew for the abolition of all selection and the establishment of a single structure of comprehensive secondary schools for all.

This demand became identified with the Labour Party, but the concept of one kind of school for all can be traced back far earlier both in Britain and abroad (see for instance, Halsall, 1973). Indeed the Labour Party only gradually took up the idea. Rodney Barker (1972) argues that Labour education policy was not primarily derived from basic socialist principles but was a response to the social and economic opportunities its members had experienced. 'The chief desire which emerged in the party's approach to education was not for the destruction of the old order . . . but for the broader dissemination of a tradition which, by and large, was accepted, envied and admired.' When therefore the case for common schools for all children over 11 was first presented in Labour Party circles by the Bradford ILP in 1929 and the National Association of Labour Teachers in 1930, the party was not immediately won over. Labour interest in such schools was indeed probably roused more by the Spens Report of 1938 which discussed but rejected them except on an experimental basis. There was, indeed still is, substantial pro-grammar school feeling in the Labour Party and in the 1930s and, for some time thereafter, priority was accorded to improving access to grammar schools, for instance by abolishing fees. While, therefore, the multilateral school (as the common secondary school was then termed) was much discussed in the Labour Party in the late 1930s and 1940s, when the party came to power in 1945 it was still far from united behind the concept.

The Butler Act did not lay down any particular form of secondary school structure (perhaps because of pressure from the Labour Party on their coalition partners); the tripartite system was not thus entrenched in law. The White Paper, *Educational Reconstruction*, which preceded the Act, however, set out grammar, modern and technical schools as the expected norm, though the tone was moderate and flexible. 'It would be wrong to suppose that they will necessarily remain separate and apart. Different types may be combined in one building or on one site as considerations of convenience and efficiency may suggest. In any case the free interchange of pupils from one type of education to another must be facilitated.' The Norwood Report which followed hard on the heels of the White Paper had a less pliant approach. The tripartite system was forcefully expounded as the most appropriate organisation of secondary education; there was only grudging acceptance of the possibility of experimentation with combined grammar and modern schools and denial that technical schools could ever be included too. (Even the Norwood Committee, however, stressed the importance of easy interchangeability of pupils between types of school, at least up to the age of 13. In practice interchanges proved far from easy.) The Norwood proposals were in general accepted by the Government and in *The Nation's Schools*, 1945, it set out the tripartite system in detail.

The two Labour Ministers of Education in the Attlee administrations of 1945 to 1951, Ellen Wilkinson and George Tomlinson, did not stray far from the Norwood approach. Despite vociferous criticism from some members of their party, they applied the tripartite or bipartite system as the norm for secondary education. They permitted some limited experimentation with multilateral or bilateral schools where the LEA was taken keen to try them out. Thus the first trickle of comprehensive secondary schools appeared, notably in London and Coventry, but alongside selective schools; a fairly bold scheme by Middlesex to reorganise six secondary schools on comprehensive lines was, however, pruned by the Labour Government. In 1951 Labour suffered electoral defeat. Subseqeuently, according to Barker (1972), 'A Conservative administration applied in an open and single-minded fashion the policy which Tomlinson had pursued with a measure of confusion.' This policy was to preserve the grammar schools but to allow some building of comprehensive schools. By 1951, however, the Conservatives had become somewhat more hostile to comprehensive education. During the next thirteen years LEAs wishing to establish comprehensive schools had to press very hard for departmental permission which was by no means always forthcoming, even when no closure of grammar schools was envisaged.

As Conservative policy hardened, so did Labour in the opposite direction. The last years of the Attlee Government were marked by mounting criticism of its education policy from within the party. A conference resolution in 1950 called for implementation of comprehensive education and a year later the National Executive Committee published *A Policy For Secondary Education* condemning the tripartite system and proposing wholesale comprehensive reorganisation. Thus in 1951 as the Labour Party relinquished office it became for the first time fully and publicly committed to comprehensive reorganisation of secondary education. Disagreements were to persist about timing and methods. At the local level enthusiasm amongst party members for comprehensive education was to remain very variable. Nevertheless the overall goal was determined.

Labour returned to office in 1964 and eight months later the Secretary of State for Education and Science, Mr Anthony Crosland, issued Circular 10/65: perhaps the most famous, or infamous, ever issued – certainly the only one to become widely known and referred to well outside educational circles. The Circular announced the Government's objective of ending selection at 11-plus and of eliminating separatism in secondary education, and 'requested' LEAS to submit to him plans for reorganising their secondary schools on comprehensive lines. The Circular set out six varieties of comprehensive organisation for LEAS to bear in mind. A year later Circular 10/66 announced that no school building would be permitted which was not designed to fit reorganisation.

The Labour Government's move was hamstrung by two secret decisions which it took then but which only emerged later: no *additional* building programme allocation was to be made to encourage reorganisation and no new legislation would be introduced to compel reorganisation. The policy was to be implemented largely by persuasion. It was far from unsuccessful. The majority of LEAS decided to toe the Government's line, with attitudes ranging from enthusiasm to reluctant acquiescence. Many LEAS already had some comprehensive schools or had schemes in the pipeline, but Circular 10/65 was a major catalyst to action. In five years the number of comprehensive schools jumped from 189 to 1,145. Nevertheless, the defenders of grammar schools often contested an LEA decision to reorganise on comprehensive lines and impassioned local conflicts were frequent. Also a minority of LEAS decided to resist the Government.

The disputes were not always a simple Labour versus Conservative confrontation. Many Conservative parents were strong opponents of the 11-plus examination. Many Labour parents were unhappy about destroying the grammar schools. Some Conservative-controlled LEAS concurred with Government policy, albeit sometimes reluctantly. Some Labour-controlled LEAS were far from single minded in their support. Batley, O'Brien and Parris (1970), for instance, show how comprehensive reorganisation in Darlington was hindered because two leading Labour members of the council (the chairman of the education committee and the party group leader) were hostile to comprehensive schools. In Barnet comprehensive reorganisation plans were the subject of a protracted dispute largely because the ruling Conservative group was deeply split on the issue. The most dramatic dispute of all was, however, on party lines. Enfield Borough Council, Labour controlled by a small majority, tried to rush through comprehensive reorganisation before the 1968 London borough elections in which the Conservatives were expected to recapture the borough (as they did). The secretary of state also expedited his approval. On application by some Enfield Grammar School parents however, the courts ruled that insufficient time had been given to consider parental representations and the process had to be deferred. Perhaps the worst blow to Labour hopes was, however, the Conservative swing in the municipal elections of 1967 and 1968. A number of the LEAs captured by the Conservatives, for instance Liverpool, Bexley, Walsall, ILEA, withdrew or modified comprehensive reorganisation plans which had previously been submitted.

Eventually the Labour Government decided that legislation would after all be necessary to compel the intransigent LEAs. Benn and Simon (1972) claim that 'The failure to grasp the nettle in 1965 can be traced in part to political naivety and under-preparation by the Labour party of the necessary strategy for implementing a comprehensive school policy, but also in part to a departmental naivety in assuming that education should or could be non-controversial in this day'. When the Bill did appear some protagonists of comprehensive schools found it disappointingly mild. It would have required LEAs to have regard to the need to abolish selective schools in any reorganisation plan and empowered the secretary of state to require the preparation of reorganisation plans. In any case, as was mentioned earlier, the June 1970 election killed the Bill.

The new Conservative Secretary of State, Mrs Margaret Thatcher, as one of her first acts announced, in Circular 10/70, her withdrawal of Labour Circulars 10/65 and 10/66. Her policy was not to impose any form of secondary organisation but to permit local variation basically according to the wishes of the LEAs. They could opt to go comprehensive, to remain selective or to adopt a mix of both. Yet LEAs were often forbidden to incorporate grammar schools in comprehensive schemes, and some would argue that such prohibition undermined the validity of the schemes. The overall effect of Mrs Thatcher's regime was to slow the rate of comprehensive reorganisation.

The electoral pendulum swung again, albeit hesitantly, and Mr Wilson and his Labour colleagues returned to power in 1974. Mr Reg Prentice, appointed Secretary of State for Education, quickly made clear his passionate commitment to comprehensive reorganisation and his determination to implement it with all expedition. Within two months of taking up his duties he issued Circular 4/74, heavily reminiscent of Circular 10/65, but with a sterner tone. LEAs were required to submit plans for full comprehensive reorganisation to the DES by the end of 1974 if they had not already done so, and were given the choice of only three varieties – the all-through 11 to 18 school, 11 to 16 schools plus separate sixth-form colleges, and 8 to 12 or 9 to 13 middle schools plus separate schools for senior pupils. The Circular was sent not just to LEAs but significantly also to the managers and governors of voluntary aided and direct grant schools thus indicating Mr Prentice's determination to achieve comprehensive reorganisation throughout the publicly maintained sector. His decision to abolish the direct grant schools emanated from the same determination.

He announced his willingness to use his control over building programmes to secure the co-operation of LEAS. He also threatened voluntary aided schools with loss of their status and their public funds if they resisted comprehensive reorganisation (in a speech to the NUT conference at Eastbourne in April 1974).

Despite such tough tactics, seven LEAS – Bexley, Buckinghamshire, Essex, Kingston upon Thames, Redbridge, Trafford and Sutton – openly refused to comply. Others dragged their feet or produced schemes unacceptable to the Government. Eventually the Labour Government decided that it would need new powers to enforce its will. Legislation was promised in the Queen's Speech of 19 November 1975. The Conservative Opposition, in particular their Shadow spokesman Mr Norman St John Stevas, threw their weight behind the grammar schools and the resisting LEAS. In the long run, however, unless an election intervenes there can only be one outcome to the struggle.

Some fear that the controversy about comprehensive schools has done educational damage but there is little evidence to justify such fears. No doubt sudden changes of policy can be unsettling but one suspects that the majority of staff and pupils quickly adjust to new circumstances. In any case the frequency of changes can be exaggerated; by no means all LEAS changed political masters and even where they did it was usually at intervals of three years or longer. Moreover where genuine ideological differences exist a liberal democracy can hardly avoid a certain to-ing and fro-ing (as in nationalisation, taxation policy and so on). Comprehensive schools understandably appeal to the egalitarian principles of the Labour Party. The retention of grammar schools naturally strikes a responsive chord with Conservatives, with their disposition to preserve what is good.

There is a certain ambiguity about the concept of the comprehensive school. On the one hand it is that of the common or neighbourhood school, the one which all children attend. On the other hand the concept is of a heterogeneous school containing pupils of diverse academic levels and from mixed social backgrounds, and offering courses of all kinds; this is perhaps closer to the old concept of the multilateral school, one embracing grammar, technical and modern streams. The neighbourhood school and the heterogeneous school are not necessarily the same thing. Some neighbourhoods may be very homogeneous socially, perhaps even ethnically, and would thus produce a very unmixed body of pupils. To produce a heterogeneous school in such circumstances would necessitate measures such as Haringey's 'banding' or even American-style 'bussing' which destroy the neighbourhood concept. On the whole the neighbourhood concept of comprehensive education is the one most widely accepted in Britain, perhaps because the catchment areas of most secondary schools are thought to be reasonably heterogeneous.

By the end of 1974 there were 2,273 comprehensive secondary schools in England and Wales; there were also 909 middle schools (usually associated with a comprehensive scheme). In 1964 the figures were respectively 195 and nil. Over the same decade grammar schools halved in number from 1,226 to 675.

The dispute about comprehensive schools is a remarkable chapter in British educational history, and as yet an uncompleted one. In duration, in depth of feeling, in involvement of the public it perhaps surpasses even the turn-of-century conflict about church schools. Moreover, it throws interesting light on many facets of the political process, for instance the way political parties become committed to a policy. More important from the viewpoint of this book, it is illuminating about central–local relationships in the education service. It is clear that LEAs of any political persuasion are disposed to follow a strong lead from the DES but that, where they feel unable to, even a determined secretary of state has great difficulty in securing compliance. Despite the battery of financial and legal powers he possesses, an adamant LEA is no mean opponent.

NOTES

1 The *Guardian*, 7 September 1968, editorial.
2 *HC Deb.*, Vol. 888, No. 85 (11 March 1975), cols 271–8.
3 See, for instance, 'Freedom to Disbelieve' by Lena Jeger in the *Guardian*, 1 November 1966.

Chapter IV

RUNNING THE SCHOOLS

At least eight different parties are or may be involved in running a school: the local education authority, other local authorities, the governors or managers, the head teacher, the other teachers, the pupils, the parents and, of course, the central government either through its emissaries, especially HMIS, or through the law (prescribing for instance what may be taught). For a maintained school, the LEA and the head teacher are undoubtedly the twin pinnacles of power, with managers or governors a poor third. For voluntary aided, direct grant and independent schools the managers or governors loom much larger.

Decisions taken in the running of a school range of course from the broadest policy to the narrowest, day-to-day matters. Each of the eight parties tends to focus on different parts of this spectrum, although there is some overlap of responsibility and their respective roles are not very precisely defined. The local education authorities, for instance, are somewhat airily enjoined by the Butler Act to provide schools 'sufficient in number, character and equipment to afford for all pupils opportunity for education offering such variety of instruction and training as may be desirable in view of their different ages, abilities, and aptitudes'. The dominant role of the LEAS in the running of the maintained schools flows not from any statutory enumeration of powers but rather from their fundamental position as the bodies responsible for the whole system. They are limited only by departmental powers to override them in a few instances (e.g. on admissions) and by some legal stipulations (e.g. on religious instruction). They are also the paymasters. While some money comes from the government, all is channelled (for maintained schools) through the LEAS. They have to sign the cheques to pay for the salaries, the fuel and telephone bills, the books and equipment and so on. Clearly this provides them with an enormous *potential* lever over the running of schools. In practice LEAS do not exploit their legal and financial authority to the full; the conduct of their schools is shared with the other parties mentioned above.

Nonetheless, if they wished, LEAs could wield more power than they do.

The Head Teacher

The power of the head teacher rests by contrast less on legal authority and more on entrenched tradition. True the articles of government and rules of management (discussed below) for each school describe the functions of the head teacher, but usually in rather general terms. In any case, his or her hegemony can extend well beyond them. Both inside and outside schools there is a cultural acceptance, indeed expectation, that the head teacher will be a dominant figure. Naturally much depends on his personality, inclinations and skill as to the degree of autocracy wielded. Also there is some variation between types of school; voluntary school heads tend to be more powerful than maintained school heads, and secondary than primary. Nevertheless the pattern set by the nineteenth-century public school headmasters is deeply ingrained in the British educational tradition and has percolated through the whole system. The head teacher exercises particular sway over the pupils and the teaching staff. Ronald King (1970, pp. 94, 95) has summarised the position as follows:

'The head teacher's control over his assistant teachers extends through time and space. He may decide which teacher takes which group of pupils at a particular time in a particular place. He usually has a most important part in selecting his staff. He may initiate the proceedings that lead to the dismissal of a teacher. No such formal mechanism exists in maintained schools for teachers to initiate a movement to get rid of a head teacher. Even the official route for communications with the governors or managers is through the head teacher. He may affect the pupil/teacher relationship in the formal learning situation by the way he allocates money for books and apparatus. In this way he may encourage or discourage educational experiments which require some capital outlay. He may directly affect the pupil/teacher relationship by actually entering classrooms, interrupting and taking over lessons. He may sit silently at the back of the classroom, or simply look through the door . . . he is also in a position to influence a teacher's career prospects. This is not only referring to his distribution of allowances for special responsibility and positions of heads of department, but also to the influence he has on the careers of his teachers when they leave, or attempt to leave, for other schools. A testimonial from the teacher's present head is sometimes obligatory when seeking a new post. . . . His authority over [his pupils] is wide in scope and very pervasive. He may control their actions in most spheres of their activities, at any time they are within the school. He may use his power to regulate the length of their hair, where they may whistle or walk, even the colour of their underwear. His control may extend beyond the school, and outside of school hours. He may forbid the use of certain bus stops, purchases from certain shops, the removal of a school cap until a pupil reaches his front door.'

This does not exhaust the head teacher's powers. LEAs allocate each of their schools a lump sum, often in the form of a capitation allowance (i.e. an amount for each pupil), to be spent on books, equipment, perhaps even minor repairs. The head teacher is usually responsible for spending this sum; even where his responsibility is formally shared, his voice is invariably the most powerful.

The Other Teachers, the Parents and the Pupils

The dominant position of the head teacher is criticised by those who would like to see some of the other parties have more say in the running of schools – the other teachers, the parents, even the pupils. Indeed in some schools there are moves in this direction. Any significant erosion of the head's position is still, however, rare.

The NUT has shown increasing concern that teaching staff should participate in the running of schools. The 1971 NUT conference passed a resolution calling for the preparation of draft constitutions for staff councils in schools. Three years later a more strongly worded conference resolution called for mandatory consultation of teaching staff. The NUT's ultimate objective is more than consultation; it is to secure the participation of all the teachers in decision making. The head teacher would be expected to accept and implement the joint decisions of all the staff. His role would be more that of a chairman.

In larger schools head teachers already necessarily delegate more, especially to heads of departments, but this can simply create an oligarchy in place of an autarchy. To involve all staff more far-reaching arrangements are necessary. There are many possibilities: monthly or termly meetings of all staff to decide or express views on certain matters, staff working parties or committees on special subjects like finance or the curriculum, staff councils or academic boards elected by all the teachers as consultative or decision-making organs, or combinations of all of these. In the larger secondary schools at least there is an increasing trend to innovate on these lines – see, for instance, Valerie Perry (1974).

Pupils have had much less success with similar demands. Various small, usually radical, groups of pupils have appeared, like the

Schools Action Union in 1969; this staged an unsuccessful strike of schoolchildren in May 1972. A less ephemeral body, the National Union of School Students, achieved some respectability when invited to give evidence to a Parliamentary Select Committee; indeed its evidence seems to have had some effect since the Committee recommended in its report *Education Maintenance Allowances* (1974), that local authorities pay £1·30 pocket money per week to every pupil staying at school beyond the age of 16. Apart from demands for the abolition of corporal punishment, school uniforms and the like, these groups also press for more pupil participation in running schools. Some schools have established pupil councils, or provided for pupil representation on general school councils. There has been the odd appointment of a pupil to a school board of governors but of this more anon. In general, though, pupil power has not achieved much acceptance.

By contrast lip service has long been paid to parents' rights. The Butler Act states 'so far as is compatible with the provision of efficient instruction and training and the avoidance of unreasonable public expenditure pupils are to be educated in accordance with the wishes of their parents'. In the past parent power has been most in evidence in the choice of school for their children. LEAs try hard to select the school which the parents prefer but this is not always possible; a sprinkling of disputes is reported in the press each year. Parents can appeal to the secretary of state if dissatisfied with the school their child is allocated to. In 1972 a Staffordshire family even renounced their religion in an attempt to have their child sent to a non-denominational rather than a Roman Catholic school but the secretary of state upheld the county's decision to allocate him to the latter.[1]

When it comes to running schools, parents have generally been kept firmly at arm's length. While the NUT has long favoured the appointment of parents to school governing bodies (as in their policy statement *Into the 70's,* 1969), the involvement of parents in day-to-day administration or academic decisions would be quite unacceptable to most British teachers;[2] they are horrified at the degree of parental control which operates in many American schools. To some extent this is the resistance to lay interference common to all professionals but made more vehement in the case of teachers because they are less confident of their professionalism than, say, doctors or engineers. Parent–teacher associations (PTAs), where they exist, are traditionally arrangements for telling parents about the school's activities, or possibly for raising funds for some new facility like a swimming pool, but not to provide a channel of influence over what goes on in a school.

There are signs of some change. Parents have in the last decade been encouraged to become better informed and more active in education by such bodies as the Advisory Centre for Education (ACE) and the Confederation for the Advancement of State Education (CASE), as its name suggests a national grouping of local Associations for the Advancement of State Education. Moreover in 1967 a Home and School Council was formed jointly by ACE, CASE and the National Association of Parent–Teacher Associations to promote the acceptance of parents as full partners in the educational system. Publications guiding parents on how to become effectively involved in schools appear with increasing frequency, like Bagnall (1974). Perhaps most significant of all the major political parties have begun to make sympathetic noises about parental involvement in schools. Recent Labour Party publications, such as *Labour's Programme for Britain* (1973, p. 76), mention the need to make managing and governing bodies more representative of parents (as well as staff and students). The Conservatives have gone even further. Their party manifesto for the October 1974 election, *Putting Britain First*, included a charter of parents' rights, a set of specific pledges to increase parental power in education – mandatory representation on boards of governors or managers, improved appeal arrangements for school selection disputes, strengthening of the legal obligation to take account of parents' wishes, providing facilities for schools to publish prospectuses and other information for parents to read. All this is having some effect. In particular parental appointments to school manager or governor are becoming more common.

There has been much recent discussion of the voucher system under which parents would receive an annual cash voucher for each of their school-age children equivalent to the cost to the State of their education. Parents would be free to spend the voucher at maintained or private schools as they wished. If this system were introduced, and it is not totally inconceivable, parental influence over schools would be dramatically increased, as Boyson (1972) stresses.

School Management and Government

School managers and governors are peculiar to England and Wales. Not only are they virtually unknown overseas, but even in Scotland are confined to the independent schools.[3] Their presence reflects the long English tradition that each school should have a measure of autonomy and more recent (nineteenth-century) pressure for community involvement in school government. Howell (1967) and Baron and Howell (1968 and 1974) have produced a wealth of material on school management and government and their findings are drawn upon in the account which follows.

Government assistance to the voluntary societies' elementary schools in England and Wales became dependent by the mid-nineteenth century on their being properly managed by trustees. The school boards set up after 1870, however, generally departed from the precedent set by the voluntary societies; save for London and Liverpool, most did not appoint boards of managers for their elementary schools. When in 1902 the local authorities took over the responsibilities of the school boards, they were not obliged to appoint boards of managers (except where schools were provided by counties), although some did. Thus immediately prior to the 1944 Education Act all voluntary elementary schools and some LEA elementary schools had boards of trustees or managers.

In secondary education the tradition was stronger. The public schools set a pattern of powerful headmasters and boards of governors which was eventually imitated by the LEAs. The Public Schools Commission 1861–4 examining the nine major public schools, and the Schools Inquiry Commission 1864–8 examining the five or six hundred endowed and proprietary schools, made careful recommendations about the role of governing bodies; their principles have strongly influenced subsequent thinking about school government in both the private and the local authority sectors.

When empowered by the 1902 Education Act to establish their own secondary schools, many LEAs gave them boards of governors to demonstrate that they would have something of the status of the public schools, in particular a measure of autonomy. The Board of Education later made the existence of a governing body a condition for the payment of grant, and in 1908 issued a *Model Article of Government for Secondary Schools*. When direct grant schools were created in 1926 they had to be provided with a governing body because of their independence from LEA control. By 1944, therefore, all voluntary and direct grant secondary schools and most LEA secondary schools had boards of governors.

Boards of managers or governors were made mandatory for all schools by the Education Act 1944. This provision was largely, thus, an entrenchment of the existing tradition. In the case of voluntary schools (especially the new category of voluntary controlled) it was also a means of ensuring adequate representation of denominational interests.

The Education Act 1944 lays down that all primary schools must have boards of managers and all secondary schools boards of governors. The constitution of the body of managers or governors is contained respectively in instruments of management or government made by order of the LEA in the case of LEA schools, and of the secretary of state in the case of voluntary schools. The Local Government Act 1972 prescribes that in the non-metropolitan counties one third of the managers of a maintained primary (but not secondary) school must be appointed by the relevant parish or parishes (or community or parish meeting), or in the absence of such by the district council.

Every secondary school is conducted according to articles of government which in the case of voluntary secondary schools are made by the secretary of state and in the case of LEA secondary schools are made by the LEA and approved by the secretary of state. Every primary school (LEA and voluntary) is conducted according to rules of management drawn up by the LEA without reference to the secretary of state.

No obligation to submit rules of management to the secretary of state for his approval was included in the Act, probably because the administrative load would have been too much for the department.[4] In respect of secondary schools the department issued both a White Paper, *Principles of Government in Maintained Secondary Schools*, in 1944 and model articles in 1945 (bearing much similarity to those of 1908). Nevertheless the department seems to have approved virtually all articles of government even where they departed from the spirit if not the letter of the White Paper and the model articles. Baron and Howell (1968, pp. 49–53 and 1974, pp. 49–55) describe protracted disputes between two LEAs and the department over articles of government, but in one case the reasons for the department's uncharacteristically tough stance are obscure and in the other the department eventually gave way. Articles of government may be revised at any time with the department's approval.

It is not obligatory for every school to have a *separate* board of managers or governors. LEAs are specifically allowed to group two or more schools under a single governing body; the groupings may be all primary, all secondary or even primary and secondary combined. Voluntary schools may be included in a grouping if their managers or governors consent. LEAs widely availed themselves of this provision in the past, and many still today group at least some of their schools for purposes of management or government. It was particularly common in the old county boroughs and still tends to be more frequent in the urban LEAs (London boroughs and metropolitan districts) than in the counties. Moreover in some LEAs *no* proper managers or governors are appointed; instead the management or government of *all* local authority schools is vested in a subcommittee of the education committee. (Since there is no statutory limit to the numbers of schools in a group, this is technically legal.) Where there are no school managers or governors some LEAS (e.g. Haringey) appoint to each school an individual member of the education committee as a 'visitor'. The role of 'visitors' is rather shadowy but involves showing a particular interest in the school and perhaps acting as someone to whom the head teacher can bring problems. All such practices are, however, definitely declining. Separate boards of managers or governors for each school are increasingly the rule.

Managers or governors are either representative or co-optative, the former being those appointed by the LEA and the latter those co-opted by the board of managers or governors themselves. Representative managers or governors need not be members of the LEA, although most are; appointments are in some cases made from universities, industry, teaching staff, parents, religious bodies, lower-tier local authorities or other sources. In a number of LEAS few or no managers or governors are co-opted; where they are, however, they may be drawn from a similarly wide field.

Party political considerations may play a part in both representative and co-optative appointments. Sometimes it is winner take all but party agreements about the distribution of managerships or governorships are quite common. In Waltham Forest, for instance, there was for a time a curious party agreement whereby all governorships in the south of the borough were at the disposal of the Labour Party and those in the north at the disposal of the Conservatives and Ratepayers; but this was later changed to a system of proportionate representation on all boards. Party agreements are very often amicable but disputes can occur. In Reading in 1967, for instance, there was some party strife when the Liberals pressed for increased representation on certain boards of governors. In a number of counties, e.g. Berkshire, party influences on appointment are present in certain areas but absent from others.

Managerships or governorships are often used to reward the unsuccessful party faithful or even (as, for instance, with the Reading Labour Party) as a training ground for aspirant councillors. Usually, however, some neutral, for instance university, appointments are also made. Sometimes indeed such neutral appointees serve for longer than their political colleagues if the latter are periodically dislodged by the swing of the electoral pendulum. Even party political appointees tend, however, to enjoy extensive periods of office.

The appointment of teachers, parents and pupils to governorships and managerships is even more contentious than party political nominees. For many years it was unusual for teachers to be appointed to boards of managers or governors either of their own school or even of other schools in the same LEA. It was generally felt that it would undermine the head teacher's authority and produce awkward problems when matters like promotions or appointments were discussed, especially when a teacher was manager or governor of his own school. Attitudes are, however, changing. The vogue for participation, the NUT campaign for teacher representation on boards of managers or governors, the move to staff representation on governing bodies of colleges of education and polytechnics, caused some LEAs to think the unthinkable. Increasingly, LEAs now appoint teachers to managing and governing bodies of their own schools or others schools in the same LEA. By 1975 forty LEAs had amended the instruments of management or government of some or all of their schools specifically to provide for staff representation on the boards.

The story of parent governors and managers is similar, from an unusual and rather suspect phenomenon to an increasingly accepted normality. One must not exaggerate. Many teachers are still far from convinced of the wisdom of parents on the board. Baron and Howell's survey (1974, p. 84) showed how divided head teachers were on the issue. Some LEAs too are unwilling to countenance parental governors or managers. Nevertheless there is no doubt as to the direction of change.

It is far from clear whether pupil governors (pupil *managers* are difficult to conceive of) will become widely accepted. In 1972, despite the protests of the National Association of Schoolmasters and the National Association of Head Teachers, Wolverhampton and Brighton decided to appoint pupil governors to all their secondary schools. The DES expressed doubts about the legality of this move since under common law no minor can hold public office or a position of trust. There seems nothing, however, to prevent pupils *over* the age of 18 from holding school governorships and several instances have been reported. On the other hand an 18-year-old is only likely to remain a pupil for a matter of months and the point of his appointment is thus largely nullified.

The functions of managers and governors (as contained in the appropriate rules of management or articles of government) lie in three main fields: finance, staff appointments and the general conduct of schools. They have, besides, certain miscellaneous functions; most boards of governors and some boards of managers are empowered to grant a limited number of occasional holidays and to determine the use of school premises outside school hours.

Most boards of governors and some of managers are responsible for preparing annual estimates of their school's (or schools') income and expenditure. In practice their discretion is slim. All significant expenditure is either fixed, e.g. teachers' salaries, or determined by the LEA. A few LEAS give some money to each board of governors or managers to distribute as they please on facilities, equipment and the like, but the amount involved is rarely more than token. Sometimes too the governors or managers may be consulted by the head teacher in the spending of his capitation allowance. Invariably, however, he remains the prime determinant. It would be unusual if the minor repair which the head teacher thought most urgent was given a lower priority, and inconceivable for him to be forced to accept a textbook he did not want, on the insistence of the governors. Baron and Howell conclude (1974, p. 124): 'It can be said, and without qualification, that governors' financial powers are negligible, and that there is no prospect of any significant increase.'

The appointment of head teachers is unquestionably the most important function of governors. Procedures vary. In some cases the LEA (in practice an official, often the chief education officer) prepares a shortlist of applicants and the governors are allowed to make the final choice; in others the governors both prepare a shortlist and make the final choice with the LEA merely retaining a right of veto. Joint arrangements are, however, commonest, a committee of governors and LEA, advised by officials, often either draw up the shortlist or make the final choice or both. Managers are less often given real powers in such appointments; sometimes indeed they are merely consulted.

Responsibility for appointing other teachers usually depends on the level of the post.[5] In secondary schools the head teacher is often responsible for appointing to grades one, two and three, perhaps in consultation with the chairman of governors; there tends to be a larger involvement of governors in grade four appointments, and appointments over grade four are the responsibility of the governors in consultation with the head teacher. If adamant the latter can often get his way. In primary schools, with their smaller grade range and fewer staff, managers tend to be involved in lower-level appointments. Caretakers, cleaners and other non-teaching staff are appointed by the governors or managers in consultation with the head teacher; temporary teaching appointments are often made in the same way or by the head teacher subject to the ratification of the LEA.

The majority of LEAS follow the department's Model Articles in giving their boards of governors responsibility for the 'general direction of the conduct and curriculum' of their schools; some boards of managers are given a similar responsibility. Nevertheless this reponsibility means little. LEAS are invariably responsible for 'determining the educational character of each school and its place in the local educational system'; head teachers are usually responsible for 'controlling the internal organisation, management and discipline' of their school and for supervising both teaching and non-teaching staff. It is hard to see what is left for the governors' 'general direction'. Indeed Baron and Howell mention (1968, p. 101) that in some cases this situation '. . . leads to demarcation disputes, and attempts by governors to exercise what they regard as their rights'. More commonly however, governors are diffident about interfering in curricular decisions.

Governors have thus rather few significant functions. Managers generally have fewer; even Howell, a strong supporter of school managers, was forced to conclude (1967, p. 611) that in terms of their formal powers 'there does not seem to be any overwhelming justification for their existence'.

In the past, chief education officers in county boroughs have tended to be less enthusiastic about school managers or governors than their county counterparts. The difference is probably largely the result of geography; in urban communities education staff feel generally in close enough contact with all their schools; education staff at county headquarters (but not divisional offices) sometimes feel a little remote, and value the local knowledge which managers and governors can supply, especially in rural areas. Much, however, depends on personal predilections.

Head teachers' views are equally mixed. On the one hand, virtually to a man (or woman) head teachers resent any attempt by managers or governors to intervene in any detailed way in the running of their schools. Few head teachers would tolerate for long a situation in which they were not substantially masters of their own domain. On the other hand, head teachers often feel a little isolated and welcome the interest and support of managers or governors. Governors or managers, especially if they are also councillors, can be an effective lobby for the school with the LEA. Peschek and Brand (1966, p. 98), for instance, describe cases in Reading where through governors' intervention head teachers were able to secure additional telephones, a special science allowance, greater attention to some disrepair and similar fairly minor but not unimportant matters. Also managers and governors can help to take the heat off of the head teacher in any dispute with parents or any substantial public controversy, especially if the press become involved. For instance governors are usually required to endorse major disciplinary action like suspensions or expulsions and so share reponsibility with the head teacher if there is a critical reaction.

Baron and Howell (1968, pp. 106–7) found that the relationship between head teachers and their governors or managers was most likely to be satisfactory where the latter were given some guidance about their role. A number of LEAs now do this, producing booklets for new managers or governors, sometimes even sponsoring conferences or courses. The National Association of Governors and Managers also plays a part in this work, again especially through literature and conferences.

The case for managers and governors is the case for lay participation and responsibility at the level of the individual school as well as the LEA. This case is by no means overwhelming, certainly little greater than that for other individual local authority institutions – police stations, libraries, children's homes, etc. Perhaps these *should* all have their boards of governors. On the other hand it could be argued that it is the role of the elected member to provide the lay participation in local government services, as opposed to the professionalism of the permanent officials. There is some validity in the line of thought that as many citizens as possible should be directly associated with the control of local services; this is the argument for, to use that overworked term, 'participation'. There is, though, a penalty to pay in terms of extra paperwork, cost and administrative complexity; the penalty is particularly evident in the case of managers since there are four or five primary schools to every secondary. There certainly was not room for both governors or managers and divisional executives. With the abolition of the latter, managers or governors can be more easily justified.

On the whole LEAs which make a genuine attempt to give governors and managers a credible role find them worthwhile. Current trends are to give them increasingly such a role. In 1975 the Labour Secretary of State, Mr Reg Prentice, announced the setting up of an independent inquiry into the government and management of schools in England and Wales.

Religious Instruction
In every LEA and voluntary school the day must commence with an act of collective worship, attended, unless the premises make this impractical, by all the pupils. This obligation was a new one imposed by the 1944 Act although previously most schools had in fact held such a morning assembly. In addition, every LEA and voluntary school must provide religious instruction. Indeed, this is the only subject which must by law be taught. As has been mentioned, in voluntary aided and special agreement schools religious instruction is denominational except where parents request otherwise; in voluntary controlled schools it is only denominational where the parents so request.

c

In LEA schools, however, neither the act of worship nor the religious instruction may be denominational. The latter must be on the basis of an agreed syllabus drawn up for each LEA by a conference of four committees appointed by the LEA to represent respectively the LEA itself, teachers' associations, the Church of England (except in Wales), and, finally, such other (invariably Protestant) denominations as the LEA consider appropriate. The original series of conferences was completed in the 1940s and the syllabuses produced were basically a non-denominational form of Bible teaching. (If the local conference failed to agree the *minister* had to appoint a similarly representative body to prepare a syllabus.) LEAS were empowered to convene further local conferences whenever they felt that the syllabus should be revised; few in fact did so and many syllabuses are over twenty years old. The 1944 Act also included provision for LEAS to set up, if they wished, a standing advisory council on religious matters, to make suggestions on, for instance, teaching methods and books; few such councils were established.

When new or substantially changed LEAS have appeared – the reorganisation of London government in 1965, the odd creation of a new county borough in the 1950s and 1960s, and above all the major reorganisation of 1974 – they have usually started afresh on their religious education syllabus. In recent years some have adopted a radical approach.

The ILEA was particularly bold; its agreed syllabus, *Learning for Life* (1968), makes deliberate allowance for teaching the subject in a multi-religious setting. The syllabus took three years to appear and was the product of a conference containing Jewish, Moslem, Roman Catholic and Greek Orthodox representatives as well as those of the Church of England and the Free Churches. Birmingham was even more controversial. In 1974 the city voted to introduce a new religious education manual for schools which not only covered all the main world religions as well as Christianity, but included substantial sections on humanism and communism.

Parents may withdraw their children entirely from religious worship or religious instruction or both. They may also withdraw their children during such periods as are reasonably necessary for them to receive denominational instruction, as long as there is not in the vicinity a denominational school of the desired persuasion that their children could have attended in the first place. Moreover, where there are no suitable premises nearby in which denominational instruction can be given (in rural areas for instance) then LEA *secondary* schools (but not for some strange reason *primary* schools) may provide facilities.

Given Britain's strong liberal traditions, most overseas visitors are surprised at the heavy public subsidies given to denominational schools and astonished at the compulsory provision of religious worship and instruction in the LEA schools. Since 1944 these statutory provisions have provoked comparatively little contention but there are signs of a heated debate in the offing. The prospect of a new Education Act, while it has receded again in the 1970s, was much discussed in the late 1960s and stimulated those, principally humanists, who oppose religious worship and instruction in LEA schools into fighting a determined campaign to rouse public opinion to their support. An important move was the establishment in February 1969 of a Campaign for Moral Education to press for the abolition of compulsory religious education.

The bulk of opinion within the churches favours broadly the status quo – on four main grounds. First, it is claimed that children would suffer an enormous deprivation if they were not given a sound understanding of the faith upon which the way of life, culture and traditions of Britain so largely rest (how could they even appreciate Handel's Messiah?). In any case it is alleged that no satisfactory syllabus of religionless moral instruction has yet been produced. Surveys have revealed, moreover, that the vast majority of parents and teachers (and indeed children) wish to retain religious instruction and worship in LEA schools. Finally, since parents have the right to withdraw their children from both, no one's conscientious scruples need be compromised.

The humanists and their allies argue, on the other hand, that there is a distinction between information and indoctrination. Children should be informed about Christianity (together with other religions and ideologies) but not persuaded as to its truth. The right of withdrawal is not entirely satisfactory; rarely more than a handful of children are withdrawn from any one class; these stand out as different from their fellows and most children hate to be different. The claim that most parents favour religious instruction is also disputed; the validity of the opinion polls is doubted on the grounds of the phrasing of the questions, the selection of the sample, and so on. This is probably the least telling of the humanists' arguments. As with all statistical evidence it is easy to attack opinion polls but there is no reason to think that those in question are particularly defective.[6] Unless the evidence of opinion polls is to be discounted entirely there can be little doubt that most parents want their children to receive some religious education.

Some *Christians* also oppose collective worship and religious education in local authority schools. They claim that school assembly can be an empty ritual more likely to bore or antagonise children than arouse their interest in the Christian faith. Religious education too can be of dubious benefit to Christianity. Since the subject *has* to be offered, head teachers are obliged to use whatever staff resources they possess, often teachers with no special training, sometimes indeed no interest, in the subject. Some Christians would prefer no teaching to bad teaching. This is, however, a minority reaction. Most Christians argue that the teaching could be improved by producing more satisfactory syllabuses and encouraging more trainee teachers to specialise in the subject.[7] In October 1967 the Church of England set up a commission under the Bishop of Durham to examine the aims and methods of religious instruction in schools. Its report three years later, *The Fourth R,* proposed a host of changes. The main theme was that worship and religious education become part of the normal curriculum and that the legal compulsion to provide them be repealed.

In practice, though the law remains unaltered, changes have occurred in many schools. A growing number of secondary schools find it impractical to hold a school assembly because of their size or dispersal amongst several buildings. Religious education often takes the form of discussion of moral themes without specific reference to Christian doctrine. Heads of religious education in large secondary schools are often allowed to draw up their own curriculum, irrespective of the agreed syllabus.

In 1969, the then Secretary of State for Education and Science Mr Edward Short, promised in a speech at Alnwick, Northumberland, that compulsory provision of both religious instruction and the daily act of worship would be retained in any new Education Act.[8] Much water has flowed under the bridge since then. Nevertheless one suspects that still today governments will be reluctant to stir up a political hornet's nest by abolishing compulsory provision. Actual practice will increasingly diverge from the legal formality. There might perhaps be some minor changes. Children over 16 may, for instance, be allowed to decide for themselves whether to attend religious instruction.

Secular Instruction

In contrast to religious education, the secular curriculum is not closely regulated by law. Indeed the Butler Act specifically gives control to the LEAs: 'In every county school . . . the secular instruction to be given to the pupils shall, save in so far as may be otherwise provided by the rules of management or articles of government for the school, be under the control of the local education authority.' Moreover 'secular instruction' is defined broadly to include determining the length of school terms, the starting and finishing time for the school day and the power to require attendance at classes not held on the school premises.

True there are certain broad requirements for LEAs to observe: they must provide effective education so as to further the spiritual, moral, mental and physical development of the community; education must be suitable for the various ages of pupils; sufficient regard must be paid to the wishes of parents. These are not very restricting conditions. Otherwise the LEA has complete discretion in controlling secular instruction in all LEA and voluntary schools (except aided *secondary* schools where the governors are the controlling body). Indeed the governors of *all* secondary schools (although not the managers of primary schools) are invariably delegated control of their school's curriculum. In practice, however, neither the LEA nor the governors operate the real control over the school's curriculum, but rather the head teacher.

The power and discretion of the head teacher in the British educational system has already been described. A head teacher with any strength of personality can normally get his own way in respect of the curriculum. Of course if he were to propose a ridiculous change, say the abolition of all mathematics teaching, no doubt his governors or LEA would veto the proposal. Short of this, however, the dropping of existing subjects or the introduction of new ones is very largely up to him, as is the introduction of new teaching methods. Ideas for change often originate with one of his staff, or less commonly a governor or LEA official, but without the head teacher's support they are rarely implemented. New subjects can only be taught by teachers trained in the particular discipline; again, however, a head teacher may ask his LEA to send one of his existing staff on a course to train him in some new teaching method. Most LEAs would try to meet such requests.

Curriculum control is, therefore, highly decentralised, most discretion being exercised not even at LEA level but at that of individual schools. This situation is traditionally a source of pride in Britain and the more centralised arrangements of other countries are viewed with horror. It is asserted, for instance, that the French Minister of Education can glance at his watch and know what every schoolchild is being taught at that time.

In recent years, however, there has been a growing current of feeling that perhaps curriculum control is too decentralised and that a modicum of co-ordination would be desirable. The first expression of this feeling was the establishment in February 1962 of a Curriculum Study Group in the Ministry of Education, bringing together HMIs, academic educationists, teachers and LEA officials to study curriculum and examination problems. There was, however, some resentment at this ministry initiative and some pressure for the Group to be widened. Accordingly in July 1963 a meeting was held of representatives of a wide range of educational interests under the chairmanship of the Minister, Sir Edward Boyle. This meeting agreed that new co-operative machinery in the field of school curricula and examinations be established, and a working party under Sir John Lockwood was appointed to consider what form this should take. On the recommendation of this working party, there was set up in 1964, the Schools Council for the Curriculum and Examinations – usually abbreviated to 'the Schools Council'; the Curriculum Study Group was dissolved and the former Secondary School Examinations Council absorbed. The Schools Council is a large body; today it has seventy-five members – a chairman appointed by the secretary of state, and representatives of teachers' associations, private schools, local authority associations, denominational educational bodies, technical colleges and universities, professional associations of education officers and local inspectors, examining boards, the Council for National Academic Awards, the National Foundation for Educational Research, the National Confederation of Parent–Teacher Associations, the TUC, the CBI and the DES. Practising teachers (school, college and university) are in a majority with forty-two representatives; the NUT has the largest single block with seventeen.

The work of the Schools Council is conducted primarily through a series of committees, subcommittees and working parties. It also has a considerable staff, some of them seconded from the DES, LEAS, schools and other educational bodies. Today the Schools Council is financed by equal contributions from LEAS and the DES.

The job of the Schools Council is to consider what children should be taught, how they should be taught and how examined. The Council provides advice and assistance but has no power to compel individual LEAS or schools; it is also a forum of discussion. As its chairman explained in its first report, *Change and Response* (1965), 'In fact, though we have no right or wish to lay down laws on anything, we are a kind of Parliament of Education, each of us (except the Chairman) owing his membership to the wish of his constituents'. The Council produces a wealth of literature – working papers, research studies, examinations bulletins, curriculum bulletins and others – which has a wide readership both in Britain and abroad. It supports a large number of research projects. It sponsors a host of conferences, workshops, lectures and discussions. Its field officers are closely linked to the network of LEA teachers' centres which now covers most of the country. The Council provides information in response to numerous postal inquiries and personal callers at its London offices, and in 1973 opened a regional information centre in Newcastle upon Tyne.

Perhaps its most controversial activities have been in the field of examinations (responsibilities taken over from the old Secondary Schools Examinations Council). In 1970, for instance, the Council decided in favour of the introduction of a single examination for young people at the age of 16-plus to replace the Certificate of Secondary Education (CSE) and the ordinary level General Certificate of Education (GCE). Subsequently it sponsored a number of feasibility studies and trial schemes so that it could make a detailed recommendation to the secretary of state. The Council has also been concerned with examinations beyond 16-plus and has long favoured replacing the advanced level GCE with broader, more flexible tests. After much internal debate and several working party reports, especially two influential ones known after their respective chairmen as the Butler and Briault Reports (1973), the Council has moved towards acceptance of a two-level Certificate of Extended Education (CEE) for sixth formers. Such reformist activity on examinations is highly contentious. Many fear that the proposed new examinations would lower standards. The Schools Council has no power itself to change the examinations system; this is for the secretary of state to decide. One would expect, however, Schools Council proposals to be influential.

In the constitution of the Schools Council its object is defined as '. . . the promotion of education by carrying out research into and keeping under review the curricula, teaching methods and examinations in schools, including the organization of schools so far as it affects their curricula'. The constitution also provides that '. . . regard shall at all times be had to the general priniciple that each school should have the fullest possible measure of responsibility for its own work . . .'. At present the Schools Council does not compromise the individual responsibility of LEAs and schools for curricula and teaching methods. Schools Council spokesmen, like Caston (1971), claim that it is a powerful force for decentralisation and pluralism in British education. It could conceivably contain, however, the seeds of future restriction. Since it reflects the weight of professional opinion its collective views already have great force. It is not an unthinkable step from consensus to compulsion. The Schools Council might one day be given statutory power to lay down curricular standards.

Conclusions

The British educational system is still a very decentralised one so far as the conduct of schools is concerned. LEAs and head teachers are very much in control. There are signs of change. Parent and teacher power is decidedly on the increase. Managing and governing bodies, too, show signs of growing strength, partly indeed because of greater parent and teacher involvement. Power is a zero sum game. If these groups have more, someone must have less; the obvious candidates for diminution are head teachers and possibly LEAS. Nevertheless this would still be a system in which educational power was dispersed. The central government is a sleeping giant when it comes to running schools. The Schools Council is a cloud no bigger than a man's hand on the horizon.

NOTES

1 See 'Act means boy must go to Catholic School' in the *Daily Telegraph*, 5 January 1972.
2 See for instance 'Heads baulk at parental "monster" in classroom' by Richard Bourne in the *Guardian*, 28 May 1969.
3 Musgrave has pointed out that scholastic autonomy in Scotland has been achieved without the need for a buffer of governors between schools and public authorities; the high professional status of the dominie and the great public respect accorded education have been sufficient to protect the schools from excessive external interference. P. W. Musgrave, *The School as an Organisation* (Macmillan, 1968), pp. 20, 21.
4 When this point was raised during the Committee stage of the Education Bill Mr Butler said it 'would mean that the actual management instrument for the primary shool would have to come, in every case, before the Minister, which would be a quite intolerable position and a reversal of the existing practice. I do not think it is necessary to take out of the purview of local authorities the setting up of the ordinary governance of primary schools throughout the country.' *HC Deb.*, Vol. 397, col. 2251 (9 March 1944).
5 There are today seven grades or salary scales for schoolteachers: scales one, two, three, four, senior teachers, deputy heads and heads. Within each scale there are a number of incremental points and the one occupied by a teacher depends primarily on his or her qualifications and length of service. Thus a newly qualified teacher with a good honours degree might start at point 4 on scale one. For deputy heads and head teachers salary is also related to the size of the school. There are also various special allowances, for instance, for teaching in a special school. Movement between scales is, of course, primarily a matter of promotion but LEAS have considerable discretion in determining what scale is appropriate for a certain post.
6 See, for instance, Research Department Odhams Press, *Survey of Young People 16–25* (1962); Institute of Christian Education, *Survey of Parents of Sixth Formers* (1964); National Opinion Polls, *Survey of Five Religions* (1965); P. R. May, *Attitudes to Religion in Schools*; (Durham University, 1967). For humanist objections, see M. Hill, *R.I. and Surveys* (National Secular Society, 1968).
7 For a reasoned exposition of a moderate Christian viewpoint see the series of articles entitled 'Religion in Our Schools' by Roger J. Owen in *Life of Faith*, 1, 8, 15, 22 February, 1, 8 March 1975, Nos 4455–60.
8 See the *Guardian*, 11 January 1969.

Chapter V

EDUCATING THE HANDICAPPED

Children who suffer from mental or physical disabilities, or both, have special educational requirements. Provision for them is today called 'special education'; the older term 'special educational treatment' is going out of favour.

Under the Education Act 1921 local education authorities were required *as a separate duty* to ascertain which children of 5 years of age and above were better suited to education in special schools because of mental or physical defect or severe epilepsy. Handicapped children (other than the blind and deaf) began compulsory education at the age of 7 not 5 as with normal children. The most unhappy principle of all was that children had to be be certified as mentally or physically defective before they could attend special schools. As Dent (1971) points out, schools for children certified as mental defectives acquired a reputation as 'looney' schools, obviously distressing to the parents and perhaps even the teachers involved.

The Education Act 1944 made many improvements, especially in its greater flexibility. *As part of their general duty* to provide primary and secondary schools in sufficient variety to meet the different ages, abilities and aptitudes of the children attending them, local education authorities are required to have regard '. . . to the need for securing that provision is made for pupils who suffer from any disability of mind or body by providing, either in special schools or otherwise, special educational treatment, that is to say, education by special methods appropriate for persons suffering from that disability'. Thus, not only are the handicapped brought into the mainstream of education, but local education authorities are not restricted to special schools in catering for them. LEAs are required to ascertain which children of 2 years old and over need special educational treatment. Compulsory education commences at the same age as for normal children and used to carry on for a year longer. With the raising of the general school-leaving age to 16 in 1972 it is now the same for all children. Moreover, there is no requirement for the prior certification of children as mentally or physically defective.

Categories of Handicap

The secretary of state is empowered to make Regulations defining the categories of pupils requiring special educational treatment and setting out appropriate provision for each. At present there are ten categories: blind pupils, partially sighted pupils, deaf pupils, partially hearing pupils, educationally subnormal pupils, epileptic pupils, maladjusted pupils, physically handicapped pupils, pupils suffering from a speech defect and delicate pupils.[1]

There was until 1970 another category of handicap. This was the child '. . . suffering from a disability of mind of such a nature or to such an extent as to make him incapable of receiving education at school'.[2] Such children were known as severely subnormal (SSN), to distinguish them from the educationally subnormal (ESN), and sometimes crudely and inaccurately as 'ineducable'. Such children were reported to the local health authority by the LEA as being unsuitable for education at school; their education was the responsibility of the local health authority. Most of them were educated in junior training centres, formerly known as occupation centres, run by the local health authority (local health authorities also ran *adult* training centres for persons over the age of 16). A number of SSN children were also committed to hospitals for the subnormal.

Parents could appeal to the secretary of state against the designation of their children as SSN. The number of children reported as SSN fell from just over 3,000 per annum in 1950 to just over 2,000 per annum in 1970. In the 1960s there were 200 or so appeals each year and something over 20 per cent were successful.

The division of responsibility for ESN and SSN children was attacked for many years, but supported by the Royal Commission on the Law Relating to Mental Illness and Mental Deficiency in its Report in 1957. The Commission rehearsed the arguments for and against LEAs being made responsible for SSN children. It was argued that this change would reduce the distress to parents who would not have to bear the stigma of their child being ascertained ineducable; it would make for easy transfer between institutions for SSN and ESN children as their condition or diagnosis changed; it would enable SSN children to benefit from the school health services – free milk, dental care, medical examinations, and so on. Against the proposition it was argued that no child was diagnosed as SSN without careful examination and that the instruction of such children, consisting principally of habit training, could not be considered as education 'in any normal sense of that word'.

The Commission concluded that the most serious criticism of the existing arrangements was of the distress caused to parents. It recommended therefore that the procedures and terminology be revised and a more positive approach adopted. Thus for instance the term 'training centre' should be used rather than 'occupation centre' and no child should be labelled 'ineducable'. Moreover children in training centres should receive equivalent health services to those in LEA schools. The administrative responsibility for SSN children should, however, remain with local health authorities. The Government accepted this advice.

Nevertheless many continued to call for a change. Segal (1976) claimed,

'. . . the exclusion of certain groups of handicapped children as "unsuitable for school" . . . can only be acceptable to those who believe that (a) such children are "ineducable", and (b) that "care" has more to offer the child than has education'.

Mrs Margaret Crozier of the National Society for Mentally Handicapped Children argued (1960) in a similar vein:

'The severely subnormal child's well-being is a problem of education and the old division that makes the Ministry of Education responsible for the ESN teacher and the Ministry of Health for the occupation centre still obscures it. No single change would contribute more to the treatment of severe subnormality than an improvement in the recruitment and training of those who teach the child. Until his teacher is part of the field of education, has the same standard of training, the same status, and remuneration as other teachers, the educationalist in the occupation centre works under appalling difficulties, which purpose built premises, however desirable, do not put right. He is cut off from the main field of education to which he has a contribution to make and from which he needs the stimulus of interchange with colleagues working in other types of schools.'

Gradually these kind of arguments gained increasing acceptance and were reflected in a growing tendency to integration at the local level.

Gloucester City, for instance, had by the mid-1960s a special school for ESN children and an adjacent junior training centre with a common headmaster, interchangeable staff and a virtual absence of formal ascertainment. In Birmingham the LEA administered the City's junior training centre on behalf of the local health authority with the latter retaining only financial responsibility. Moreover, even where integration did not go as far, there were often co-ordinating arrangements to mitigate the inconvenience of the division –

joint committees, case conferences, informal admissions, an active interdepartmental role for educational psychologists, and the like. Nevertheless, in a minority of local authorities, relationships between the health and education departments were not so close and cordial. Indeed, personal and professional incompatibilities could lead to the statutory division assuming the proportions of a Berlin Wall.

The Government eventually succumbed to the overwhelming weight of informed opinion. By the Education (Handicapped Children) Act 1970, responsibility for children who had, or would have, been deemed unsuitable for education in school was transferred to the LEAS. The junior training centres became part of the educational system, most of them being transformed into special schools. Most of the staff were transferred to the education service on terms which protected their interests; the majority became fully accredited teachers. The LEAS also became responsible for the education of children in hospitals for the mentally handicapped. They can provide individual tuition or, where the caseload so warrants, establish hospital special schools; in the latter case the LEA can either provide suitable premises itself, or lease property from the hospital authorities.

Despite the switch in responsibility a distinction is still made between moderately and severely subnormal children ESN(M) and ESN(S). Nevertheless it is wholly to the good that both are now an educational responsibility. It facilitates the application to the severely subnormal of *educational* techniques, recognised today as more beneficial than the more restricted concept of training. The staff responsible benefit from the higher status and pay of teachers and from the easier contact and interchange with teachers of other kinds of handicapped children.

The demise of the SSN category still leaves ten and the need for *any* statutory categorisation is debatable. As CASE (1967) claimed, 'This division into categories though periodically revised is no longer representative of the children the system is meant to help and can too often result in children being made to fit into the nearest appropriate category regardless of real needs.' Similarly the Plowden Committee (1967) argued:

'However useful the categories may be administratively they are inevitably somewhat artificial and children do not necessarily fit neatly into them. An acute and prolonged difficulty in learning to read, which does not appear in the list at all, may spring from a variety of causes. A large and growing number of children are found to have more than one disability. A deaf child may be mentally retarded; maladjustment is often a consequence of a physical or mental handicap; physical handicap can include a wider range of disabilities.'

There are three problems. First, handicaps may be discovered which do not fit properly any of the categories. Autism, for instance, a condition of withdrawal in which a child, though perhaps intelligent, shows little inclination or ability to communicate, has only received serious attention in the last decade or so. Autistic children fit easily into no existing category. Secondly, a known disability might become more prevalent or might be found to be better treated as a separate handicap even though it falls into an existing category. Children suffering from *spina bifida*, for instance, a congenital deformity of the spine, are surviving in greater numbers and though they fall into the physically handicapped category are arguably better educated separately from other physical handicaps. Finally there is the problem of multiple handicaps. Again it is not in the best interests of a child who is, say, both mentally and physically handicapped to be classified as only one or the other.

The department and the LEAs are, of course, aware of these problems. Nevertheless, the statutory categories impose a straitjacket upon the system. There seems to be no convincing reason why handicaps should be statutorily categorised at all. It may be argued that this allows for statutory provisions, for instance, maximum class sizes to be applied to different categories, but this could be done informally. Indeed statutory maximum class sizes were withdrawn in 1973. In Circular 4/73 the DES admitted that actual class sizes were often well below the statutory maxima. In the light of this and other developments the secretary of state announced that the rigid concept of class sizes would be replaced by the more flexible one of staff–pupil ratios. During the actual school day the instruction group might range from one to twenty or more depending on the subject and other circumstances. Moreover, staff–pupil ratios were not imposed statutorily but as advisory standards. This move to flexibility and advice from rigidity and control seems to remove one of the major arguments for categorisation.

Moreover in the past the department's predilection for precise classification, occasionally even tighter than the statutory categories, has sometimes been positively harmful. In its 1946 pamphlet *Special Educational Treatment*, for instance, it narrowed down the definition of ESN and SSN children to intelligence quotient (IQ) terms by suggesting the IQ range 55 to 75 as broadly defining the ESN child, and below 55 the SSN. The pamphlet was withdrawn in 1953 but the damage was done. IQ had become entrenched as a primary criterion for determining the existence and the extent of mental retardation in children.

Doubts about what reliance should be placed upon IQs have become even stronger. Segal (1967) quotes evidence showing that IQ does not necessarily remain constant, and that it can be significantly affected by factors like pre-school education; he also points out that international differences in the levels of IQ regarded as educable demonstrate how arbitrary the dividing lines are. The DES is on Segal's side. It too prefers now to define educational subnormality in broad, general terms. As early as 1964 its publication *Slow Learners at School* described ESN children as part of a much wider problem of children failing in some way at school. It preferred the term 'backward' or 'slow-learning' to describe children of any degree of ability unable to do work commonly done by children of their age. The term 'dull' was then applied to children with limited mental potential and the term 'retarded' to those performing poorly because of some factor other than limited ability. ESN children were then simply those with 'pronounced educational backwardness', the lower end of this much larger group of slow learners. Despite such departmental efforts, for many LEAS IQs still play a central role in ascertainment, although they are increasingly supplemented with other criteria – home environment, teachers' opinions, the contentment or unhappiness of the child himself at his existing school, and so on.

The DES displays a similar cautious and flexible approach today to the definition of maladjustment. In its 1965 pamphlet *The Education of Maladjusted Children* it was careful to stress that the definition of maladjustment in the Regulations was not '. . . to provide criteria for identifying this handicap, but was designed to provide a legal cover for the provision of this kind of special education'. The Underwood Report's six groupings of symptoms considered to indicate maladjustment were employed – nervous disorders, habit disorders, behaviour disorders, organic disorders, psychotic behaviour and educational and vocational difficulties. The pamphlet stressed, however, that only when such symptoms were excessive or abnormal should they be thought to indicate the possibility of maladjustment. That the department now employs such vague, ambivalent language underlines the case against any statutory categorisation of handicaps.

In 1970 the Younghusband working party of the National Bureau for Co-operation in Child Care produced a report on the problems of handicapped children. In it the statutory classes of handicap were strongly criticised, but the working party merely proposed replacing them with a set of its own: visual handicap, hearing impairment, physical handicap, speech and language disorder, specific learning disorder, intellectual handicap, emotional handicap, severe personality disorder, severe environmental handicap, and severe multi-handicap. Though it was stressed that these were broad groupings, the arguments against classification would still apply to them. The working party asserted 'In our view there is a place for some form of categorisation chiefly perhaps because those concerned with planning and providing special education require some indication of the variety of needs to be met but also because delineating a category helps to focus attention upon it and promotes the provision of the necessary resources.'

This argument is specious to the point of perversity. Categorisation, far from indicating the variety of needs, obfuscates it. For instance to classify *spina bifida* children merely as physically handicapped is to obscure their *specialised* needs, as DES Circular 11/69 recognised. Also, delineating a category is far from the only or even the most effective way of focusing attention upon it. Autistic children do not fit unmistakably into any of the categories yet they have received increasing attention. Partly this reflects publicity they have received in both the general and specialised press. Partly too it is a result of concern shown by the department reflected in various publications, including Circular 6/71 urging LEAs to devote special care to the needs of the autistic.

The regulations defining the ten categories of handicap should simply be withdrawn. This would remove unnecessary obstacles to the identification of new handicaps or to the new treatment of existing ones. It would allow the DES to be as selective as it wished in promoting treatment. It would leave LEAs freer to experiment.

Ascertainment

The term 'ascertainment' is applied to the process of determining which children need special education. The department today stresses that it involves three stages: discovery (finding out which children have disabilities calling for special help), diagnosis (identifying the nature and causes of the disabilities) and assessment (determining the effect of the disabilities on the child and the nature of any special education required).

Any child of 2 or more may be examined to see whether he or she needs special education. Parents may request their LEA to conduct such an examination, but more usually the LEA is the initiator, requiring parents to present their child for examination. Indeed parents are liable for prosecution if they fail to comply. They may, however, appeal to the secretary of state against any decision about their child's education following the examination. No details of the number or outcome of such appeals have been published. The DES has, however, records of appeals in respect of physically handicapped, delicate and ESN children from 1961 which it discloses in confidence to *bona fide* inquirers. These show that the number of such appeals is small and declining. Since 1961 the highest number of appeals in any one year has been forty and in recent years the annual total has fallen to well under twenty. The majority of appeals were unsuccessful.

The law does not prescribe in detail how ascertainment is to be carried out, except that the examination is to be by a medical officer. Moreover government guidance on ascertainment has usually been very generalised. When in Circular 14/61 the DES urged the use of audiology clinics for the full investigation of hearing defects, this was exceptionally precise advice. Ascertainment procedure has been left largely to the discretion of LEAs. The one broad principle which the Government has consistently emphasised is the desirability of a many-sided approach to ascertainment. As early as 1946 for instance the Ministry of Education pamphlet *Special Educational Treatment*, while explicitly leaving LEAs to settle their own approach to ascertainment, suggested that a number of people might be involved – parents, teachers, head teachers, educational psychologists and perhaps others, as well as the legally necessary medical officers. The same message was still being preached twenty years later in Circular 7/66. In a field of flux and experimentation like ascertainment of handicaps there is much to be said for this approach by government departments, setting out only broad principles and allowing local authorities to adapt them to local circumstances and wishes. Nevertheless, after some years, a consensus usually emerges as to what has proved most effective. At this point a government department can become more specific in its advice, promoting what informed opinion accepts is the best practice. The DES can be criticised for being slow to move to this position. Not until 1975 was a Circular issued, Circular 2/75, which gave clear, comprehensive, forceful guidance on ascertainment. For the first time authoritative pronouncements (instead of rather tentative advice) were delivered on a whole range of issues (instead of only one or two). In particular the circular covered the use of informal procedures, early diagnosis, continuous assessment (and the link between special and mainstream education), the role of parents, the role of teachers, and the relationship between the medical and the educationally psychological.

While the department had long expressed a preference for informality, many LEAs were still uncertain about when to use formal procedures, especially the issue of certificates to require the attendance of a child at a special school. The 1975 Circular was crystal clear: certificates should only be employed where parents would not agree voluntarily to send their child. The Circular admitted that informality had dangers. Parents after agreeing to co-operate sometimes changed their minds following an informal examination; to compel their compliance involved certification which meant a second formal examination. Nevertheless the Circular insisted that the risk of having to repeat the process was outweighed by the benefits of being predisposed to use informal procedures. For instance, where a child's handicap is complex or borderline informal ascertainment permits more flexibility: also re-examinations of a child are likely to be deterred if each has to be fully formal.

Circular 2/75 was also strong in the role of parents in ascertainment. While the 1944 Act contained certain safeguards for parents, such as the right to attend medical examinations, it was too easy for LEAS to view them negatively, only as potential disrupters to be mollified. The 1975 Circular adopted a positive approach. It insisted that parents be involved in all stages of ascertainment because they had information to impart, because they contributed to their child's development and because their support smoothed the path of their child's education.

Similarly the Circular placed a new emphasis on the involvement of teachers. It did not merely repeat the conventional wisdom that their opinions be sought in ascertainment. It urged that teachers be trained both to detect and to help children who had disabilities of a mental or physical nature, and that effective channels of communication be installed so that teachers could refer such children for investigation without delay.

The timing of ascertainment, as well as its character, is, of course, crucial. The earlier in the life of a child that handicaps can be correctly diagnosed, then the greater the child will benefit from special treatment. This was, for instance, one of the primary conclusions of the major Carnegie Inquiry of 1964 *Handicapped Children and Their Families*. 'The evidence shows that early ascertainment and counselling of parents would greatly help to combat handicaps from early babyhood, to postpone, or shorten, or even avoid separation and keep many more handicapped children in the main stream of school life.' While children may be ascertained from the age of 2, most have to wait until they reach school. Generally only the most obvious handicaps are detected early. This unsatisfactory situation did not provoke strong language from the Circular; for once its advice was too muted. It merely commented favourably on the developmental screening of children from birth until 5 years of age.

A number of local authorities operate 'at risk' registers on which are entered children predisposed to disability (because of parents' medical history or other reasons) or actually suffering from a handicap; such children are roughly one in ten of all live births. The information is usually provided by general practitioners, midwives and hospitals. Children on the 'at risk' register can be carefully watched, examined early, parents advised and medical and educational provision planned well in advance. There seems no reason why all LEAs should not operate such registers, and the department could do more to encourage this practice. It would be of inestimable value too if *all* children could be examined at least once between the ages of 2 and 5. If this were imposed by law, it would place strain upon LEA and area health authority staff resources, and their co-ordinating machinery. Perhaps though such considerations should not be decisive.

Circular 2/75 was much more satisfactory in its coverage of continuous assessment. There has long been a demand from some eminent quarters for the continuous assessment of handicapped schoolchildren. It was included, for instance, in the recommendations of the Thomas and Plowden Committees. The case for continuous assessment rests partly on the risk that a single diagnosis may be incorrect, and partly on the fact that even correctly identified conditions can change.

Some of the more progressive LEAs already operate such continuous assessment schemes. Durham County, for instance, have a scheme whereby all children in special schools are annually re-examined and if necessary transferred. The majority of LEAs, however, fall short of this standard. Known borderline cases are regularly reviewed in some LEAs but in most re-examinations are on a rather *ad hoc* basis. The stimulus for the re-examination of a child may come, for instance, from teachers or parents. Shortage of staff is a factor in this situation. Nevertheless many LEAs could be more systematic in their re-examination; some seem almost random.

Circular 2/75 at last provided a strong lead. It asserted that the progress of all handicapped children, wherever placed, should be subject to regular and systematic (though not necessarily formal) review, and that this review should be annual. Indeed the Circular went further and argued that ascertainment, treatment and education were all closely interrelated. A child should be continually re-assessed because his response to education or treatment could alter his condition.

Finally Circular 2/75 tackled the thorny issue of the relationship between the various expertises involved in ascertainment, especially the medical and the psychological. As was mentioned, the law only specifies examination by a medical officer but the Government has long suggested that others be involved too. Until 1974 the medical officer in question was invariably the local authority's medical officer of health, wearing his other hat of principal school medical officer.

In the 1950s and 1960s most local authorities tried to adopt an interdepartmental team approach to ascertainment but the shortage of certain specialists often made this difficult. Moreover even in a mixed team the medical view often in practice predominated, and in a minority of local authorities the medical officer of health and his staff, following the letter of the law, retained exclusive responsibility for ascertainment.

The position has been much complicated by the reorganisation of the National Health Service and the transfer to it of the former local authority health services, including the school health service. From 1 April 1974 local authorities lost their medical staff. Nevertheless LEAS remain responsible for the ascertainment and special education of handicapped pupils. While the new area health authorities have a statutory duty to make available to LEAS the staff required for ascertainment and special education, horrendous co-ordinative difficulties are involved. The past problems of securing satisfactory co-operation between different departments of the same local authority are obviously magnified many times when two separate public agencies, a local authority and an area health authority, are involved. There is a danger, now that the doctors are no longer local government employees, that the medical view will become increasingly dominant.

Medical hegemony in this field may well be considered undesirable. As CASE (1967) points out, as long ago as 1952 the UNESCO Report on Education and Mental Health argued that ascertainment should involve medical, psychological and educational opinion, all carrying equal weight. This ideal is all the harder to achieve because of the inadequate supply and uneven distribution of child psychiatrists, educational psychologists and psychiatric social workers.

Circular 2/75 stated unambiguously that a sound ascertainment decision on a child had to be based on a full diagnosis of disability and an assessment of skills and development. This in turn necessitated the involvement of many people: even in the medical field, besides the school doctor, the GP, the health visitor, other medical specialists and therapists had to be consulted; outside, psychologists, social workers, parents and teachers had to be involved. The Circular drew attention to the multi-disciplinary comprehensive assessment centres established in some district general hospitals. These are designed to bring together the GP, the hospital and specialist services, local authority education and social services and perhaps voluntary agencies. The Sheldon working party reported on these centres in 1968 and there has been some guidance about them from the Department of Health and Social Security. Until now most have been preoccupied with the under-5s but they are extending their range. There is a danger that their hospital base will give them an overly medical orientation and Circular 2/75 urged that teachers and educational psychologists play a full part in these centres.

The Circular also stressed that medical examination should usually precede the psychological, that the educational psychologist should normally conduct any intelligence tests and that the educational psychologist should be responsible for recommending to the LEA the nature of any special education required. Whether any child needs special education and the kind required is an educational issue. Yet in the past doctors had often been expected to make the recommendation. In short the Circular attempted to reduce the medical element in ascertainment to equality with the other elements. Whether this will occur is doubtful, given the doctors' separate agency base in area health authorities and their control of the comprehensive assessment centres.

In general it is clear that much has been learned since the war about ascertainment, and considerable advances made. One can only regret that a Circular on the lines of 2/75 did not appear a decade earlier.

Ascertainment Standards

The numbers and proportions of children receiving special education, by category of handicap and by regions, were once set out in the biennial reports of the chief medical officer of the DES. The regional variations revealed up to 1968 (the last year for which data were published) were disturbing because they were unlikely to reflect the real incidence of handicaps. Certain regions, such as Greater London, had a high proportion of almost all kinds of handicapped children. Others such as Wales and south-west England generally had a low proportion. It is difficult to believe that handicapped children are heavily concentrated in certain regions. The department's chief medical officer commented in his Report for 1964–5: 'The lower ascertainment rates in some areas were probably due largely to shortage of professional staff, insufficient special school accommodation, or both.' According to CASE (1967), 'Informed comment from a less official source has said that the incidence of handicap tends to be correlated to an authority's willingness to spend money on it'.

The DES has later figures which it claims are too unreliable to publish but which it makes available in confidence to researchers. These show that between 1968 and 1974 the extent of regional variation was reduced for certain categories – partially hearing, physically handicapped, maladjusted, epileptic, speech defect – but widened for others – blind, partially sighted, deaf, delicate, ESN(M). The situation is not satisfactory. A certain regional disparity is perhaps tolerable but some of the variations are much too large. A handicapped child's chance of discovery and proper education treatment should not rest so hugely on his place of residence. The long-term solution is obviously improved staffing and greater provision of facilities. In the meantime, however, the department could do more to encourage a more uniform approach to ascertainment.

A surprisingly low incidence of some handicap should provoke an inquiring letter or telephone call from Elizabeth House or a visit from the district HMI; this does not seem to happen often. The DES courses, run each year for special school staff, school health service staff, educational administrators and others, should provide a medium for achieving some commonality of approach to ascertainment. The persistence of wide regional variations in the incidence of certain handicaps implies that the DES is not fully utilising such opportunities for influence.

Provision
Handicapped children may be educated in special day schools, special boarding schools, special classes in ordinary schools and even *ordinary* classes in ordinary schools; LEAs may also make provision for the home tuition of handicapped children. LEAs are responsible, too, for the education of children in hospitals.

At one time there were many statutory requirements concerning provision. In the 1945 regulations the epileptic and physically handicapped were so defined as to imply that they could not be educated in ordinary schools. More, LEAs were obliged to obtain a determination from the Minister of Education before they could educate blind, deaf, physically handicapped, epileptic or aphasic children in other than special schools and blind or epileptic in other than *boarding* special schools. All this was withdrawn in 1953 and replaced by a requirement that ministerial permission be obtained before educating blind or deaf children other than in special schools. Even this was withdrawn in 1959. Similarly regulations used to prescribe the maximum size of classes in special schools and of special classes in ordinary schools but, as was mentioned earlier, these were revoked in 1973. Indeed the only statutory safeguard left in the 1959 regulations is 'there shall be in every school a head teacher, who shall take part in the teaching, and a staff of assistant teachers able to provide full time education suitable to the ages, abilities and aptitudes of the pupils'.

The department has, however, issued a number of Circulars and other publications giving LEAs the department's policies on provision. The central feature of these policies today is the department's conviction that wherever possible handicapped children should be educated in ordinary schools; where this is not appropriate or possible they should be educated in special *day* schools unless the nature of their handicap or their home conditions militate against it; only in such exceptional cases should *boarding* education be resorted to. This policy was firmly enuciated as early as 1954 (Circular 276). Subsequently these views have been reiterated a number of times by the department, often in even more forcible terms. In Circular 4/73, for instance, it asserted: 'The great majority of children requiring special education can receive it in primary and secondary schools, either in special classes or in ordinary classes.'

The department's views on home tuition are less clear. The implication behind several departmental statements is that it should be employed sparingly but that in certain cases it may be preferable to boarding education. In 1956, for instance, in Circular 300 on physically handicapped children, the view was expressed that parents should rarely be forced to send their children away from home and, if suitable, home tuition was an acceptable substitute.

Another important theme in departmental policy pronouncements is the need for regional provision. In 1947 a number of regional conferences of local authorities and voluntary bodies were held to consider how they could co-operate to provide special education. In some areas permanent inter-authority machinery was established. In Circular 276 of 1954 the department urged the establishment of such regional machinery everywhere to review regularly the provision of special education. Regional committees involving voluntary bodies as well as local authorities were subsequently set up in most parts of England and Wales. On many occasions subsequently the department has stressed the value of a regional approach to special education, especially boarding education. Such a course has been advocated, for instance, in relation to physically handicapped children (Circular 300), maladjusted children (Circular 348), ESN and maladjusted children (Circular 11/61) and more generally (Circular 10/67). Nevertheless, the regional machinery varies enormously in efficacy, depending largely on the degree of commitment of the component LEAs. In some parts of the country the machinery is moribund or ineffective, and despite its Circulars the DES has done little about it.

In general, therefore, local authorities are allowed very considerable latitude and hardly surprisingly vary considerably in their provision. LEA policies may reflect deeply held beliefs on the part of officials or members, but also the exigencies of particular situations – the size and density of population, the number of voluntary institutions, the co-operativeness or otherwise of neighbouring LEAS and similar factors.

For ESN children the clearest division is between LEAS favouring separate special schools and those preferring special classes within ordinary schools; some of course have both. In Cheshire, until 1966, ESN children were all educated in *ordinary* classes in ordinary schools. Probably for most ESN pupils the ideal system, and the one preferred by the DES, is of a special class within an ordinary school with its own less strenuous timetable and atmosphere. That such a variety of provision persists in LEAS indicates the loose rein of the department. To some extent, however, it is also due to the sheer need for ESN provision. Since 1944 the greatest need in terms of numbers has been for ESN places, and the addition of the former SSN category in 1971 has swollen demand still further. In his Report for 1971–2 Sir George Godber, the department's Chief Medical Officer, estimated that in the special school population one child in five was ESN(s). Despite a massive increase in ESN provision since the war a substantial waiting list has persisted, reflecting ever higher ascertainment. The provision of more ESN places remains a top building priority of the department. Perhaps when the basic need for places has been more fully met, the department will devote greater efforts to trying to iron out the widest variations in *type* of provision among LEAS.

After ESN, the greatest need is for more places for maladjusted pupils. Indeed some claim that maladjusted children are the greater numerical problem, if only ascertainment were effective at discovering them.

The department's views on provision for the maladjusted are very similar to those on provision for ESN children. These views were most comprehensively set out in 1959 in Circular 348; the department announced its agreement with the recommendations of the Underwood Committee, that if possible maladjusted children should live at home during treatment and attend an ordinary school. If a special school is necessary, than a day school is normally preferable. Where a maladjusted child has to be treated away from home, he should be returned as soon as possible. The whole emphasis of the department is upon day provision.

In practice LEAS also vary widely in their provision for the maladjusted. Some are strong advocates of special boarding schools for maladjusted children in order to remove them from home stresses. Other LEAs firmly support the department's preference for day schools. A third group are attracted to the idea of hostels for maladjusted children; these provide a child with special care and treatment away from his home environment whilst at the same time allowing him to attend an ordinary school.

Knowledge and understanding of maladjustment is less than of educational subnormality and there is greater scope for debate about provision. As with ESN children, however, the principal factor is the need for more places – of any kind.

Until recently it was thought indisputable that blind children had to be educated in a special school. Moreover, they are such a small numerical problem that no LEA can maintain a school of reasonable size solely for its own blind children. All schools for blind children, therefore, serve a wide area, whether run by LEAs or voluntary bodies, and inevitably most children have to attend as boarders. This distribution of such schools is, moreover, very uneven and blind children from the north of England, for instance, have to attend schools in the south or midlands. There has been some recent challenge to the assumption that blind children could not attend ordinary schools, perhaps in special classes, but much professional opinion still firmly rejects this.[3]

Partially-sighted children, who were first defined as a separate category in 1945, make better progress, it is generally agreed, if not educated with blind children. Partially-sighted children range widely in the gravity of their visual defects. Those with relatively small handicap it is possible to educate in ordinary classes in ordinary schools, with a little special attention and perhaps some special equipment – for instance a reading lens. Where, however, more than a small amount of special equipment is necessary the department's view is that partially-sighted children should be educated in special classes or special schools. The DES tends to favour the latter because the age range in special classes would be too wide; while more numerous than blind children, the partially-sighted are still only 5,000 in the whole of England and Wales. Few local authorities are able to fill a partially-sighted school entirely with their own children. Also in many cases boarding education is unavoidable simply because there is no school within daily travelling distance of the child's home.

Deaf children are slightly fewer in numbers than partially-sighted. Again, depite some argument for integration, majority feeling is that they must be educated separately and again, given their small number, only the largest LEAs can provide a school of adequate size (according to the DES eighty pupils) for their own children. Boarding places. whether in LEA or voluntary schools, constitute the bulk of provision.

Partially-deaf children, like partially-sighted, were first separately categorised in 1945. They differ from deaf children in being able in some measure to benefit from oral methods of instruction, and vary widely of course in the severity of their handicap. The department emphasises (see Circular 24/61) that where possible these children should be educated in an ordinary class, given some special attention. Where their impairment precludes this, however, then special schools or special classes within ordinary schools must be provided. The department prefers the latter.[4] Increasingly, however, the term and concept of special classes has been discarded in favour of 'units' for partially-hearing pupils.[5] Each unit is a group of such pupils educated in a school which also has normal children; a unit may be one special class, or several, or several pupils distributed throughout ordinary classes. The LCC was the first to establish such units with four in 1947; Salford set up one the following year and other LEAs have copied their example.

At one time the department had very firm views on the education of epileptic children; it advocated that all epileptic children requiring special education should go to special boarding schools. Indeed, as was explained, this was a statutory requirement for a time. By 1956, however, the department's views had been totally reversed. It then accepted the conclusions of medical research that epileptic children should be enabled to live as normal a life as possible. Thus, wherever practicable, they should attend ordinary schools, leaving special schools to cater for children with frequent or severe fits or extreme behaviour difficulties. LEAs in general concur with these later views of the department, but sometimes teachers are reluctant to accept epileptic children in ordinary classes.

The separate category of diabetic pupils was abolished in 1953 and since then it has been included in the wider one of delicate pupils. The traditional provision for delicate pupils – children physically debilitated due to illness or home conditions – is the open air school with its emphasis upon exposure to the elements, hygiene and a nutritious diet. The health of school children has, however, so improved since the war that the earlier kind of physical debility is less of a problem. Open air schools today are often, therefore, used for children who find the ordinary school regime too strenuous, for instance asthmatic children. Indeed to some extent they are even used for physically handicapped children. Diabetic children have very specialised dietary and medical needs. Nevertheless most today can receive this at home and attend ordinary schools. For the few hundred who cannot be given proper treatment at home, special hostels are provided (principally by voluntary organisations) from which the children attend local schools.

The children suffering from speech defects constitute a very small and specialised problem. These defects are, moreover, not the same but include aphasia (a condition of severe difficulty in oral and written expression not stemming from defective hearing), stammering, voice and articulation problems. Most children with such handicaps are provided for in special classes or by special tuition; there is one special boarding school. The major problem is a shortage of speech therapists.

Physically handicapped is perhaps the most variegated category of handicapped pupils. Included within it are children obliged to stay in hospitals or sanatoria for long periods, or even convalescing at home, together with those suffering from all types of physical disability not categorised elsewhere. Perhaps the commonest of these latter are children suffering from cerebral palsy, usually known as spastics.

This variety of condition necessitates diversity of provision, and provides scope for dispute. The department's preference, as with so many categories of handicap, is for day provision. In Circular 300 in 1956 the department urged specifically the employment of small day units for physically handicapped children – perhaps even as small as ten pupils with a teacher and assistant. In fact many of the more mildly handicapped children should, in the department's view, be educated in ordinary schools. Most LEAs approve of this emphasis.

Some separate provision is, however, inevitable. From necessity or principle, or both, many LEAs mix categories of physically handicapped pupils in special schools or classes. Much informed opinion supports the separate education of certain kinds of physically handicapped children. For instance some separate schools and units for spastics and for *spina bifida* children have been founded to cater for their specialised needs.

Finally there is the problem of handicapped children not adequately covered in the statutory categories. For instance, despite efforts in recent years, provision for autistic children still lags behind demand; a report from the National Society for Autistic Children in 1975 claimed that only 900 special school places existed for Britain's estimated 6,000 autistic children. Above all there is the problem of multi-handicapped children. According to Circular 4/73, a quarter or more of handicapped children may suffer from two or more disabilities. There are so many combinations of handicap that specialised provision is extraordinarily difficult to organise. Very few boarding institutions specialise in children with multiple disabilities, and for most LEAs special day provision is rarely practicable. Many thus have to attend schools designed to cope with only one of their disabilities. Home tuition is also fairly common. The position is far from satisfactory, and departmental initiative seems to be rather weak in this field.

Voluntary Provision
Education generally is rich in voluntary bodies, but in special education they are particularly numerous. There are professional associations (like the College of Teachers of the Blind and the Association of Educational Psychologists), research groups (like the Midland Society for the Study of Mental Subnormality and the National Foundation for Educational Research), pressure groups (like the National Society for the Prevention of Cruelty to Children) and others; of course many groups combine two or more roles. Not all offer special educational provision themselves. Many are concerned rather to bring the needs of particular groups of children to the attention of LEAs and the department, to encourage more *public* provision, and to inform parents about existing facilities. In fact, however, few LEAs are conscious of lobbying from these bodies. It is rare for an LEA's provision to be influenced by pressure from the local branch of some national voluntary society; most LEAs would indeed welcome more attention from such bodies.

On the other hand a number of voluntary bodies provide special education in some form. A significant proportion of LEA children are educated in facilities run by such bodies.

Most of the longest established bodies, founded in the nineteenth or early twentieth centuries, have a religious basis – the Church of England Board of Education, the Roman Catholic Education Society, the National Children's Home (Methodist), Dr Barnardo's Homes and others. In many cases these led the way in certain kinds of provision; the first school for epileptics, for instance, in 1903 was a Roman Catholic establishment.

Secular bodies now, however, outnumber the religious ones. Most were founded later, a significant number since the Second World War, and most are concerned with one handicap or homogeneous groups of handicaps. The most prominent include the Royal National Institute for the Blind (1930), the Royal National Institute for the Deaf (1948), the National Society for Mentally Handicapped Children (1946), the Society for Autistic Children (1962) and the Spastics Society (1952). All these provide facilities; in fact the first two and the last provide a high proportion of the facilities for the education of the kinds of handicapped children with which they are concerned.

There are, besides, a number of bodies of a more localised nature running perhaps one school or very few facilities. One can mention, for instance, the Lord Mayor Treloar Trust (a college for physically handicapped children), the Poplars Special School (adolescent ESN and maladjusted) and the Ravenswood Foundation (mentally handicapped children).

Voluntary provision is enormously important. Without it the work of LEAs would be immeasurably more difficult. There is indeed some suggestion that in a few areas LEAs try to place their more difficult cases in voluntary schools. On the other hand LEAs complain that some independent schools are too exclusive in their admissions policy and refuse to admit any but the simplest or safest kinds of handicapped children – no dual or multiple handicaps for instance. The department has no power to alter the admissions policy of independent schools. Once such a school is recognised as efficient by the department, LEAs can place their children there freely, and controls of admissions is entirely at the discretion of the body controlling the school. Permission has to be obtained from the department for placements in schools *not* recognised as efficient, but even here there is no control over admissions *policy*. This is however only a minor problem. A more important one is the need for co-ordination of LEA and voluntary provision on a regional basis. In general where regional arrangements among LEAs are effective the voluntary bodies are involved too, and co-ordinated provision is achieved – but this is far from the case throughout England and Wales.

Staffing
Ordinary qualified teachers are entitled to teach any handicapped pupils with the exception of the blind, deaf and partially-deaf. Teachers of these need special qualifications – diplomas issued respectively by the College of Teachers of the Blind, and the National College of Teachers of the Deaf, and involving one-year full-time courses at the Universities of Birmingham, Manchester or Dublin. The prescription of these exceptional qualifications can perhaps be attributed to the strength of the professional associations involved, anxious to maintain high status and standards. Teachers of other kinds of handicaps are not yet as well organised. There are no obligatory additional qualifications for these, although there are certain voluntary ones. A number of courses are now run by colleges and departments of education, polytechnics and technical colleges, LEAs, voluntary bodies, and the DES; some of these are one-year courses; some are shorter; some are for experienced teachers, others for less experienced. Together these cover the teaching of most kinds of handicapped children. The department encourages the establishment

of new courses for handicaps not previously covered. Similarly the department tries to ensure a fair range of courses in all regions; where a region lacks some fairly common course a suitable institution may be approached to lay it on.

In 1955 a White Paper proposed that all such teachers be statutorily obliged to obtain additional qualifications. This followed the recommendations of the fourth Report of the National Advisory Council on the Training and Supply of Teachers. These proposals have never been implemented. The NUT has long held that mandatory additional training be prescribed for the teachers of all handicapped children, not just the blind and deaf; the NUT also argues that teaching in special schools should normally be undertaken only by those who have served for some time, say five years, in ordinary schools, and that *all* teachers during their professional training should receive some instruction in diagnostic and remedial methods for handicapped children. None of these policies has been achieved although there has been some movement in their direction.

In the past, demand for teachers of most kinds of handicapped pupils has considerably exceeded supply. This has been the main obstacle to requiring additional qualifications or experience. The shortage of teachers of maladjusted pupils for instance has been particularly acute. Boarding school staff are also often in short supply, especially domestic staff, partly because of the location of some of these schools and partly because few people are prepared to work at weekends. Only when teachers are in adequate supply can higher qualifications be insisted upon. This day may not be too far distant. If the increasing signs that teachers in general are becoming sufficiently numerous for the needs of British education are realised, this general sufficiency may well spill over into special education.

Special Education: The Future

Despite the massive post-war achievements of special education, by the 1970s many special education teachers felt that it had settled into a rut. They wanted a radical reappraisal of the whole system. Accordingly they began to lobby the Government to set up a major committee of inquiry. It was only after prolonged pressure that Mrs Margaret Thatcher eventually agreed. In November 1973 she announced the appointment of Mrs Mary Warnock, Talbot Research Fellow in Philosophy at Lady Margaret Hall, Oxford, and former headmistress of Oxford High School for Girls, to chair the inquiry. The terms of reference were 'to review educational provision in England, Scotland and Wales for children and young people handicapped by disabilities of body or mind . . . to consider the most effective use of resources for this purpose and to make recommenda-tions'. The inquiry was exceedingly slow to get under way, partly, it is true, because of the intervention of the February general election and change of Government. The other members of the committee of inquiry were not appointed until July 1974 and the first meeting was not held until September.

At the time of writing it is impossible to predict what will emerge from the Warnock Committee. Some expect an authoritative pro-nouncement on the growing controversy between those advocating the integration of handicapped children's education with the ordin-ary system and those preferring separate facilities. Another idea gaining increasing currency is that there should be some form of positive discrimination in favour of the handicapped, akin to the Plowden version for educational priority areas. Mr Alfred Morris, MP for Manchester Wythenshawe and Minister for the Disabled, publicly expressed the hope that the Warnock Committee would embrace this concept.[6]

NOTES

1 The Handicapped Pupils and Special Schools Regulations 1959 (SI No. 365 1959), as modified by the Handicapped Pupils and Special Schools Amending Regulations 1962 (SI No. 2073 1962).
2 Education Act 1944, s. 57 as amended by Mental Health Act 1959 s. 11 and 2nd sch.
3 See, for instance, 'Integration not good for blind, say heads' in *Times Educa-tional Supplement*, No. 3089 (9 August 1974), p. 7.
4 A survey by an HMI showed, however, that the transfer of deaf children from special schools or units to ordinary schools was generally detrimental to their academic progress, especially below the age of 5. See *A Report on a Survey of Deaf Children Who Have Been Transferred from Special Schools or Units to Ordinary Schools* by Miss E. M. Johnson (Department of Education and Science, 1963).
5 See *Units for Partially Hearing Children*, Education Survey 1 (Department of Education and Science, 1967).
6 See *Special Education*, Vol. 1, No. 3 (September 1974).

Chapter VI

ATTENDING TO THE HEALTH AND
WELFARE OF SCHOOLCHILDREN

The school health and welfare services form a heterogeneous and rather ill-defined group. Their origin is usually traced to two pieces of Edwardian legislation: the Education (Provision of Meals) Act 1906, which allowed local authorities to provide school meals for necessitous children, and the Education Act 1907, which obliged them to arrange the medical inspection of all schoolchildren. These Acts were not a totally unexpected innovation but rather a logical extension of developments which can be traced well back into the nineteenth century – public health and factory legislation, activities by philanthropic voluntary societies, initiatives by progressive local authorities. Moreover the impact of the 1906 and 1907 Acts was not immediately radical; many local authorities implemented their provisions grudgingly. Nevertheless they constitute a landmark for this group of services. Subsequent legislation including the Butler Act has elaborated, added to and varied the services which they established.

The prinicipal services involved today are: the school health service; the child guidance service; education welfare; school meals and school milk.

The school health service proper is operated by three main professions – school doctors, school nurses and school dentists. Various auxiliary specialists (speech therapists, physiotherapists, audiometricians, orthoptists, remedial gymnasts, occupational therapists) are used in a small proportion of cases. Until 1974 although the school health service was an LEA responsibility most of the staff were technically employees of the local health authority. Nevertheless, every English and Welsh LEA, except for the ILEA, was also the local health authority, (i.e. all counties, county boroughs and outer London boroughs). School health and education staff were thus employees of the same local authority. Only small numbers of specialists from hospitals or other agencies not controlled by local government were used under arrangements made with their employers. In 1974, following the National Health Service Reorganisation Act 1973, most of the school health staff were transferred from local government to the employ of the reorganised national health service. Responsibility for the service remained, however, with LEAS. Area health authorities have the duty to make available to LEAS the requisite staff and services. Nevertheless the situation is far from ideal and joint committees and other complicated co-ordinating arrangements have been unavoidable. The Bavin working party set up to recommend on these produced a note of dissent questioning the wisdom of the division of responsibility. 'We feel that there are reasonable doubts as to the degree of priority which the NHS will be able to accord to the school health service and as to whether in all areas the high degree of co-operation required will be obtained'. The dissentients wanted LEAS to have concurrent powers to employ their own medical staff. They were not successful. These problems underline the absurdity of creating an *ad hoc* national health service structure separate from local government – as the author has argued elsewhere (Regan, 1970).

Traditionally the basic function of the school health service is to conduct medical and dental inspections of school children and to ensure that any requisite treatment is provided. This traditional work has become less crucial since the war, however, because the national health service began to provide free medical and dental aid to children from 1948. Routine inspections are still an important aspect of the service but the emphasis is less on detecting *any* ailment (say a minor bout of chicken pox) than on identifying conditions which could adversely affect a child's education (say audial or visual defects). In 1970 1,786,329 English and Welsh schoolchildren were given routine medical examinations (about 22 per cent of those on the roll), and there were besides 1,179,315 special or re-inspections. There is a school of thought which advocates dropping routine examination of all children in favour of examining only those suspected of suffering from some disability. Many LEAS now adopt a more selective approach. Obviously though there is a greater danger of needy children slipping through the net of a selective system and in any case it does not seem to effect great saving of staff resources, as Godber (1972, Chapter 2) points out.

The school health service performs a miscellaneous group of other functions too: immunisation, health education, counselling of parents and teachers, home visiting of children with health problems or handicaps, treatment of verminous children, deciding which children have a medical case for free school milk. The role of school health service staff in ascertainment for special education has already been stressed. Indeed generally their work is increasingly focused on the medical aspects of educating handicapped children, even to some extent on the medical aspects of provision for handicapped school leavers.

Child Guidance

The child guidance and related school psychological services are not specifically mentioned in law and the only legal warrant for their existence are the references in the Education Act 1944 to ascertainment for special education and to the provision of medical treatment. The LCC was the first LEA to establish a child guidance service in 1913 and other LEAs were very slow to follow suit although since 1945 they all have. The main focus of the service is to detect and treat children with serious emotional or behaviour problems; often maladjustment or educational subnormality is involved. The school psychological service is more recent, indeed has only become fully established in the last decade. Its main purpose is to assist children, and to advise their parents and teachers, when there are psychological obstacles to learning.

Behaviour problems and learning problems are usually related and it is a pity that they are not embraced in a single service. The Underwood Committee in 1955 and subsequent departmental Circulars (347 and 3/74) have emphasised the need for close co-operation between the two services. Nevertheless the erection of administrative boundaries is regrettable. Professional and departmental tensions seem to lie behind the split. While educational psychologists are the lynchpin of both services, in one (school psychology) they are in total command whereas in the other (child guidance) they share the task with other professionals. The Underwood Committee recommended that the basic child guidance team should consist of one consultant child psychiatrist, two educational psychologists and three psychiatric social workers; the Committee also wanted the school health service staff to be involved, but a decade and a half later it was still exceptional for the school doctor to be a member of the child guidance team (Godber, 1974, p. 19). The problem is not just that child guidance is multi-disciplinary but that each discipline has a different professional base – education, medicine, social work. This professional ambiguity was previously expressed in organisational variety: sometimes the director of the child guidance clinic was a psychiatrist, sometimes a psychologist, sometimes even the principal school medical officer; sometimes the staff were employees of the education department, sometimes of the health department, sometimes shared between several departments. The school psychological service developed separately partly because it was clearly rooted in education and the responsibility of educational psychologists.

D

The child guidance service today is unambiguously the administrative responsibility of LEAS. Nevertheless the staff to operate it are still split three ways: educational psychologists are invariably in education departments, psychiatric social workers in social service departments, and child psychiatrists outside local government altogether in the national health service. Thus while the situation may be somewhat clearer it is still decidedly fissile. Official reports and publications tend to assert confidently that each specialist working from his professional base will have no difficulty in contributing to an interdisciplinary effort. One must hope that they are right.

An even graver handicap to the child guidance and school psychological services than administrative complexity and professional tension has been, however, the shortage and maldistribution of staff. The Underwood Committee considered that the basic child guidance team of one psychiatrist, two psychologists and three psychiatric social workers was appropriate for a school population of 45,000 and hoped that this standard might be achieved in a decade. In 1960 the Royal Medico-Psychological Association claimed that such a team could serve no more than 35,000 schoolchildren adequately and the Summerfield Committee (1968) wanted a ratio of one psychologist to 10,000 children. Even the Underwood Committee's standards had not, however, been attained by 1972. The gravest difficulty was, and is, with psychiatric social workers: in 1972 they were only about one third of the Underwood target; child pyschiatrists were still about 15 per cent under, whereas educational psychologists had surpassed it. Moreover the situation was exacerbated by uneven distribution; while psychologists were spread fairly evenly, psychiatrists and psychiatric social workers were unfairly concentrated in the south (Godber, 1974, pp. 7, 8).

Some attention has been paid to increasing the supply of staff. The recruitment and training of child psychiatrists was the subject of a report from the Royal Medico-Psychological Association in 1960. The Summerfield Report of 1968 contained a number of recommendations for expanding training facilities for educational psychologists. Indeed educational psychologists today are in reasonably healthy supply, although still below the Summerfield target. Curiously less effort seems to have been devoted to psychiatric social workers.

Education Welfare

The education welfare service is even less clearly defined than the child guidance and psychological services although its origin is clear enough. When school attendance was first made compulsory in 1870 the school boards were empowered to appoint staff to enforce it.

These school attendance officers were the precursors of today's education welfare officers. The latters' duties, however, range much wider. They are concerned with a whole series of problems which might prevent children from benefiting from their education: truancy (again a major problem in some areas), parental attitudes, material shortages (clothing and financial assistance can be given), mental and physical difficulties, general liaison between school and home, and child employment. Also their duties are related to facilitating a child's attendance at school: census records, school transport, nursery school placement, advice on catchment areas, free school meals. Nevertheless, while this indicates the range of responsibilities, by no means every education welfare service undertakes the lot, as was discovered by a Local Government Training Board survey (1974). 'The survey shows conclusively that the functions which education welfare officers perform vary widely throughout the country and that there is no clearly defined and nationally accepted role apart from that relating to school attendance.'

The main reason for this situation seems to be that the widening of the scope of the service from purely school attendance matters has been entirely a local government initiative. The central department has evinced little interest in the service. One of the foremost pioneers in the broader approach was the LCC. Not only did it extend the responsibilities of its school attendance officers from an early date but also founded a unique school care service. Care committees of voluntary workers, trained and advised by qualified social workers were attached to each school, and promoted the welfare of schoolchildren by maintaining liaison between school and home, and with statutory and voluntary welfare agencies. Curiously the LCC never merged the school care service with its school inquiry service, responsible for school attendance and related matters. Nor indeed did its successor, the ILEA, until 1969 when at last a unified education welfare service was established in inner London.[1] While the LCC was perhaps the most eccentric, other LEAs experimented with their education welfare service and, without any lead from the centre, the result was very heterodox.

In 1972 the Local Government Training Board set up a working party under the chairmanship of Dr (later Sir) F. Lincoln Ralphs, Chief Education Officer of Norfolk, to examine the role and training of the education welfare officer. The working party found that the potential of the service had been neglected. 'The picture which emerges from this study is that of an undervalued and under-developed service which has nevertheless played a valuable role in supporting the main educational function.' Nevertheless the Ralphs

Committee acknowledged that the service had a somewhat ambiguous orientation. While its work was largely of a social work nature there were distinctive methods and attitudes. For instance education welfare officers place high priority on getting a child back to school, whereas social workers regard school attendance as less important than the treatment of underlying problems. Education welfare perhaps occupies an intermediate position between education and the social services.

In 1972 there were 2,380 established posts for education welfare officers and 2,310 were filled. Their training and career prospects are poor, reflecting the low priority accorded the service. Unsurprisingly there is a considerable loss of staff, especially to social service departments.

Clearly there is scope for debate as to whether the education welfare service should be staffed by social workers seconded from social service departments or whether its personnel should be recruited separately by education departments as at present. There is, however, no case for letting it drift on in its present unsatisfactory state. The Local Government Training Board has urged LEAs to adopt the Ralphs Committee recommendations for strengthening training. One awaits their reactions.

Meals and Milk

School meals and milk are tremendous success stories in the field of school health and welfare. While they cannot be given the whole credit for the improvement in nutritional standards of children this century, they must be given a substantial share. Winifred Foley (1974, p. 47), for instance, describes the staggering impact of the introduction of free school meals on impoverished Forest of Dean children. Some local authorities, led apparently by Rousden in Devon (Armytage, 1970, p. 152), began to supply cheap meals to schoolchildren in the nineteenth century but the service only really became established after the Education (Provision of Meals) Act of 1906. This permitted LEAs to provide premises for the provision of school meals either by themselves or voluntary agencies. Today the school meals service is entirely a local authority operation. The cost of school meals to parents is subsidised by the government, and even these charges may be partially or wholly remitted on the basis of parental income.

School milk is a more recent introduction. A scheme to supply milk to schools was inaugurated by the National Milk Publicity Council in 1927 and extended by the Milk Act 1934 when the government contributed a subsidy. Children could purchase one third of a pint for $\frac{1}{2}$d and in special circumstances could receive it free. It became free for all children in 1946 and remained so for more than two decades. In 1968 this concession was restricted to primary and special school children by Mr Wilson's Labour Government. While some disquiet was aroused by this cutback, public opposition was muted; perhaps the gravity of Britain's economic crisis was so apparent to all that economy measures even in education were accepted as inevitable. Three years later, however, a major controversy broke out when Mr Heath's Conservative Government imposed further restrictions. From 1971 only children *under 7* and special school children were allowed free milk as of right; children *over 7* were only permitted free milk where school doctors certified that they had medical grounds for doing so. LEAS were also empowered to sell milk but only a minority have done so. There was a hostile reaction from many quarters to the new restrictions and the Conservative secretary of state was especially singled out for attack ('Margaret Thatcher milk snatcher'). Several LEAS threatened to disobey the law and to continue to supply free school milk to all their primary schoolchildren. Only Merthyr Tydfil tried to carry out its threat and was prevented by the refusal of the borough treasurer to sign the cheques; *he* was not prepared to be a martyr and suffer surcharge by the district auditor for illegal expediture, even if the councillors were. In retrospect one of Mrs Thatcher's junior ministers, Mr Norman St John Stevas admitted that the restrictions were a mistake in that the saving achieved was not worth the political obloquy.[2]

To sum up, the school health and welfare services, though essentially creatures of the twentieth century, can already be credited with remarkable achievements. Indeed their very success has made them redundant in certain repects, or certainly changed their emphasis. Since children are in general so much healthier and better nourished than fifty years ago, the main thrust of their provision is increasingly towards children with minority needs and difficulties, in short special education.

The most serious current problems of the school health and welfare services are first shortages of skilled staff, and secondly organisational complexities. To some extent the latter are inevitable, given the ambiguous position of these services as adjuncts of education but with strong links elsewhere. Nevertheless doubts must persist about their present structure. Certainly it places a heavy premium on interdepartmental and inter-agency co-operation. On staff supply there is room for mild optimism. The numbers of most kinds of specialists have been substantially increased since the war, though admittedly some more quickly than others. Uneven distribution of staff is a distinct problem but a general adequacy of supply would help to ease it too. The DES could direct more attention to trying to alleviate the worst regional imbalances.

NOTES

1 The ILEA commissioned a report from Bedford College on its school welfare services – *The Social Welfare Services of the ILEA*, 1967 – and on its recommendation set up a unified service; see *Inner London Education Service: Proposals for an Education Welfare Service*, duplicated document issued with ILEA Press Notice, 7 January 1969.
2 See 'Tory Admits School Milk Mistake' in the *Daily Telegraph*, 4 October 1974.

Chapter VII

INSPECTING THE SCHOOLS

Whereas in France Napoleon established a highly centralised system of local administration held together by the corps of prefects, in Britain, in the first half of the nineteenth century, a more decentralised system was developed, but with provision for a measure of central initiative and supervision. A principal feature of the British system was, following the priniciples of Jeremy Bentham and his disciples, the employment of government inspectors to ensure that legal provisions were adhered to and that government funds were being spent effectively. The first full-time, professional inspectors were the four factory inspectors appointed under the Factory Act 1833.

In that same year Parliament resolved, as Harris (1955, p. 78) notes, 'that a sum, not exceeding twenty thousand pounds, be granted to His Majesty, to be issued in aid of private subscriptions for the erection of school houses, for the education of the children of the poorer classes in Great Britain, to the 31st day of March 1834'. Although this subsidy to the voluntary education societies was a small one, it was soon obvious that it would be a continuing commitment, and therefore that Parliament would want to see that it was spent wisely. Accordingly in April 1839 a Committee of the Privy Council on Education was set up to administer the grants and to consider all other matters relating to education. In its very first minute this Committee resolved to appoint two inspectors of schools. Later that same year in an Order in Council the Committee recommended that no grants should be paid except where inspection was permitted.

The voluntary societies were not, at first, happy about government inspection of their schools. Indeed the two societies then active, the Anglican National Society and the non-denominational British and Foreign Schools Society, appointed their own inspectors. Societies founded later followed their example. The National Society was only persuaded to accept government inspectors (in addition to its own) after a very generous 'concordat' with the Committee of the Privy Council on Education in 1840; this provided that the

Archbishops of Canterbury and York should be consulted about the appointment of government inspectors for schools in their respective provinces, that the Archbishops should be able to suggest persons for the post of inspector and should be able to veto any proposed government appointee. The other societies sought and obtained similar privileges. Consequently the government inspectors were organised on the basis of the particular society's schools they inspected; there were appointed separate inspectors for Church of England, Roman Catholic, Wesleyan, etc., schools. Moreover the individual societies retained their own inspectors as well.

Partly because of the delicacy of relations with the voluntary societies, the first HMIS were less a medium for control than for affording assistance and stimulating local efforts. Sir James Kay-Shuttleworth, a very able first Secretary to the Committee of the Privy Council on Education, insisted that HMIS should in no way displace the authority of the school committees. Edmonds (1962, p. 49) quotes the committee minutes of 1846:

'The inspector will act under instructions restraining him from all interference with the discipline and management of the school. He will have no authority to direct, and will not be permitted even to advise unless invited to do so by the school committee. With these precautions against the exactions of authority, he will not fail to be useful to all schools which he may visit, by skilfully planning under the light of a searching examination, conducted in the presence of the managers, the actual condition of the school. The results of his experience will be available for their instruction and guidance.'

This positive, rather informal approach by HMIS underwent a violent change in 1862. In that year, following the recommendations of the Newcastle Commission, a new grants system was introduced which came to be known as 'payment by results'. All grants were merged into a single capitation grant, payable in respect of every pupil who attended for a minimum number of days each year and who passed an examination in reading, writing and arithmetic conducted by an HMI. Thenceforth HMIS were no longer primarily beneficent advisers but rather annual examiners who had to be satisfied if grant was to be forthcoming. The impact of this change upon relationships between HMIS and school authorities, especially the teachers themselves, was considerable. The 'payment by results' system was eventually dropped (in stages between 1895 and 1898) but its influence persisted far longer and, as a House of Commons Select Committee Report on the inspectorate (HC 400–I) noted in 1968, 'may even have some effect today'. Some school-teachers and head teachers still do not regard the visit of an HMI as an event to be welcomed for the advice and new ideas he may have to offer, but as an event to be dreaded during which a good impression must at all costs be made.

During the 'payment by results' period Forster's great Elementary Education Act of 1870 was passed. This had immediate repercussions upon the inspectorate. It would have been possible for a separate groups of HMIs to have inspected the new school board schools just as there were separate groups for the various voluntary schools. Instead the 'concordat' was revoked, and all HMIs organised on a territorial basis; England and Wales were divided into eight divisions each under a senior inspector, and within each division eight to ten districts. In each district all schools, voluntary and school board, were inspected by the same HMI. The voluntary societies, however, retained their own inspectors in addition, and a number of the school boards also appointed their own inspectors. When, following the 1902 Education Act, the school boards were abolished and their responsibilities taken over by local education authorities, many of these too created their own inspectorates.

HM Inspectorate Today

Basically this system has persisted ever since – HMIs organised territorially, supplemented by inspectors employed by LEAs and voluntary bodies. The most important changes in the last half-century have been a major increase in the numbers of HMIs and, especially in the last few decades, less emphasis by them upon formal inspections. The numbers of local inspectors have also grown considerably.

Far more radical changes seemed in the offing in the late 1960s, largely because the Select Committee of the House of Commons on Education and Science decided in its first inquiry to examine HM Inspectorate. The Committee recommended some fundamental reforms. The response of the DES was decidedly cool; while no Committee recommendations were flatly rejected and some were accepted, the department made plain in their *Observations* (1968) on the Committee's recommendations that the more radical proposals would require careful consideration. Apparently this still continues since no subsequent public announcement was made. Nevertheless a few changes have been quietly introduced which seem to move the inspectorate gently in the direction the Committee envisaged.

Status

The status of HMIs is both controversial and elusive. Theoretically they have a large measure of constitutional autonomy. They are not an integral part of the Department of Education and Science, but are appointed by the Queen in Council, (on the recommendation of the secretary of state). This direct appointment by the Crown arose in the first instance because in 1839 there was no central education department (only a Committee of the Privy Council), but the persistence of this method of appointment has been much prized by the HMIS themselves. Most of them strongly resist any suggestion that they are merely emissaries of the department. On the other hand, outside the ranks of the HMIS themselves, they are undoubtedly regarded as essentially departmental officials; LEAS, for instance, often consult them to discover the department's viewpoint on some issue.

The Select Committee came down heavily in favour of the latter view. HMI witnesses examined by the Committee maintained stoutly their independence of the department, arguing that they were not an executive or administrative body and therefore not a channel of departmental decisions; further, one HMI insisted that if he had reservations about comprehensive education he would not become a wholehearted advocate just because this was departmental policy. On the other hand a maverick ex-HMI painted a quite different picture to the Committee.

'Once appointed HM Inspector becomes a member of the Department, and, as such, is subject to normal Civil Service procedures and departmental regulations in such basic matters as probation, leave, pension rights, subsistence rates, and removal expenses. More important still, it is the Department, and not the Queen in Council, who has the right and the power to terminate his appointment before establishment and, in certain circumstances, to dismiss him thereafter.'

Later, in oral examination, the same witness said of his experience as an HMI, 'I would feel that I would have to keep within the policy laid down by the Minister . . . It was always impressed upon us that independence in no sense meant embarrassing the Minister.' Sir Herbert Andrew, Permanent Secretary to the Department, also played down the special status of the HMIS. He compared them to other persons with professional knowledge like architects, quantity surveyors and heating engineers who could not be instructed as to their professional judgement. Sir Herbert Andrew denied that any memoranda on policy were issued to HMIS from the department although he admitted that advice went out from the headquarters HMIS to those in the field, based on conversations with administrative civil servants. The net result seems the same. This 'advice' is, moreover, sometimes an 'instruction'. The department mentioned, for instance, in its reply to the Select Committee recommendations, that HMIS were *instructed* in April 1968 not to conduct formal inspections without special reason.

The Committee concluded:

'We do not consider appointment by Her Majesty in Council to be of any great significance, although we recognise that it "delights the people who enjoy it". That HM Inspectorate is wholly independent of the Department is a myth: "The Department and the Inspectorate are a very integrated body". We noticed that the Divisional Inspectorate represents the Department on the Regional Economic Planning Boards and we believe that Inspectors are generally accepted as spokesmen of the Department . . . We do not, however, feel that the relationship of the Inspectorate to the Department prejudices the independence of an Inspector where he is clearly expressing a personal judgement.'

The DES today publicly adopts this line, soft-pedalling the autonomy issue. According to its pamphlet *HMI Today and Tomorrow* (1970):

'HM Inspectors are a body of men and women who are ultimately answerable to the Secretary of State for Education and Science. They may well be given direct instructions by him. Their appointment is made on his recommendation . . . It is the duty of inspectors, as of other civil servants, to assist the central government in discharging the responsibilities that successive parliaments have laid upon it. It has become accepted, however, that whatever instructions they receive, their professional status and advisory function should not be impaired. There are therefore things which the Secretary of State would not wish, in the course of their duties, to instruct them to do.'

HMIS are, in practice, the department's professional territorial force, not dissimilar from such forces in other departments – for instance the regionally-based engineers of the Department of the Environment. It is true that HMIS are sometimes looked upon by LEAS as allies against the department; HMI support is often sought in a dispute with Elizabeth House. When, for instance, a school building allocation is considered too meagre, the LEA will commonly ask their district HMI informally if he will throw his weight behind an appeal for an additional allocation. Indeed certain district HMIS identify so closely with their LEA that they come to be regarded in the department almost as its proponents. Again, however, all this is not unique to HMIs.

Present Organisation

HM Inspectorate in England is divided into eight divisions each under a divisional inspector; the Welsh Inspectorate is semi-autonomous under its own chief inspector. Within each division all HMIs are of equal rank; each acts in one or more of the following capacities: general inspector, divisional specialist inspector, divisional advisor and district inspector. The role of district inspector is not to inspect any educational establishment but to liaise between the Department of Education and Science and *one* local education authority and to give general advice and assistance; for each LEA there is one district inspector for further education and one for primary and secondary. District inspectors invariably serve also as general inspector or in one of the other capacities. The headquarters establishment consists of a senior chief inspector, a deputy senior chief inspector, and five chief inspectors, each with a special responsibility for, respectively, primary education, secondary education, further education, teacher training and external relations, counselling, guidance. Fifty or so staff inspectors with special subject responsibilities (art, modern languages, and so on) assist the chief inspectors. The Chief Inspector for Wales, assisted by eight staff inspectors, combines all these responsibilities. A handful of HMIs are seconded to organisations like the Schools Council, the Centre for Curriculum Renewal and Educational Development Overseas and the Central Youth Employment Executive; a few others have assignments abroad connected with overseas aid, services education, international conferences or study tours. The great majority are based in the divisions although many sit on various committees and working parties as well as performing their divisional responsibilities.

As may be seen from Table 7.1 the strength of the inspectorate has fluctuated somewhat since the war but is still higher than the inter-war level. The recent fall in numbers is not so dramatic as to indicate a significant change of government policy; indeed it may be primarily due to recruitment difficulties.

The vast majority of HMIs are recruited from teachers in schools and colleges. Advertisements are placed in the educational press and the choice is made from the applicants by a board composed of HMIs and civil servants. It is clear sometimes HMIs advise persons to apply, although the department denies that this is common (HC 400–I, 1967–1968 questions 7, 8, 1098). The average age on entry

Table 7.1   *Numbers of* HM *Inspectors England and Wales for Selected Years 1840 to 1974*

	England	*Wales*	*Total*
1840	*	*	2
1870	*	*	108
1880	*	*	255
1890	*	*	316
1900	*	*	378
1910	337	5	342
1920	358	28	386
1930	295	23	318
1939	348	28	376
1950	515	43	558
1960	473	43	516
1970	496	47	543
1973	451	45	496
1974	438	47	485

Note: The separate Welsh Inspectorate was created in 1907.
Sources: There is no consistent published source for numbers of HMIs nor do the DES have such statistics. The above table was compiled from a variety of publications including Reports of the Board and Ministry of Education, Imperial Calendars, Report of the Select Committee on Education and Science HC 400–I, 1967–8 and annual Lists of the Inspectorate and Inspection Arrangements.

has remained consistent for several years at just over 41 (*HMI Today and Tomorrow,* p. 10). The department claims that it deliberately recruits from all educational fields, but it has adduced no evidence of the educational background of HMIs. It is certainly true in some areas that HMIs with only grammar or even public school experience are advising and inspecting secondary modern or comprehensive schools but unless the department produces hard figures it is impossible to know how widespread this is. It would be administratively impossible and perhaps undesirable to guarantee that HMIs only inspected schools of a kind in which they had taught. Nevertheless an inspectorate drawn preponderantly from grammar and public schools, the smallest educational sectors, would clearly be unsatisfactory.

Once recruited, HMIs receive little training. There are a number of short courses run by HMI Inspectorate each year for their own personnel, largely to keep them abreast of developments in specialised educational fields. They can also attend courses offered by univerities, colleges and other bodies. Otherwise the new HMI has to learn on the job, although he has a more experienced colleague as his mentor during a probationary period (Blackie, 1970, pp. 36, 37).

Attendance at special courses is particularly important for HMIS in further education, given the vast range of subjects, the difficulty of recruiting people with experience in them all and the high rate of obsolescence of knowledge. For all HMIS, however, there is a clear case for more systematic training not only to ensure that they are kept up to date with facts and ideas but to equip new entrants with a sound approach to their work.

The Work of HMIs

The law says little about the functions of HMIS. The secretary of state has a statutory duty to cause inspections to be made of every education establishment; so that he can perform this duty, the Queen is empowered by the Butler Act to appoint inspectors on his recommendation. The work of HMIS is, however, far wider than just inspection.

First they are the professional educational advisers to the department. The HMIS specialising in the various educational sectors – further education, special education and so on – work with the administrative branches concerned with the same topics. HMIS are also involved with departmental working parties and the Central Advisory Councils. It is clear, however, that they are not always used as effectively as they could be. While some branches like further education have close and long-standing working relationships with HMIS, other branches have not developed these as fully. To involve the HMIS more in planning, a Joint Planning Committee composed partly of members of the planning branch and partly of HMIS was established in 1966; it co-ordinates the supply of information and assessment. Nevertheless there still remains a problem of comunication between the HMIS and the rest of the department. A former Senior Chief Inspector, Mr Cyril English, in his evidence to the Select Committee claimed that HMIS were consulted enough about policy decisions but that they lost sight of what happened to their advice (HC 400–I, question 182). Sir Herbert Andrew seemed to place the blame for this state of affairs upon the inspectorate itself; he remarked acidly that the methods of diffusion of information within the inspectorate seemed to some of his colleagues on the administrative side 'a bit primitive' (ibid., question 122).

Apart from giving the department the benefit of their educational expertise, HMIS also act as its ears and voice in the field. Whenever any issue arises in respect of a particular LEA – school building programme, comprehensive reorganisation difficulties, etc. – the district HMI is asked for information. Where too a complaint is received about the actions of a LEA, the appropriate HMI will usually be asked to investigate.

HMIS also play a part in the department's publications. A number of the department's educational pamphlets are written by HMIS and they also contribute articles to the department's journals. They are permitted too to write for other learned journals and to appear on radio and television programmes.

The department's short courses (seven to ten days) for teachers are organised and largely staffed by HMIS. A large number of these are held each year; in 1966/7 there were 113 courses for 7,000 teachers and in 1967/8 175 courses for 9,500 teachers.

Outside the department HMIS are members of a large number of committees – examination boards, regional advisory councils for further education, committees of the Council for National Academic Awards and many others. They are deeply involved in the Schools Council. In 1967 there were 215 English HMIS involved in 1,189 outside committees. A number of HMIS also have, as was mentioned, overseas responsibilities, in respect of United Nations agencies, the Council of Europe and similar bodies, armed services education abroad, and individual foreign countries when requests for help are received.

Finally, HMIS have their basic function of advice and inspection in respect of educational establishments. They advise and inspect both LEA and independent schools and colleges. Moreover they proffer considerable advice and assistance direct to LEAS, not only through one of their educational institutions. The HMIS principally involved in this latter role are the district HMIS; as has been mentioned, they are important agents of liaison between LEAS and the department; they channel departmental thinking to the LEAS and LEA reactions in the reverse direction. They are not, however, the sole channel of communication; there is much direct contact between the LEA and Elizabeth House. District HMIS are in any case much more than the voice and ears of the department in the locality; they are educational experts in their own right and as such may be valuable to LEAS in several different contexts. They may, for instance, be asked for their views on the plans of a new school or college, especially if it contains some novel feature; they may be asked to participate (or arrange for HMI colleagues to participate) in a refresher course run by the LEA for its teachers; they may be asked for their comments on some new teaching method.

The most time-consuming and controversial function of HMIS is still, however, the inspection of schools and colleges. According to the department, about 300 HMIS are responsible for inspecting 30,000 LEA schools and, together with two small teams of twelve and twenty-seven specialised HMIs, 3,300 independent schools (ibid. p. 3).

Inspections range from a short, informal visit by one HMI to full formal inspections involving a number of inspectors and a written report. Each school and college is allocated a general inspector who visits at fairly regular intervals to give general advice and assistance. They are now advised in a written note from head-quarters to aim at a visit once every five terms (roughly three times in five years), although it is not always possible to achieve this frequency (ibid., question 69). Routine inspections by the general inspector rarely last for more than a day and do not involve a written report; they can, nevertheless, be fairly rigorous. Sometimes one or more specialist HMIs call (either alone or in company with the general inspector) to inspect the teaching of one or more subjects, say, music or English or domestic science. Occasionally an inspection is requested by the school or college itself – perhaps advice is sought regarding the teaching of some subject – but more usually the initiative comes from the HMIs.

The full formal inspection of a school is a very elaborate under-taking. The LEA and head teacher are warned well beforehand and the latter in turn warns his staff and pupils. Generally special effort is made to ensure that the appearance and conduct of the school is at its best; preparations may last for weeks and go to extra-ordinary lengths; pupils may be given special coaching and even instructed to make sure that their hair is combed, their shirt-collars clean and their shoes shining. Schoolteachers sometimes claim that HMIs never see their school as it normally is; as for a Royal Visit, everything is perfect. Occasionally, however, no at-tempt is made to present a favourable picture to the HMIs. Where a school occupies old premises, for instance, the head teacher may wish to make clear to the visiting HMIs the difficulties under which the school operates, in order to underline the case for new build-ings. Indeed a little exaggeration of the difficulties is not unknown. In this way an LEA can put pressure on Elizabeth House to increase its school building allocation; sometimes indeed the head teacher parades his school's difficulties before the HMIs not so much to help his LEA put pressure on Elizabeth House but rather to put pressure on his own LEA to take a more urgent view of his problems.

The actual inspection is conducted by a team of inspectors and lasts several days if not weeks. Before it commences the head teacher supplies the HMIs with the basic statistical information they request. When the HMIs appear each concentrates on one or more subjects – history, mathematics, music, domestic science, and so on. The techniques of inspection vary considerably; an HMI may simply observe a class or he may participate himself by, for instance, asking questions or he may examine written work. The school's administrative arrangements, premises and equipment are also assessed. The HMIs discuss their findings among themselves, and also with the head teacher, his staff and usually the governors; indeed it is a long-established policy that, where an individual teacher is to be criticised in the report, it must be discussed with him beforehand.

Eventually the report is drawn up by the HMI who has acted as chairman of the team (and been designated for this purpose the reporting inspector) and submitted to the secretary of state. This report, according to a former senior chief inspector, is the primary purpose of the whole exercise (ibid., question 200). Yet generally the report is simply read and then filed away. The department can take no action unless the very gravest circumstances are revealed, necessitating, for instance, the immediate closing of a school. Even where an individual teacher is heavily criticised any action against him is left entirely to the LEA. The HMIs themselves make rather greater use of the report, reappearing at the school after a decent interval to see whether the weaknesses reported have been tackled.

The reports are most careful documents in which the HMIs strive to be as positive as possible. A free copy is sent to the head teacher, to every manager or governor, and twenty copies to the LEA, which may obtain additional copies at a small charge. Undoubtedly they are sometimes useful to the LEA and school authorities. Nevertheless, as the Select Committee pointed out (ibid., p. viii), not all reports 'seem to serve any purpose commensurate with the time spent on them'. It is clear that the department itself was beginning to question the value of these formal reports even before the Select Committee raised the issue. Sir Herbert Andrew said (ibid., question 56), 'It is not necessary, if you inspect something to have an enormous report which takes weeks to write up and is then solemnly buried in the cellars at Curzon Street.'

The Select Committee were informed that formal inspections used to be held at five-yearly intervals but that these had grown more protracted. Harris (op. cit., p. 127), writing in 1955, claimed that the intervals between formal inspections were from seven to ten years. It is not difficult to find schools that have not had a full formal inspection for fifteen years or longer. If only because of sheer inability to cope with the increasing numbers of schools, HMIs have been conducting ever fewer formal inspections. The Select Committee recommended that they should be discontinued altogether, save in exceptional circumstances, and that HMIs should rely almost entirely upon informal visits. In effect the department has accepted this recommendation. HMIs were instructed in April 1968 only to undertake them for some special reason (see *Observations*, 1968, p. 2).

Informal is, however, too loose a term to describe *all* other inspections; as has been mentioned, some routine or *ad hoc* inspections, although narrower in scope than a full formal inspection, can nevertheless be exacting. There is recently a growing tendency to produce area reports embracing a number of schools or colleges. These usually consist of a main section assessing the educational system in general and then a separate appendix for each school or college.

HMIs *and Local Inspectors*

Following the example of some of the voluntary societies and school boards, LEAs (some from very early days) created their own local inspectorates. These inspect their own schools and colleges with a frequency which varies considerably between LEAs and, more important, give frequent advice and assistance. Indeed the very title 'inspector' is falling increasingly into disfavour and these personnel tend now to be called 'organiser' or 'adviser'. Broadly they are of two kinds: general organisers and specialist organisers. The former have responsibilities in broad fields (like further education or primary and secondary education), the latter in one or more subject specialisms. Apart from inspection and advice, local organisers usually play a major role in staffing matters. They are often concerned with the recruitment, placing and promotion of teachers; and in a number of LEAs they write regular reports on each teacher.

The increase of local inspectorates obviously implies a certain redundancy of the role of HMIs. It can be argued that the functions of local inspectors are rather different from those of HMIs; the latter offer advice based on a wider experience and unlike local inspectors rarely make reports on individual teachers. Nevertheless it cannot be denied that to a large extent their jobs overlap; basically both are concerned as educational experts to help ensure high standards of teaching. The department recognises this; its witnesses before the Select Committee admitted that the local inspectorate might eventually take over all inspection of schools from HMIs, say fifty years hence (HC 400–I, 1968, questions 62, 63, 70). Lord Alexander, Secretary of the Association of Education Committees, gave fifteen as the minimum number of local inspectors to provide sufficient specialist coverage (ibid., question 275). Following the reorganisation of local government most LEAs now have local inspectorates of this size.

Even so it is unlikely that HMIs will completely disappear, although they might well be reduced further in number. The department will still require a certain number of education experts to assist in preparing publications and to give educational advice. Moreover, no matter how large LEAs have become, there is still a case for a number of HMIs, eminent in their particular fields, to keep LEAs abreast of latest developments on a national or international scale.(HMIs, e.g. Blackie, 1970, p.29, stress the width of their network of contacts and information compared to local inspectors.) Lord Alexander argued the need for a *corps d'élite* of this nature some 200 strong (HC 400–I, 1968, question 259). To perform such a role HMIs would not only have to be recruited from amongst the foremost educationists, but trained intensively. Also, given the amount of central finance poured into education it is difficult to see the government forgoing all *right* to inspect educational establishments. HMIs would be needed for occasional inspections. Indeed the Select Committee, while urging that the statutory obligation imposed on the secretary of state to cause inspections to be made of educational establishments be repealed, also recommended that the *right* to do so be retained.

The Select Committee also recommended that more inspection be left to the local inspectors and that HMIs should work more closely with them. Already there is a good deal of co-operation, but the department accepted that it could be improved (*Observations*, 1968, p. 2). Local inspectors in their evidence to the Select Committee pointed out, however, that while they were able to co-operate with HMIs in advising teachers they found it difficult to carry out joint inspections with them. The difficulty is that local inspectors feel a certain responsibility for their own schools and cannot be entirely impartial. Moreover, many schoolteachers are far from enthusiastic at the prospect of local inspectors taking over work from HMIs. Local inspectors are sometimes thought to be less experienced than HMIs. More importantly, local inspectors are employees of the same LEA, often with an influential voice in the promotion of teachers. While an adverse report from an HMI is certainly to be avoided, it is a far less likely occurrence than falling foul of a local inspector. Similarly, an HMI's advice may be ignored fairly safely but a local inspector's must be treated with greater care if a teacher wishes to safeguard his career (HC 400–I, 1968, pp. 161–78). Teachers would probably prefer an amalgamation of HMIs and local inspectors under a semi-autonomous public body like the Schools Council. LEAs would certainly, however, resist the loss of their inspectors and it is hard to see that there would be much advantage thereby. LEAs would still need some personnel to advise them on staffing matters.

Relations Between HMIs *and* LEAs

Apart from local inspectors, HMIs have important relationships with the three other groups of LEA personnel – members of the education committee, the administrative staff and teachers, including head teachers.

The chairman of the education committee, and perhaps his deputy, may come to know the district inspectors fairly well but they rarely consult them in the absence of the chief education officer. The ordinary members of education committees, both elected and co-opted, have little contact with HMIs. If education committee members are also school governors or managers they may have slightly more; at least they are sent copies of any inspection reports. It is difficult to generalise about attitudes of members of education committees to HMIs; one unfortunate experience with an HMI may sour a member's attitude for life; nevertheless on the whole HMIs are regarded favourably and their advice treated with respect.

Relationships between HMIs and administrative staff headed by the chief education officer are particularly subtle. The latter is always an important official and in many cases a most eminent one in educational circles; the district HMIs are lower paid and often of a lower status both educationally and professionally. It is difficult to see what value they can be in such circumstances except as spokesmen for the department. In small LEAs the situation may be very different; HMI advice and assistance may carry considerable weight. Indeed in 1968 when the Select Committee's criticisms of HMIs received some publicity, several chief education officers in smaller authorities expressed in private great concern at the possibility of a significant reduction in HMI assistance. Since, however, reorganisation has now eliminated the very smallest LEAs, heavy dependence on HMIs has gone; nevertheless, smaller LEAs are still likely to benefit most from their provision.

In both large and small LEAs, relations between HMIs and chief education officers (and their subordinates) are usually cordial, although much depends on personalities on both sides. Chief education officers tend to be defensive about HMI criticisms of individual schools or colleges but in practice the criticisms may well be taken to heart and acted upon.

With school teachers, relations are much more variable. A visit by an HMI may be regarded with less trepidation than that of a local inspector, but in many schools it is not greeted with joy. True, some head teachers welcome, indeed initiate, the visit of HMIs, perhaps to obtain an objective view of their school's operation or to learn of new educational developments; some teachers too welcome the advice of specialist HMIs; the impression one gains, however, is that both are in a minority. Most teachers and head teachers would be unmoved, if not glad, if HMIs never inspected their schools. Such an attitude arises not only from fear, but sometimes also from a low respect for HMI advice. Some teachers feel that they can obtain information about educational developments from other sources; HMIs have little unique to offer. Some HMIs are regarded as unreal in wanting the optimum in teaching, rather than the best practicable. And where HMIs criticise matters over which teachers have little or no control (buildings, staff shortages, etc.) this may cause irritation. Finally where HMIs have not themselves taught in a particular type of school, the teachers in it may feel that this nullifies the value of their advice. In the past HMIs were sometimes criticised by teachers for being reactionary or too wedded to middle-class values (see Blackie, 1970, p. 43). Today they are more likely to be attacked for being too trendy; HMIs may even be blamed for declining standards of literacy (Izbicki, 1975).

HMIs and Further Education

The work of HMIs in further education, while essentially the same as in schools, has certain special features and problems. Since there are far fewer further education institutions than schools but the number of HMIs involved is not proportionately less, they have a much smaller institutional caseload. Consequently HMIs in further education are on the whole better known among the teaching staffs than is the case in schools. Also the awe, fear or resentment of HMIs still sometimes found among schoolteachers seems entirely absent from further education lecturers. Partly this may be because there is no bitter folk memory of 'payment by results' in further education. More important, the prestige and status of many further education institutions and the qualifications and experience of many of their staff make them more self-confident in their dealings with HMIs. Indeed sometimes today HMIs and the staff of some institution of further education *jointly* produce a report on it.

The Select Committee devoted only a small part of its efforts to the inspection of further education but this was sufficient to reveal the distinctive nature of the issues. In contrast to the evidence urging a reduction in the numbers of HMIs in primary and secondary education, witnesses tended to want *more* HMIs in further education. They also urged that HMIs become more narrowly specialist in further education. There was also some irritation expressed about the powers of the regional staff HMI over course allocation (this is explained below in Chapter X). None of these three demands was met. In 1975 there were roughly the same number of HMIs in further education (about 100) as in 1968. The range of subject covered by each was of the same order. The inspectorate argue that their expertise lies in the *teaching* of further education subjects, not necessarily in the subjects themselves; they cannot and should not attempt to match all the subject knowledge of all further education staff. Finally the powers of the regional staff HMI were left undiminished.

The Select Committee was clearly uncertain what to think about the inspectorate in further education. Since the evidence of witnesses suggested, however, that all was not well, the Committee recommended that a working party be set up jointly by the DES and LEAs to examine the recruitment and work of HMIS in further education (HC 400–I, 1968, p. xiii). This recommendation was given short shrift by the DES. It refused to join any such working party but conceded instead an *internal* review of the further education inspectorate, (*Observations*, 1968, p. 4).

Subsequently a departmental working party was established, headed by Mr T. R. (later Sir Toby) Weaver, a senior administrator, and Mr W. R. Elliott, the Senior Chief Inspector. It seems, however, that they soon decided that the exercise was unprofitable and the working party quietly ceased operations without producing any report or recommendation.

There have thus been no significant changes in the further education inspectorate since 1968. Such 'dynamic conservatism' (Schon, 1971) is unfortunate. There is undoubted scope for desirable change. While HMIS may claim that their skills lie with teaching, not with the subjects themselves, in practice it is difficult to divorce the pedagogic from the substantive. Where an HMI's subject knowledge is clearly inadequate, further education lecturers find it difficult to value his teaching advice very highly. HMIS in further education are undoubtedly able and eminent people; most new entrants have both teaching and industrial or commercial experience. Nevertheless, each is expected to cover a considerable range of subject specialisms. Moreover in many fields the rate of change is high and HMIS can easily suffer from obsolesence of knowledge. True, in recent years, the inspectorate have increased the number of courses they arrange for their own members to keep them abreast of new developments. Most of these courses are, however, very short and do not solve the problem.

The time has come for a radical new approach. The inspectorate for further education should consist of a larger number of more specialist HMIS, serving for limited contractual periods. Instead of appointments being for life they should be for, say, five years and should be made from those with narrower, deeper, subject expertise. At the end of their contractual periods most HMIS should return to teaching or to industry or commerce. With a rotating body of more specialist HMIs the problems of adequacy and freshness of knowledge would be much reduced, although their number would need to be somewhat greater than at present in order to cover a sufficient range of specialisms. It may well be that such a reform would also ease recruitment difficulties. The job of HMI does not appeal to everyone and the pay differential with teaching is not so great as to constitute much attraction in itself. More people might be prepared to serve for a limited period, indeed might regard it as an opportunity for wider experience. Of course one would expect a small number of HMIs to decide to remain permanently in the inspectorate and these would eventually supply the higher ranks. The norm, however, would be limited terms of office.

The Future of HMIs

At present HMIs fall unhappily between a number of stools. They are too few to carry out frequent formal inspections and yet rather too many if formal inspections are to be virtually abolished and more functions left to the local inspectors, as the Select Committee recommended. The Select Committee explicitly pointed out (HC 400–I, 1968, p. xiv) that the acceptance of their recommendations would involve 'an appreciable decrease in the numbers of HM Inspectorate'. Lord Alexander's *corps d'élite* 200 strong may not be far wide of the eventual mark.

HMIs also fall between two stools in respect of their recruitment and training. On the one hand they are not given intensive training to equip them for their job. On the other hand they do not possess a sufficient range of educational experience. There seem too few HMIs with a background in secondary modern, comprehensive and perhaps also special schools. In further education HMIs seem often too broad in their subject orientation to command sufficient respect with those whom they are advising.

Even where an HMI has appropriate experience when recruited either for schools or further education, he can become stale and perhaps unreal unless his teaching experience is periodically refreshed. Secondment of HMIs to teaching posts was rare in 1968 but on the recommendation of the Select Committee the DES agreed to consider extending it (*Observations*, 1968, p. 4). In practice there has been only marginal change. There are of course practical problems, like salary differentials, but given sufficient will these could no doubt be overcome. Indeed the inspectorate should go farther than increasing the opportunity for secondment to teaching posts. A strong case can be made for transforming the inspectorate for further education, and perhaps for schools too, into a primarily *temporary* body of men and women.

Since 1968 the inspectorate have made some changes in the direction advocated by the Select Committee – formal inspections have been reduced, the number of HMIs has been cut (though not dramatically), in-service training has been increased (but not transformed). One feels that the changes have been cautious, if not grudging. The inspectorate are unconvinced of the need for radical change. Without it they will no doubt remain indispensable as the professional educationalists in the DES, but one suspects that the value of their advice to schools and colleges, LEAs and voluntary bodies will progressively decline.

Chapter VIII

BUILDING THE SCHOOLS

Since the war, school building has been dominated by the need to provide sufficient schools to accommodate all children – a policy termed 'roofs over heads' or basic needs. This need has of course grown enormously in the last three decades swelled by the increasing population, especially the baby booms of the 1940s, the raising of the school-leaving age and the tendency for ever more children to stay at school voluntarily beyond this age. School building for other purposes, for instance to effect educational reorganisation or to replace obsolescent stock, has had to take second place to the 'roofs over heads' priority.

While 'roofs over heads' has never ceased to loom large in departmental thinking, the 1950s were particularly the decade of the 'Battle of the Bulge'. The great majority of new schools built then were to house additional children resulting from the high birth rates of the 1940s or to keep pace with new housing developments. There was little replacement of existing schools. There was, however, some improvement, especially through the minor works programme; particular attention was paid to remedying bad sanitation in village schools. The elimination of all-age schools (the former elementary schools, containing both primary and secondary children) was also a high priority. The proportion of senior children in such schools fell from 14·8 to 3·5 per cent between 1950 and 1960. This was achieved largely as a by-product of building for 'roofs over heads' although a few special projects to reorganise all-age schools were permitted. Another departmental policy at this time was to permit, where possible, building to accommodate the growing numbers of children staying beyond the age of 15, especially science laboratories for sixth forms.

It was bold for an official publication to claim (Morrell and Pott, 1960) 'by the end of 1959, the race against time had been won'. Nevertheless school building entered then a new phase, heralded by the White Paper *Secondary Education for All – A New Drive*. This announced a five-year programme to improve secondary schools by remodelling or replacing obsolescent buildings and by eliminating the remaining all-age schools. In improvement special emphasis was again placed on facilities for scientific and technical subjects. While the main thrust was directed at secondary schools, primary education was not totally neglected and the worst schools were replaced or modified. A great increased minor works programme was especially useful for the primary sector. Even during this quinquennium, however, a high proportion of the programme had to be devoted to 'roofs over heads'.

The three policy priorities which the department announced in Circular 12/63 to follow the five-year programme were: first, 'roofs over heads'; secondly, provision for pupils staying beyond the age of fifteen; thirdly, facilities for science teaching. Three years later Circular 10/66 specified first 'roofs over heads' and secondly the improvement of obsolescent primary schools. A Labour Government being in power, the department also stressed that all new secondary provision had to be conducive to non-selective education. The same Government announced a special, four-year, £100m. programme to cover the extra places needed for raising the school-leaving age; when this measure was later postponed the special programme had to be deferred for two years. The Conservative Government elected in June 1970, in the person of Mrs Margaret Thatcher swung the investment emphasis heavily on to primary schools. Still, however, 'roofs over heads' or 'basic needs' remained the overriding priority. In 1974, with economic difficulties once more besetting Britain, Circular 8/74 announced that *only* projects to meet 'basic needs', plus special schools, would be permitted.

Similar policy continuities can be traced in other fields of educational building. Only about £1m. annually could be devoted to *special school building* until the end of the 1950s. The department reported in its memorandum *Educational Building in England and Wales* (1961): 'This was sufficient to make adequate provision for most handicapped children, but not for those who are educationally subnormal or maladjusted.' When increased allocation became possible high priority was given to increased provision for these two kinds of handicaps (Circular 10/66) but the need to expand provision generally, especially because of the increased numbers of handicapped children surviving infancy, was also stressed (Circular 10/67). Finally the department urged concentration on day, as opposed to boarding, provision to avoid unnecessary separation of children from their families. These three policies still basically obtain – the department still places major emphasis on expanding special educational provision, especially day places, the lion's share being for ESN and maladjusted children.

Nursery school building was severely restricted until 1973, successive Governments considering it a low educational priority. In 1964 the department decided to permit the establishment of new nursery classes where they enabled married women to return to teaching, but any expansion of basic provision was still forbidden. This was the sole concession (save for the urban programme about which more anon) until Mrs Thatcher announced the first post-war expansion programme for nursery education in *Education: A Framework for Expansion* (1972). Her policy was to provide by 1982 nursery education for all 3- and 4-year-olds whose parents sought it. The department estimated that only 15 per cent of 3- and 4-year-olds would require *full-time* education but 35 per cent of 3-year-olds and 75 per cent of 4-year-olds would want *part-time* education. To provide the 250,000 additional places necessary, a building programme started in 1974; £15m. annually for the first two years was earmarked. This start coincided with an economic crisis and a change of Government. Although the new Labour Government was as keen as Mrs Thatcher to expand basic nursery provision, her programme had to be curtailed.

Building for *the youth service* was, like nursery schools, long considered a low priority. The first significant building programme did not commence until after the Government accepted the recommendations of the Albemarle Committee. Considerable investment in both LEA and voluntary provision was subsequently authorised (see Circular 3/60), starting in the financial year 1960–1. Youth service building has, however, tended to be an early target for the pruning knife in times of economic stringency, as in 1974.

Building for *further education and teacher training* has been more fortunate. In both sectors there has been a steady (at times rapid) increase in authorised investment. No special investment priorities have been urged upon LEAs in departmental circulars or other publications.

Besides these basic investment areas there have also been three special programmes. First, there was one for *educational priority areas* – the concept devised by the Plowden Committee. The department announced in Circular 11/67 an authorised investment of £16m. for the two years 1968/9 and 1969/70 for schools in educational priority areas. LEAs were asked to identify such areas on the basis of multiple social deprivation (overcrowding, large families, high turnover of teachers, etc.) and poor physical environment (old, poorly maintained houses, etc.). They were then to identify schools within such areas which would particularly benefit from investment. The additional authorisation could be used for a wide variety of purposes – school replacement, school remodelling, improvement of staff amenities, and so on. On a national basis the department wanted about half the programme devoted to major projects and half to minor, with the emphasis on primary rather than secondary schools, but was happy to adapt to the needs of individual LEAs. Voluntary aided and special agreement schools benefited from the programme as well as maintained schools.

The second special programme was the *urban programme*. This had a more complex origin in the general anxiety about the problems of city life in the late 1960s, given increased currency by the American urban riots of the period. In Circular 19/68 a special investment authorisation was announced to assist areas of urban stress – poor physical environment, high concentration of immigrants, and so on. In the first phase thirty-four urban local authorities were selected by the Government as beneficiaries, but subsequently the programme was thrown open to any local authority that could make out a case. The programme was a joint one between the Home Office, the Ministry of Health and the Department of Education and Science and was thus devoted not just to educational purposes but to health and welfare too. The first phase was restricted to the building of new nursery schools and classes (DES) plus children's homes (Home Office) and day nurseries (Ministry of Health). Later phases were not so restricted but in the education field the nursery sector was undoubtedly the principal beneficiary of the programme. In 1968 the Government envisaged a programme of £20m. to £25m. over four or five years but this target has not yet been attained.

Finally there was a special programme of £100m. to cover additional investment needed in connection with the raising of the school-leaving age in 1972.

Thus, to sum up, national building policies have been characterised more by continuity than fluctuation; even the special programmes have tended to complement, rather than contradict, existing policies. Most policies persist for many years. For instance the emphasis on provision for sixth formers, especially science facilities, had a long run in the 1950s and 1960s. There was also the sustained (and successful) campaign to eliminate the all-age schools. In special education the priority given to provision for ESN and maladjusted children still continues. Above all the 'basic needs' or 'roofs over heads' criterion has never ceased to predominate. Nursery schools and the youth service both experienced prolonged periods of parsimony but later began to receive a moderate share of investment. Teacher training and further education were more fortunate in that their allocation grew almost constantly throughout the period, although the rate of acceleration varied.

Departmental policy emphases are not necessarily all scrupulously followed by every LEA, if only because local circumstances vary. Thus counties with scattered, rural populations tend to concentrate on boarding provision for certain kinds of handicapped children, despite the department's preference for day schools. Similarly local priorities may emerge which have not been a focus of departmental attention. For instance when LEAs took over responsibility for SSN children in 1971, the facilities they inherited from the health departments varied considerably in adequacy. Where they were unsatisfactory LEAs naturally felt the need to devote high priority to improving them. The department only stresses in an undifferentiated way the need to expand ESN provision generally. Major policy conflicts between central and local government on school building are, however, rare save for the massive exception of comprehensive education. A policy lead from the department usually provokes a willing response from LEAs.

The Building Programmes

Today there are four educational building programmes: primary and secondary schools; nursery education; special schools, including child guidance clinics and hospital schools; institutions for further education and teacher training. This list is not a constant one. Nursery schools are a recent addition. Some formerly separate programmes have been dropped or amalgamated. Perhaps the most interesting of these was for primary and secondary school *minor* works, that is for projects costing less than a certain amount each; in 1973 the limit was under £40,000. Separate minor works allocations are, however, still made for further education and teacher training, for projects costing individually less than £25,000. The investment totals for each programme for particular financial years are settled basically by negotiation between the Treasury and the DES and involve the PESC procedure which today characterises British government financial decision making (see Heclo and Wildavsky, 1974, Chapter 5). When each total is determined, the DES allocates it among the English LEAs and the Welsh Office among the Welsh LEAs.

It is important to stress that this allocation is not an allocation of money but merely of permission to spend a specified amount on educational building. (The granting of financial aid is an entirely separate operation. For educational purposes most today is paid through the Rate Support Grant as described in Chapter XI.) The purpose of the building programmes is to control public investment in educational capital whether funded from local or central government or both.

The building programmes are of 'starts'. Thus a programme of, say, £50m. for a particular financial year would mean, not that the whole sum was to be expended in the twelve-month period, but that projects which would total this amount to complete were to be *started* in the year.

Until 1974 the building programmes, *with the exception of minor works*, were allocated not as lump sum authorisations but as a list of specified projects. Thus an LEA would not be given permission to spend, say £½m. on major school projects starting in a particular financial year. Rather would such an LEA be given permission to start, say, two new named secondary schools, three named primary schools and a major extension of a named fourth. The costs of all the projects would be estimated so that the department would know the value of each LEA's programme and the total value for the whole country. Nevertheless, the allocation would be on a project-by-project basis.

The procedure was for the department to invite LEAS to submit proposed projects for the next programme. The LEAS had to rank their proposed projects in priority order and to accompany each with a statement explaining and justifying the need for it. Since the global total of proposals invariably exceeded the figure agreed with the Treasury, the department would select a proportion of the submissions as the programme for LEAS to undertake. In selecting projects the department would examine the justifications and pay regard to the LEAS' own priorities. Nevertheless the department would take independent advice and quite commonly override the LEAS' own priorities.

This degree of intervention and control occasioned some resentment from LEAS and some criticism by observers (Griffith, 1966, pp. 159–63). It could not be defended as a means of ensuring *standards* since these were (and are) subject to statutory regulation no matter how the projects were selected. It could only be justified as a means of enforcing *national investment priorities* – replacement of all-age schools and the like. LEAS left to pick their own projects within a capital allocation might not always have followed them. Basically the issue is one of national versus local priorities.

For nearly three decades the department insisted on retaining project selection. In 1974 there was a change of course. The department announced in Circular 8/74 that for the 1974/5 building year school projects to meet the basic need for additional places (but not other purposes) would be allocated to LEAS in the form of lump sum authorisations. This was the way the minor works programme had always been operated. The present procedure is discussed below.

Cost Limits

Cost-per-place limits were one of the most characteristic features of the post-war educational building programmes, until these were swept away by the raging torrent of inflation in 1974. They prescribed the *maximum* that schools (and other educational buildings) were to cost, as calculated primarily upon the number of children for whom the building was designed. There were different limits for primary and secondary schools, large and small schools, schools with and without kitchens and other similar variations including special latitude for difficult sites. The whole point of these cost limits was economy. In the euphoric aftermath of the war, school building had sometimes been extravagant. Thenceforth, LEAs were compelled to eradicate all waste in construction.

Cost limits were first announced in 1949 to be applied the following year. They were set at £170 per place for primary schools and £290 for secondary. The intention was to achieve a reduction of $12\frac{1}{2}$ per cent on the average costs of school building in 1949. The following year the limits were reduced to £140 and £240 respectively to screw down costs even tighter; indeed this involved some reduction in the area possible per child. The cost limits remained at this basic level for three years, although the system was elaborated to take account of the higher unit costs incurred by small schools and by schools with kitchens as opposed to those with sculleries only.

In 1953 it was proudly announced in Circular 264 that schools started in the second half of 1952 were 45 per cent more economical than those started in 1949. It was recognised, however, that with a 35 per cent rise in building costs in two years, the lid could not be sat on further without risk of severe deterioration of standards. Accordingly a 4 per cent rise in the basic limits was permitted. Two years later a further small increase was allowed, but this level was then held for five years. Then a flurry of rises ensued in 1960, in 1961 and 1963. In 1966 the cost limits were raised by a further $8\frac{1}{2}$ per cent, but this level was then held for four years. Then began, however, the inexorable annual rise by ever greater increments in an attempt to keep abreast of the great waves of inflation foaming over the British economy. In 1970 the cost limits were raised by 10 per cent, in 1971 by a further 13 per cent, in 1972 by a further 15 per cent and in 1973 by no less than 22 per cent.

Even this proved insufficient. LEAs were quite unable to keep within the limits. The department had to permit increasing numbers of projects to exceed their appropriate costs. The system collapsed. The abandonment of cost-per-place limits was announced in Circular 8/74.

'Although the Secretaries of State will retain the right not to approve projects on cost grounds there will be no formal cost limits. The controlling factor overall will be the lump sum authorisations, not the list of projects based upon them, and it will be for local education authorities to secure the best value from these resources in the light of local conditions.'

Cost limits for other educational buildings were dropped even earlier. Youth service projects, for instance were freed from cost control in 1971. Despite the ultimate demise of the cost-per-place system, the department is on the whole, proud of its achievements and the Treasury very satisfied. It would be difficult to find another important field of public expenditure with as effective a history of economy. It was no mean feat to hold the limits unchanged for long periods in the 1950s and 1960s. At the end of the 1960s the basic cost-per-place limits for schools with kitchens were £206 and £367 for primary and secondary schools respectively, compared to £170 and £290 when first introduced in 1949 – a very modest rise indeed. Of course thereafter the balloon went up to reach £361 and £691 by 1973.

On the other hand LEAs have always had a more ambivalent attitude to cost-per-place limits. Many chief education officers and education committee chairmen felt that they imposed a legitimate financial discipline on constructional activities but, when they lagged seriously behind inflation as sometimes occurred even before the 1970s, they caused LEAs serious difficulties. And in the twelve months before suspension they were an impossible hurdle. Some LEAs, for instance Kent, designed projects to the absolute minimum statutory standards but still could not obtain tenders within the limits. It is still not certain whether the banishment of cost-per-place limits is temporary or permanent. Presumably much depends on whether national economic policy is successful in controlling inflation.

The cost-per-place system undoubtedly achieved great economy in school building and was the spur to considerable ingenuity in constructional techniques. Yet cheap initial construction sometimes led to higher maintenance costs. Also the rigorous exclusion of all frills perhaps induced a certain architectural bleakness, arguably not conducive to education in its fullest sense. Whether the net effect was good or bad, LEAs certainly felt ground between the upper and nether millstones of cost-per-place limits and minimum standards for school premises.

Statutory Minimum Standards
The department and its predecessors have long had an interest in

the standards of accommodation which schools provide. Building regulations for public elementary schools and for secondary schools were issued separately in 1914. They were not statutory, however, but according to the department's account, *The Story of Post-War School Building* (1957), 'were intended as a statement of the general principles of school planning and the best current practice in applying these principles'. Both sets of Regulations were eventually superseded by *Handbooks of Suggestions*. Statutory minimum standards were a post-war phenomenon. The Education Act 1944 required the minister to prescribe such standards; draft standards were published in November 1944; the instrument came into force as the *Standards for School Premises Regulations* 1945, commonly referred to as the 'Building Regulations', They have been amended several times since and the current set are the *Standards for School Premises Regulations* 1972.

They apply not only to primary and secondary schools, but to nursery schools and classes, special schools and boarding accommodation. The standards vary somewhat between these categories. The regulations prescribe the minimum area of school sites, playing fields and teaching accommodation, minimum standards for dining, cloakroom, sanitary and washing facilities, minimum levels for lighting, heating and ventilation, and a host of other aspects of school accommodation and construction. Some of the regulations are very detailed and specific (e.g. a primary school with twenty-five children must have 3·7 square metres of teaching accommodation per pupil); others are much more general (e.g. 'sufficient and suitable facilities shall be provided in or near the teaching accommodation, for the storage of apparatus, equipment and materials required for teaching'). Nevertheless the net effect is to lay down a very demanding rubric for LEAs to adhere to.

The regulations prescribe *minimum* standards; LEAs are free to exceed them. In the past, however, cost limits often made it difficult to exceed the minima by much, and even today costs cannot be discounted. There is a recurring danger that minima will in fact be maxima.

Post-War Development of the School Building Programme
Until 1975, as was mentioned, there were two programmes for primary and secondary school building – one for major works, one for minor. The major works programme was always by far the biggest of the building programmes and now that it has absorbed minor works too, its primacy is even more pronounced.

From the cessation of hostilities until 1949, school building was in an emergency phase. The halt to new construction during the war, the considerable destruction of school buildings by enemy action, the raising of the school-leaving age and the increased numbers of children meant that speed and quantity had to take precedence over careful planning and quality. Many prefabricated temporary classrooms were erected. With the emergency contained, the first effective annual building programme began in 1949. LEAS were instructed in December 1947 to submit proposed projects to be started in 1949, and the programme selected from these was announced in August 1948. This extent of forward planning was fairly typical of the many annual programmes that were to follow.

Until 1958 the major works programmes were annual although the department always tried to give as much advance notice of its allocations as possible. In that year, however, the Government announced in *Secondary Education for All: A New Drive* a five-year building programme for the financial years 1960–1 to 1964–5. For the whole quinquennium projects to the value of £300m. were to be permitted, with £55m. allocated in the first year and £60m. in the second. Five-year planning proved, however, somewhat unwieldly and thereafter the department tried to find a happy mean by employing two- to three-year programming. In 1963 the department invited LEAS to submit their proposals for school building for the three years 1965–6 to 1967–8 and promised to announce the allocation for the first two years and part of the third in the spring of 1964. The next two and a half years to 1969–70 were to be allocated in 1965 but the change of Government disrupted these arrangements. The size of the programme was not fixed and the bids were not invited from LEAS until 1966.

It was not only changes of Government, however, which caused this style of major works programme to creak at the seams by the late 1960s. Sometimes projects included in a programme could not be started in the appropriate financial year and had to be carried over to the next. The department itself admitted that this weakened the programme's credibility. It also argued that the old-style major works programme was not entirely suited to the increasing scale and complexity of educational building and its need to be co-ordinated with urban development. The system which the department announced as a replacement in Circular 13/.68 was a rolling programme – a common arrangement in public administration whereby investment in some field is settled firmly for the next one or two years and tentatively over a longer period, say five years, and then is rolled forward annually so that it constantly covers the next five years. It was to apply to 1969–70 and subsequent years.

The rolling programme was given three phases – preliminary list, design list and starts programme. The *preliminary list* was to be of major works reasonably expected to be needed within the next five years. LEAS were to propose additions to the preliminary list which the DES might or might not accept. Once entered on the preliminary list the LEA could begin initial work on a project – acquiring the site, obtaining planning permission, drafting the architects' brief and the like. Appearance on the list involved no commitment, however, as to the year in which a project could start.

The next stage was to be the *design list*, like the preliminary list drawn up by the DES in response to submissions by LEAS. Projects were to be transferred from the preliminary to the design list when preparatory work was completed and the year for construction to start more certain. Appearance on the design list for a particular year implied that building would commence the next; thus the design list for 1971–2 was of projects to start building in 1972–3. A project was only to start the following year, however, if detailed planning was finished and the LEA still wanted it to.

The final stage was to be the *starts programme* consisting in the main of projects promoted from the previous year's design list. The department promised to try to finalise the starts programme at least six months before the building year it applied to begun.

These arrangements were intended to combine coherent programming with a degree of flexibility. While the majority of projects could follow the logical sequence of preliminary list, design list and starts programme within a quinquennial time-scale, other possibilities were not excluded. Educational forecasting being about as reliable as the meteorological variety, the size or urgency of need is sometimes over- or under-estimated. Projects could, however, stay longer than five years on the preliminary list or longer than one year on the design list. On the other hand, an exceptional emergency could lead to projects jumping one stage or even two.

The rolling programme began to operate with a fair measure of success but even it proved insufficiently elastic to accommodate the stresses of galloping inflation and retrenchment of public expenditure. The counter-inflationary measures taken by the Government in the autumn of 1973 included rephasing public building over a longer period to relieve pressure on the building industry and to moderate prices. Thus LEAS were informed in Circular 12/73 that no more final approvals for major or minor projects would be issued before the end of 1973 and that only projects already blessed with such approval could be started. So a giant-sized spanner was thrown into the careful machinery of the rolling programme. Approvals were resumed in 1974 but only for 'roofs over heads' and special schools. Also, as was mentioned, the department finally dropped all project selection in the case of basic needs. This left the programme consisting of lump sum authorisations like the minor works programme.

In late 1974, however, the Labour Government announced (Circular 13/74) that a modified version of the three-stage rolling programme was to be restored. The aim is to give LEAS progressively firmer authorisations either as lump sums (nursery, primary, secondary schools) or for specific projects (special schools, institutions of further education or teacher training) at regular intervals before the beginning of the starts year. The stages selected are 'provisional' (two and a half years before the starts year), 'planning' (fifteen months) and 'final' (six months).

When fully operational the cycle will begin with LEAS sending 'priority building lists' of their primary and secondary school projects two and three quarter years before they are intended to be started. The DES will then make a provisional lump sum allocation to each LEA, taking account of these lists, government policies and resources available. LEAS are next to send in a provisional list of the projects they intend to undertake within their allocations; the DES emphasises that it will not allow any projects inconsistent with secondary reorganisation to reach the provisional list. LEAS next are to receive their planning allocations and will be asked to submit planning lists; the process is to be repeated with final allocations and sending in of final lists six months before the starts year.

It will be noted that, although there is emphasis on lump sum allocations, the department intends to peruse LEA lists of proposed projects at no fewer than four stages before any construction takes place. No doubt heavy pressure will be put on LEAS to omit projects which the DES considers undesirable or premature. The difference between this system and the old one of individual project selection seems paper-thin.

It is intended that the nursery education programme will consist of earmarked additions to the lump sum authorisations for primary and secondary schools. There will not be the same four-hurdle project vetting; instead the department will keep in touch only informally with LEAS on their nursery projects.

On special schools, allocations will continue to be made for individual projects. The DES and the Welsh Office are to start, for England and Wales respectively, registers or provisional lists of LEA and voluntary projects suitable to be started within five years. Proposals for additions to these lists will be considered at any time. Further education and teacher training projects will also be subject to individual project selection, although there will also be a three-stage process. A provisional list of projects will be drawn up which the department agree to be suitable to start within five years. Subsequently the *DES* will select from it a planning list eighteen months, and a final list six months, before the starts year. There will be two separate minor works programmes (one for England, one for Wales) for further education and teacher training projects costing less than £25,000 each, allocated to LEAs on a lump sum basis.

Once again therefore the DES is struggling to find a formula which will preserve some coherence in a fluid situation, yet will not impose an unreal rigidity. One feels that the department is still trying to retain too much detailed intervention and will have to move towards even broader investment controls.

Construction and Approval of Individual Projects

In the past, departmental interest in a project did not cease once it had been allocated to a starts programme. Projects were subject to the dual statutory regulation of *minimum* standards and *maximum* costs and the department was concerned to ensure that actual project planning and construction accorded with the regulations. Today, although in most cases the department has dropped project selection in favour of lump sum authorisations, it maintains interest in the planning and construction of individual projects. Statutory cost limits have been abandoned but structural standards certainly have not. The department must still satisfy itself that each project fulfils the requirements of the *Standards for School Premises Regulations*

This stage of the process starts with the receipt by an LEA of a lump sum authorisation from the department. It is the LEA's responsibility to decide which projects to undertake within the sum allocated, although as was stressed if there has been repeated departmental scrutiny of lists of projects, there are unlikely to be many surprises. In any case, in all programmes and at all times the main determinant is invariably need, especially where new housing developments necessitate 'roofs over heads'. The chief education officer and his staff are the best equipped to assess such factors and thus have usually the major voice in project selection. Occasionally a particularly powerful councillor or group of councillors may be able to promote some project they favour to a slightly higher priority than it warrants but *gross* unfairness is unlikely. Most projects are in the pipeline for several years and the case for each widely known. It would be too blatant to select a project which clearly did not merit it. At the very least this would provoke outraged resistance from councillors interested in other projects.

Similarly, since need is the prime criterion, assessed on a professional basis, party political factors do not usually loom large in project selection. They are most likely to arise where a ruling group

for ideological reasons wishes to accelerate or decelerate comprehensive reorganisation of secondary schools with obvious repercussions on building priorities.

Eventually the list of projects to be undertaken is settled. Next
the LEA must decide whether to use its own architects or a private
firm. With the increased average size of LEAs following the reorganisation of local government, most have substantial architectural
staffs of their own and can be expected to rely increasingly on them.
In any case sketch plans are produced, approved by the LEA and
usually go to the DES for perusal, although it is not obligatory at
this stage. Final plans, though, have to receive departmental sanction. Speedy departmental approval can usually be obtained by the
LEA completing a certificate of compliance with building controls.

Since projects are often in the pipeline for several years, they
may be at an advanced state of planning before an allocation is received in which they can be included. Some may even have had
their plans approved by the department.

The department does not, however, restrict itself to this negative,
vetting activity. First, the department itself undertakes some inno-
vatory building. There is a Development Group of Architects and
Quantity Surveyors in the DES who each year build one or two projects in co-operation with a local authority to try out new technical
or educational ideas or both. For instance the Development Group
designed a science block for a large boys' grammar school in Oxford.
This enabled the Group both to investigate the requirements of
modern science teaching in terms of buildings and to fulfil a number of technical objectives – to test a dimensional control system
proposed by the Building Research Station, to develop a rapidly-
erected, dry form of construction, to carry farther the application
of permanent supplementary artificial lighting of interiors, to gain
experience with the use of modern management techniques for pro-
cessing the bill of quantities. Similarly a sixth-form centre for a
girls' school in Epsom was designed by the Group in association
with Surrey County Council. Not only was it an opportunity to plan
for new styles of sixth-form teaching but also to use a new kind of
system building developed by the South Eastern Architects' Collaboration and to pay special attention to the problems of heating.
The Group undertook the construction of new buildings and the remodelling of existing ones for a college of further education in
Preston in collaboration with a private firm of architects. Educationally the task was to design for increasing numbers of students and
diversity of courses; technically the main problem was to provide
planning, mechanical services and equipment. Many other examples
could be quoted.

Secondly, the department publishes a series of *Building Bulletins* which give advice on educational building. Fifty have been published since 1949, covering a range of topics from design of school kitchens to minimising fire risk in school design. Some *Bulletins* also describe and assess projects built by the Development Group; the three projects mentioned in the last paragraph were described in *Building Bulletins* 29, 39 and 41. Thirdly, the department sponsors occasional building conferences, both with local education authorities and with voluntary school authorities. These may be regional or national.

This kind of positive activity on the part of the DES has not only helped to foster a spirit of co-operation and mutual respect in central–local relations but has stimulated creativity and innovation in educational building. Of course some LEAs are more influenced by departmental advice and publications than others, but all welcome the department providing it and them.

Chapter IX

PROVIDING THE TEACHERS

No one can teach in a maintained primary or secondary school in England and Wales unless approved by the DES as a qualified teacher. The only minor exceptions are for instructors in specialised activities like sport or playing musical instruments, a small number of uncertified teachers active before 1945 and 'student teachers' (people over 18 who intend to enter a teacher training course and have the requisite entry qualifications and who may be used in a limited and temporary capacity, for instance while awaiting entry to college). To secure qualified status from the DES all teachers have since 1973 had to undergo an approved course of teacher training. Before 1973 graduates and holders of certain other specialist qualifications could become qualified teachers without further training. Only a minority took advantage of this loophole, however, and its closing in 1973 was not a dramatic change. Unlike school teachers, teachers in institutions of further education are not obliged to undergo teacher training.

Teacher training has undergone fundamental changes since the war, and the pace of change has accelerated in the last few years. The very term 'teacher training' has now generally been discarded in favour of 'teacher education'. Despite the changes, however, there still remain two basic avenues of training or education for new schoolteachers – the non-graduate and the post-graduate – although they are tending to converge. The former used to be provided mainly by specialist institutions first called teacher training colleges and later colleges of education. Following the government reorganisation scheme announced in 1974 (discussed below) the colleges of education have progressively lost their specialist identity, many being merged with universities, polytechnics and other institutions of further and higher education, and others diversified into colleges of higher education. Post-graduate teacher training or education was once the almost exclusive concern of university departments of education, but increasing numbers of colleges of education, polytechnics and technical colleges began to offer it too; by the mid-

1970s more graduates were attending teacher education courses outside universities than inside.

The usual length of course at training colleges became, by the 1930s, two years for young men and women following secondary school. The McNair Committee (1944) urged that the college course be extended to three years for the normal 18-year-old. This was finally achieved in 1960. Successful students were awarded a certificate of education, called popularly the teachers' certificate. In 1963 the Robbins Committee proposed that college students be allowed to proceed to a degree to be known as the Bachelor of Education (B.Ed.). The proposal was accepted. There are several different course patterns for the B.Ed.; some involve four years of study, some three. For a decade the B.Ed. and the teachers' certificate existed concurrently but following the James Report, as is discussed below, the Government decided that the teachers' certificate should be phased out.

Aspirant teachers who follow the other avenue, degree plus post-graduate teacher education, usually take four years. This has changed little over the years. Most first degrees in English and Welsh universities require a three-year course. Post-graduate teacher education (whether in university departments of education, or polytechnics or colleges) invariably lasts a year. Successful candidates receive a post-graduate certificate of education.

There has always been a tension between the academic and the vocational in teacher training. In general teachers have constantly urged that greater emphasis be placed on the academic. To some extent the history of this part of the education service can be seen as a gradual victory for their view, symbolised by today's use of the term 'teacher education' in place of 'training'. There has however been some reaction against this trend in recent years. The NUT, for instance, in its policy statement *The Reform of Teacher Education* (1971) stresses that equal importance be accorded to the professional element.

The first coherent theory of teacher training was the monitorial principal under which older pupils were instructed by the teacher and then passed on the instruction to younger pupils. This was superseded in the 1840s by the pupil-teacher system associated with Sir James Kay-Shuttleworth. Under this a boy or girl of 13 could become apprenticed to a teacher. At the end of a five years' apprenticeship some pupil-teachers went on to training college, others took an examination to qualify immediately as a teacher. After the Education Act 1902 pupil-teachers were replaced by student-teachers who devoted only part of their last year at school to preliminary training before going on to training college. Not until the 1920s was it finally decided that all prospective teachers should complete normal secondary education before undertaking any training.

Obviously the Kay-Shuttleworth pupil-teacher system involved rather low academic standards and extensive practical instruction. Today the position is almost directly reversed, especially for graduate teachers (three years of university and only one of teacher education). The extension of the college course to three years and the introduction of the B.Ed. also represent successes for the viewpoint favouring greater academic emphasis.

Even in the normal course today for non-graduates, academic instruction seems to predominate. There are four elements in the course: the main subject or subjects, the theory of education, curriculum or professional studies, teaching practice. The NUT claims (op. cit., 1971, p. 19):

'The inclusion of a main subject in the curriculum of colleges of education stems very largely from a desire to give intellectual and academic weight to the teacher's certificate, in place of the preponderance of a large number of low level courses in the past. Based on the concept of the traditional university degree, the main subject in colleges of education has come to be recognised as the academic side of the teacher's education, whilst the remaining courses are seen as his professional training.'

The pattern varies somewhat between colleges. Some have two main subjects, others one main one but one or more subsidiaries. Nevertheless this major academic element is common to all.

Educational theory is also a compulsory feature of all such courses. This brings to focus on education a range of disciplines but especially psychology, philosophy and sociology. If successful, this part of the course should be of both intellectual and practical value. It should combine the academic and the professional.

This is also true of the third element, curriculum or professional studies. These are designed to equip a teacher with the knowledge and skills needed for teaching. They involve the study of subjects, partly for their content but primarily with a view to learning how to teach them. Such curriculum studies are particularly important for those intending to teach in primary schools. They have to be equipped to teach a wider range of subjects than their secondary colleagues; consequently study of the two or three main subjects is insufficient.

Finally there is teaching practice, that is, actual school teaching under supervision. For the NUT (op. cit., 1971, p. 22) it has 'a position of *primus inter pares* with the other elements'. Today a trainee teacher spends at least 140 half-days (the equivalent of fourteen weeks) on teaching practice during the three-year course. There is much argument about teaching practice: how it should be supervised, how assessed, whether it should be in short or long bursts, and so on. Nevertheless, its indispensability is unquestioned. Yet it is a very abbreviated modern version of the five years' apprenticeship of Kay-Shuttleworth's pupil-teachers.

Of the four course elements, therefore, one is wholly academic (the main subject or subjects), one is wholly professional (teaching practice) and the other two have a mixed purpose. This balance between the academic and the professional is by no means universally acceptable, as is discussed below in the context of the James Report.

All this applies to the usual courses. There is, as has been mentioned, a range of special courses either in the normal colleges or in specialist institutions. The most important include courses for teachers of physical education, of home economics, of handicapped children, of immigrant children, and full-time or part-time courses for older people wishing to take up teaching as a career. Also art teachers are usually trained in colleges of art. All such courses likewise contain both academic and professional elements in varying proportions. Even in the universities which now offer combined degree courses in two or more subjects with education as the principal or subsidiary component the professional side is not omitted. If they are three-year courses, graduates must take a further year to obtain the usual post-graduate teaching certificate. If the courses are four years in duration, they are for a combined degree and teaching certificate.

The four colleges of education (technical) provide training for prospective teachers in further education institutions. The usual course is a full-time one of a year's duration but part-time and sandwich courses are also offered. In all the emphasis is heavily professional.

Administration of Teacher Training and Education

The separation between the training of graduates and non-graduates is reflected in a division of administrative responsibility. The colleges of education (apart from the minority provided by voluntary bodies),[1] the polytechnics and the other colleges are of course part of the local authority sector. The universities are not. Sir Edward (later Lord) Boyle termed this division 'the binary system' and the term has stuck. Its roots are, however, far older than his term of office.

In the early nineteenth century the various voluntary educational bodies began to establish training colleges to train teachers for their own schools. Government financial assistance towards the establishment of such colleges was first provided in 1842, and towards their maintenance in 1846. The government also began to contribute to the salary of teachers trained in such colleges. In return the government acquired the right to inspect the colleges, prescribe courses, conduct examinations and award its Elementary School Teachers Certificate to successful candidates.

The monopoly of the voluntary training colleges was broken in 1893 when the government permitted the establishment of grant-aided day colleges attached to universities. The third strand in teacher training came in 1902 when the Education Act of that year which created LEAs allowed them to set up their own teacher training colleges. Thus by Edwardian times teacher training could be voluntary, local authority or university based with a strong government interest in all three.

The government's direct responsibility (exercised through the Board of Education) for college curricula and examinations was modified in 1930. The training colleges were arranged into ten groups and brought into an examination relationship with the universities by the creation for each group of a joint examination board, consisting of university and college representatives. The joint examination boards took over responsibility for conducting examinations and drawing up curricula subject to overall government approval. The government tried to maintain some national parity of qualification in consultation with a Central Advisory Committee. The government also retained direct responsibility through its HMIs for testing whether the colleges were imparting adequate practical (as opposed to academic) training.

McNair And After

In March 1942 Mr R. A. Butler, as President of the Board of Education, appointed a committee under Sir Arnold McNair, Vice-Chancellor of Liverpool University, 'to consider the supply, recruitment and training of teachers and youth leaders'. The Report of the McNair Committee had a profound influence on the post-war organisation of teacher training and indeed right up to the present.

There were two crucial recommendations of the McNair Committee. One was that a central training council be established to plan the detailed structure of a teacher training service and to advise the government on its operation. The other was that all training institutions and interests be closely integrated on an area basis.

In response to the first recommendation the government set up in 1947 two Interim Committees for Teachers, one for England and one for Wales, to advise the government. Two years later the two Interim Committees were replaced by the National Advisory Council on the Training and Supply of Teachers. This was not really the small, powerful, planning body which McNair had envisaged. Nevertheless, it became an important advisory organ. Its terms of reference were to keep under review national policy on the training and conditions of qualifications of teachers and on their recruitment and distribution; it was not concerned with pay, superannuation or conditions of employment.

The National Advisory Council had a membership of forty, which later grew to fifty-five, appointed from the various bodies concerned with education – local authorities, teachers' unions, universities, the DES and area training organisations. The National Advisory Council issued nine reports, some general and some on specific issues, and provided an important forum of discussion. The government, however, gradually became disenchanted with the body. It was felt that it added little to departmental knowledge. Moreover the DES was embarrassed when major disagreements arose on the National Advisory Council about the future demand for teachers and the best way to meet it. Profound differences of opinion and judgement were particularly manifest in the ninth and last report of the National Advisory Council in 1965. Shortly afterwards its chairman, Mr A. C. L. (later Lord) Bullock, Master of St Catherine's College, Oxford, resigned. He was never replaced. The National Advisory Council was not formally dissolved, but like an old soldier it faded away.

The demise of the National Advisory Council may have been welcome to the DES but it was decidedly unwelcome to many others. Teachers, especially, felt the lack of a forum for collective discussion of teacher training. Willey and Maddison (1971, p. 18) expressed very strong sentiments about the National Advisory Council's disbandment.

'It is difficult to exaggerate the importance of the central weakness in the structure of teacher training. There is no other profession which lacks an effective body-representative of the interests concerned and responsible for the maintenance of standards, the consideration of training methods, and the co-ordination of national policy.'

In 1973 Mrs Margaret Thatcher quietly resurrected the National Advisory Council in new, more modest guise – an Advisory Committee on the Supply and Training of Teachers with a membership drawn, like its predecessor, from the various sectors of the education world. The Advisory Committee has been much consulted by the DES on the numbers, quality and deployment of teachers but seems deliberately to be adopting a 'a low profile', and at the time of writing has not published any report.

The history of the McNair Committee's first recommendation has not therefore been altogether happy. Its second recommendation concerned the regional bodies. The Committee was dissatisfied with the old joint examination boards. Training colleges in the same group did not necessarily have closer relations with one another except in the matter of examinations. The joint examination boards were not, for instance, designed to promote co-operation on staffing or amenities. Nor, even on examinations, was there co-ordination between the training colleges on the one hand and the university departments of education on the other. The McNair Committee wanted much more effective regional co-ordinating machinery.

The Committee was itself divided as to the exact form this machinery should take. Half of the Committee wanted a complete integration of the university departments of education and the training colleges on an area basis. Each university would establish a school of education consisting of an organic federation of all training institutions and which would be responsible for all training and assessment. The other half of the committee were less radical. They felt that the university education departments and the colleges performed different functions and should retain their separate identities. They wanted an association of equals, not the absorption of the one by the other. Accordingly they recommended merely a strengthening of the joint examination boards. They wanted the boards' membership to be expanded to include representatives of other educational interests as well as the universities and the colleges. They also wanted their functions to be expanded to include not only the organisation of all training and assessment but consultation on staff appointments.

The Government preferred the second recommendation and from 1947 established area training organisations (ATOs) as modified versions of the joint examination boards.

In 1975 there were twenty-two ATOs in England and Wales. The governing body (or delegacy) of each consisted of representatives of the colleges, universities, local education authorities and teachers in the area served together with assessors from the DES. The basic responsibility of the ATOs was to supervise and co-ordinate initial teacher training – thus they approved the standard and content of college courses, assessed and examined students, co-ordinated the arrangements for teaching practice, regulated the exceptional admission of students without normal qualifications and remitted some part of the course for students with unusual qualifications or experience. Detailed supervision of college syllabuses was conducted through a system of boards of studies consisting of appropriate college and university staff.

There was some dissatisfaction with the ATOS. It was argued, for instance, that they should have involved all English and Welsh universities, and perhaps all polytechnics. Certainly polytechnic participation should not have been confined to a polytechnic's education department. Moreover, the ATO's ranged considerably in size and their jurisdictions sometimes cut across LEA boundaries. Indeed two ATOS sometimes had an overlapping responsibility for the same area, e.g. Northampton.

A graver cricticism than their rather confused organisation is, however, that they had no jurisdiction over the university departments of education. These remained an integral part of their university, controlled in the same way as any other university department. Consequently, while universities through membership of ATOs exercised considerable influence over the colleges there was no reciprocity. In any case the ATOS were criticised as being rather feeble bodies; they had relatively little discretion. On certain matters (e.g. changes in course structure) they needed the approval of the DES, on others (e.g. the standard of B.Ed. degrees) they needed the approval of the university.

Finally, after the demise of the National Advisory Council there was until 1973 no national co-ordination of the ATOs except by the DES.

In short, the ATOS were only marginally more effective than the pre-war joint examination boards as regional organs for co-ordinating teacher training. The Robbins Committee in 1963 (like part of the McNair Committee in 1944) thought that the only solution for these kinds of problems would be to integrate the training colleges into the universities within schools of education. The colleges, renamed colleges of education, would have independent governing bodies related federally to the school of education and through it to the university. The Robbins Committee also wanted a unitary system of higher education and a single Grants Commission. Thus teacher training would have been financed by grants from this Commission through the universities to the schools of education.

Again, however, the Government would not accept the integration of teacher training with the universities. Indeed the only one of these Robbins recommendations to be implemented was the change in the name of the training colleges to 'colleges of education'.

The college of education staff were bitterly disappointed at the rejection of the Robbins proposals. The binary system was alleged to create feelings of inferiority in college-trained teachers towards their graduate colleagues. Moreover in the post-Robbins years the colleges were subjected to new pressures: to increase the supply of teachers, to introduce the B.Ed., to extend the college course to three years. Some colleges began to creak under the strain and teachers' organisations and college staff voiced growing discontent which reached a crescendo in the late 1960s.

The James Report

The first official response to the mounting wave of criticism was the decision of the House of Commons Select Committee on Education and Science to investigate teacher training. Under its chairman, Mr F. T. Willey, MP for Sunderland South, the Select Committee conducted its inquiry from July 1969 to May 1970 when it was cut short by the dissolution of Parliament for the general election. The Select Committee never thus reported. It had, however, received and published a good deal of evidence on teacher training. Moreover, Mr Willey produced a short book summarising the evidence and indicating his conclusions (Willey and Maddison, 1971).

The second official response to public anxiety about teacher training came in February 1970 when Mr Edward Short, Labour Secretary of State for Education and Science, asked ATOs to conduct detailed reviews of their courses and procedures.

Both these responses turned out to be curtain-raisers for the main event. In November 1970 the new Conservative Secretary of State for Education and Science, Mrs Margaret Thatcher, appointed a committee of inquiry into teacher training, the first since McNair. Like McNair, a university vice-chancellor was made chairman of the committee. Lord James of Rusholme (Vice-Chancellor of York University and former headmaster of Manchester Grammar School). The James Committee had a smaller membership than McNair, eight against ten; moreover several of the members were full-time. Perhaps the most innovative feature of the James Committee was that Mrs Thatcher urged it to report within twelve months – which it did.

The Report of the James Committee is one of the most contentious documents on teacher training for many a long day. Unlike McNair, which had seemed to endorse current thinking and to encourage existing trends, the James Committee challenged the consensus in some respects and indicated a different course to that expected by most informed opinion.

The terms of reference given the James Committee were curiously elaborate. Nevertheless their general impact was to accord the Committee wide discretion to investigate and recommend upon both the

organisation and content of teacher education, training and probation. The Committee was able to use all the evidence submitted to
the House of Commons Select Committee on Teacher Training, as
well as the results of the ATO surveys. Moreover the committee ener-
getically collected material itself – 500 separate submissions of
written evidence, 23 working days devoted to hearing oral evidence,
Committee visits to 50 institutions (colleges of education, polytechnics, etc.).

The James Committee's fundamental proposal was that teacher
training be organised on the basis of three successive 'cycles': 'first
personal education; the second pre-service training and induction;
the third inservice education and training'.

By 'personal education' the James Committee meant in effect
higher education. Just as in the 1920s it was finally accepted that
young men and women should complete their secondary education
before commencing any teacher training, so James wanted the principle extended in order that all prospective teachers would finish
a course of *higher education* before starting teacher training. Of
course the three-year college of education course did not permit
this; it *mixed* higher (academic) education with (professional) teacher
training. James considered that this led to a conflict and confusion
of objectives. James wanted a first cycle devoted exclusively to
higher academic education. Teachers trained via the other leg of
the binary system, that is who first read for a university degree, already fulfil this principle; thus James wanted to leave their position
basically unaltered. What of the majority then attending colleges of
education? James proposed for them a radical change – a two-year
course leading to a Diploma in Higher Education (Dip.HE) to
precede any teacher training. The Dip.HE would combine a study
in depth of one or two subjects with a more broadly based education
and would be offered by both colleges of education and other institutions (e.g. polytechnics).

James envisaged this Dip.HE as being a worthwhile terminal
qualification as well as the first cycle of training for teachers. It
was pointed out that apart from vocational qualifications there was
little short of a degree that a person desirous of higher education
could undertake. By no means all Dip.HE holders would go on
to become teachers (as by no means all degree holders). Thus the
James Committee's first cycle would be either a degree or a Dip.HE.

The second cycle – pre-service training and induction in James's
terminology – would be the professional teacher's training. James
wanted this cycle to occupy two years, but in two distinct halves.
The first year of the second cycle would be spent in a college or
university or polytechnic department of education; the second year

would be spent as a probationary teacher in a school (or further education college). James wanted the year of study to be practical and highly specialised.

'We should abandon the pretence that it is possible to train, during the initial period a "teacher". The aim at this stage should be to prepare a student to work within a defined area – an area that may, of course, be defined in a variety of ways, e.g. age of pupil, or subject. The first year of training of the modern languages teacher would, for example, include as a major element not only the techniques of language teaching but also some appreciation of the theoretical background against which those techniques must be understood and evaluated. The relevance of their training to the work they are going to do must be apparent to all students and in particular to mature students.'

Students who completed this year successfully would be known as 'licensed' teachers and would take up appointments in schools or further education institutions. They would be paid a salary and would be in most senses full members of staff. The subsequent year would, however, be an essential part of initial training. The licensed teacher would receive advice and assistance on all professional matters from his colleagues and especially from one designated his professional tutor. He would also be released for at least a fifth of his time to attend a professional teaching centre, of which James wanted a massive increase. If the licensed teacher were considered satisfactory at the end of this probationary year he would be accorded the status of a fully recognised teacher. Those holding a Dip.HE would be awarded the further qualification of a BA (Ed.).

Finally there was the James Committee's third cycle: 'inservice education and training'. There is, of course, nothing new about the concept; many serving teachers are already released to attend courses of various kinds and lengths. James, however, wanted this vastly expanded and systematised. The Committee was insistent that initial training and education was not sufficient to equip a teacher for the rest of his career. All serving teachers should be given the opportunity to extend their personal education, develop their professional competence and improve their understanding of educational principles and techniques.

The James Committee envisaged these opportunities being provided first in the schools and further education colleges themselves; they should regard the continued training of their own staffs (through evening discussions, etc.) as an essential task. Secondly, however, the Committee wanted to see a national network of 'professional centres' established. These would be the universities and colleges of education plus teaching centres operated by local authorities. Some of the latter already exist but James wanted many more and, equally important, wanted all the 'professional centres' closely co-ordinated on a regional basis.

The courses that teachers would attend during their careers would thus range from evening meetings or weekend conferences not even requiring leave to full-time courses for a higher degree, with a considerable spectrum in between. The Committee recommended that an immediate aim should be to allow every teacher the equivalent of one term's leave every seven years to pursue in-service training; ultimately the entitlement should be raised to one term in every five years. Actual take-up of the entitlement would involve 3 per cent of school teachers being absent on secondment at any one time.

The James Committee's proposals for a new pattern of teacher training required also some reorganisation of the machinery of co-ordination. The Committee agreed with much of the criticism of the old ATOS. Even if these faults had not existed, the new pattern of teacher training proposed by James would have necessitated some structural changes. In particular the major expansion of second and third cycle training would have made inevitable some adjustments in the machinery to provide for effective regional and national co-ordination.

James proposed, therefore, that the ATOS be replaced by fifteen regional councils for colleges and departments of education (RCCDEs). Each would represent and bring into partnership *all* the colleges, universities, polytechnics and LEAs in the region. A typical RCCDE would contain two or three universities, one or two polytechnics, perhaps ten colleges of education and a varying number of LEAs, depending on whether or not a metropolitan area was included. All these institutions and authorities would be represented on the governing council of each RCCDE; moreover every university and polytechnic would have two representatives – one for the institution as a whole and one for its department of education. There would besides be five representatives of school and further education teachers, plus one each from the CNAA and the Open University and finally two assessors and two full members appointed by the secretary of state. Each RCCDE would operate primarily through an academic committee and a professional committee, although there might be other committees and sub-committees.

Above the fifteen RCCDEs James wanted to see established a National Council for Teacher Education and Training (NCTET). It

would be twenty strong (half the size of the National Advisory
Council), appointed by the secretary of state from nominees of the
RCCDES.

James foresaw the NCTET and the RCCDEs performing interlocking
roles in the planning and administration of teacher education and
training and in the validation of awards. Thus on the first cycle
the RCCDEs would exercise some supervision over the teaching and
examining of the Dip.HE by the individual institutions. The NCTET
would have a primarily monitoring and advisory role. On the
second and third cycles all professional teaching qualifications,
including the BA (Ed.) and all in-service professional awards would
be dependent upon recognition and approval by the NCTET (acting
in consultation with the RCCDEs). Similarly recommendations on
the recognition of 'licensed' and 'registered' teachers would originate in the RCCDEs and would be channelled via the NCTET to the
secretary of state for final decision. The RCCDEs would co-ordinate
and plan the provision of second and third cycle facilities in their
areas; the NCTET would provide national advice on the numbers
and categories of teachers needed and the courses desired. Of
course, throughout, the NCTET and the RCCDEs would act within
the confines of government policy.

Reaction to the James Report

The James Committee's proposals provoked a stormy public debate with the critics predominating. Even the rejection by the
James Committee of concurrency of education and training was
challenged (Parry, 1972, pp. 82 – 7)). The teachers reacted particularly adversely to much that was recommended. Most teachers
wanted a system of all-graduate entry to teacher training. Only
thus, was it felt, could the profession be united and enhanced. It is
true that the James proposals would have eventually produced a
completely graduate profession but only by means of the academic-
ally rather suspect BA (Ed.) and *after* entry. The NUT, for instance,
in its evidence to the James Committee had argued strongly for
a three-year first degree course in education to be established in
universities, polytechnics and colleges of education. Thereafter
prospective teachers would undergo a year (three terms) of professional training. Where a prospective teacher read for an ordinary university degree (without any educational component), they
would require four terms of professional training. The NUT was
thus dismayed by the James proposal for a two year Dip.HE. It
failed to provide for a profession united on the basis of graduate
entry. Moreover, in the NUT's view it made too sharp a distinction
between the academic and the professional; 'education' could be

a valid component of a degree course or other advanced study.

The NUT also rejected the concept of the 'licensed' teacher since this involved a salaried teacher who was not fully qualified. It was also thought impractical for small schools with small staffs to try to supervise the progress of a 'licensed' teacher. While broadly approving the James proposals for reforming the machinery of co-ordination and consultation, the NUT wanted certain amendments. For instance it preferred the NCTET to be directly appointed by the various educational interests (on the lines of the Schools Council) rather than by the secretary of state from nominations. Also the NUT found the James regions rather large for effective teacher involvement and urged the need for sub-units to be established within each − see its *James: A Critical Appraisal* (1972).

The colleges of education and their staffs were just as hostile. Fundamentally they had hoped for a *closer* integration with the universities, ultimately perhaps for full university status. Hence their antagonism towards a Report which proposed a sharper differentiation of their role and virtually a divorce from the universities. Their feelings were demonstrated by a survey (Cortis, 1972). The principals, deputies and heads of department of 144 colleges of education were questioned about the James Report. The great majority were strongly critical; two thirds, for instance, did not believe that teaching standards would be improved if it were implemented.

University opinion too was far from enthusiastic, if only because of the feared effect on higher education generally. The general secretary of the AUT attacked the proposed Dip.HE on the grounds that it would become a second-rate form of higher education for those who would otherwise have undertaken degrees.[2] Only local authorities, especially through the medium of the AEC, gave the Report some welcome.

Government Decisions

The DES discussed the James Report with the various educational interests and issued its own conclusions within a year in a 1972 White Paper, *Education: A Framework for Expansion*. Clearly the torrent of criticism had an impact on government thinking; nevertheless, the White Paper departed fundamentally from Jamesian concepts only on the relationship between the higher education (first cycle) and training (second cycle) of teachers.

The James Committee's proposal for a strict separation between the academic (higher education) and the professional (training) was explicitly rejected in favour of *concurrent* courses. Rather than a two-year Dip.HE followed by two years of professional training leading eventually to a BA (Ed.), the White Paper explained that new teachers would undergo a three-year degree course which combined the academic and the professional. Such a course would be for an Ordinary B.Ed. degree and qualified status; students would have the opportunity to proceed to a fourth year and an Honours B.Ed. degree. The B.Ed. was to be offered in colleges of education, together with any polytechnics and universities who so wished; the normal entry requirement was to be the same as for universities. The new B.Ed. would be validated by existing awarding bodies, including the CNAA.

Having, however, thrown the Dip.HE out of the door, the White Paper brought it in again through the window. The Government accepted the case for a two-year higher diploma although not in the context of teacher training, rather as a general educational qualification for prospective local government administrators, bank clerks, etc. Thus a Dip.HE was to be instituted after all. Indeed the White Paper explained that the new three-year B.Ed. courses could be designed so that the first two years could lead to a Dip.HE for those who wished to go no farther.

The White Paper was thus a commitment to an all-graduate teaching profession. Teachers would either read for an ordinary degree and supplement it with one year of post-graduate teacher education for their certificate, as at present. Alternatively, teachers would read for the new B.Ed. and qualified status combined, taking either four years (with honours) or three years (without). Whether these arrangements would finally remove all sting from the binary system would depend upon the respect which the B.Ed. achieved. If it were regarded as inferior to other degrees, little more than a tarted up teachers' certificate, then little would be gained.

The White Paper's arrangements for the probationary year (which it termed 'induction') differed only in detail from the James Committee's. After acquiring their B.Eds or other degrees plus teaching certificates, the new teachers were to spend a year of induction in a teaching post. If their performance were considered satisfactory they would then be accorded full 'registered' status.

The White Paper admitted that serious doubts had been expressed about the concept of a 'licensed' teacher and, as before, they were to achieve qualified status before being appointed to a teaching post. Nevertheless, whatever their formal status their position during the inductive year seemed to be basically what the James Committee had in mind. Moreover, the White Paper announced the need for the designation and training of professional tutors despite objections from some quarters.

The Government's intentions for in-service training followed closely the James Committee's third cycle proposals. The Government hoped to reach the James Committee's target of 3 per cent of teachers being released for such training by 1981.

The White Paper was far from enthusiastic about the James Committee's proposed radical reorganisation of the machinery of co-ordination and supervision, especially since the RCCDES would be 'virtually divorced from the universities'. The White Paper set out a fourfold analysis of the functions of such machinery: academic validation, professional recognition, co-ordination and higher education supply. Academic validation, principally the award of qualifications, was to remain the responsibility of existing academic bodies (universities, polytechnics, colleges of education and the CNAA). Professional recognition, principally the acceptance of new teachers as full members of the profession, was to be a large (though not exclusive) extent the responsibility of the teaching profession itself. The third function, co-ordination, according to the White Paper, related primarily to in-service training, teaching practice and the distribution of teacher training courses among the various institutions. It was for this third function that the White Paper admitted the need for new regional machinery, and announced that new regional committees would be established on Jamesian lines. Fourthly and finally the White Paper talked of higher education supply, a curiously obscure term for the planning and co-ordination of the non-university sector of higher education generally. The Government wanted to combine the colleges of education with the polytechnics and other advanced insitutions of further education into some coherent system of planning and co-ordination. This vague objective in the White Paper was turned three months later into a decision to reconsider the place of colleges of education in the higher education sector. A Circular, 7/73, asked LEAS to prepare plans for the future development of their colleges including the possibility of turning them into broader-based colleges or amalgamating them with other institutions.

In this and other respects the Government had barely begun to implement the White Paper proposals when in February 1974 it fell. The new Labour Government did not, however, throw all back into the melting pot. For teacher education and training it followed broadly the course set by the Conservatives. Thus the Labour Government pressed ahead with the phasing out of the teachers' certificate and its replacement by the various forms of B.Ed., with the introduction of the Dip.HE, and with the expansion of in-service training and education. Also, after consulting the Advisory Committee on the Supply and Training of Teachers, the Labour Government announced in Circular 5/75 the replacement of the ATOS by regional committees for the education and training of teachers; these consist of representatives of employers, teachers and training institutions in roughly equal proportions plus some neutral co-optees and DES assessors, and their task is to oversee regional arrangements for in-service training, induction and teaching practice and the work of the professional teaching centres. Most important of all, the new Government continued its predecessors' reappraisal of the colleges of education. By early 1975, as the LEA plans flowed into the DES for approval, it was clear that only a minority of the colleges of education would be left as monotechnic institutions. Many were transformed, sometimes after amalgamations, into institutes or colleges of higher education concentrating on advanced level work in the arts, science, and technology while retaining a teacher training or education section. Others were merged with polytechnics or universities.[3]

The writing is on the wall for the colleges of education. Clearly both major political parties envisage teacher training and education as increasingly an integral part of higher education rather than strictly *sui generis*. The rationale for separate colleges of education has now worn very thin.

Government of the Colleges of Education

Though the colleges of education are a declining species, the debate about how they should be governed has had repercussions throughout the education system.

In a memorandum to a House of Commons Select Committee the professional association representing college of education staff, the Association of Teachers in Colleges and Departments of Education (ATCDE), registered its chagrin at the Government's refusal to federate them with the universities, (HC 182 – I, 1969-70, p. 17):

'The government of colleges of education has been the crucial problem of recent years . . . The rejection of the Robbins recommendation on the government of colleges was a major defeat of the ATCDE which was not adequately compensated by the recommendations for the B.Ed. degree.'

Most college staff aspire to university status and resent their inferior position as creatures of local government. In their view (ibid., p. 11) 'the establishment and administration and government of colleges of education by local authorities is hardly more than a historical accident . . . But these local authorities have never been more than the governors and administrators of national institutions.'

To sweeten the pill of the rejection of the Robbins proposal the

Government set up in 1965 a Study Group on the Government of Colleges of Education. The Study Group was chaired by Mr T. R. Weaver, a senior DES official, and was composed of representatives of college teachers, local authorities and religious educational interests.

In its unanimous report the Group put forward a number of suggestions for making the colleges more autonomous. In the curriculum, staffing and management of the colleges it recommended wide discretion for the governing body and the staff; in financial matters it wanted the colleges to have considerable powers of virement within five broad headings of expenditure. It also wanted the DES to set up an advisory committee to recommend the appropriate numbers and grades of non-teaching staff (supervisory, catering, housekeeping, clerical, administrative) for different sized colleges; some local authorities were thought unduly restrictive in such appointments. Most important of all it urged that the structure of government of the colleges reflect their status as semi-autonomous institutions. It proposed that every college should have an academic board representing all staff and responsible within a broad framework of policy for academic work, selection of students and arrangement of teaching practice. Moreover it insisted that the governing bodies of colleges should not consist only of local authority representatives (or in the case of voluntary colleges of representatives of the providing body) but of a wide range of interests – universities, college teachers, schoolteachers, the principal *ex-officio* and perhaps others with special knowledge. Hitherto most maintained colleges were governed by a subcommittee of the education committee of the local authority. Weaver, by contrast, wanted the local authority governors to be in a minority, although still forming the largest single group for each college.

Much of Weaver was exhortatory and addressed to local authorities and the colleges themselves. The DES, however, set up the advisory committee on non-teaching staff. The change in the structure of college government required new legislation which was also eventually forthcoming, Education (No. 2) Act 1968. Under it LEAS are required to prepare an *instrument of government* prescribing the constitution of a governing body. Each instrument has to be submitted to the secretary of state for approval. LEAS are specifically allowed, however, to create a single governing body for two or more institutions. Under the same legislation LEAS have to draw up *articles of government* laying down rules for the operation of each college. Such articles too have to be approved by the secretary of state.

The instruments and articles of government which have been

approved have followed Weaver lines although some have gone farther than others. For instance, in some cases LEA governors are in a
majority, in others a minority. The kind of impact such new arrangements have had was outlined by Alderman J. R. Coxon,
Chairman of the Durham Education Committee, to the House of
Commons Select Committee already mentioned (HC 182–I, p. 85):

'... we are now operating Weaver as fully as we can at our Neville's
Cross College and, instead of having a monthly meeting which we
did under the old regime, we do this in four meetings in the year
and rather keep the close touch with members of the governing
body. I have a bi-monthly rota of three or four members so that
the principal has two or three members to whom he can talk, and
the students can too.'

Such relaxation of control over a college of education is not confined to Durham, but the ATCDE are not satisfied. Their complaints
to the Robbins Committee about local authority control had focused
mainly on finance and the appointment of non-teaching staff (Cmnd
2154–VI, 1963, p. 204); on both some local authorities were thought
unnecessarily restrictive. Even after the Weaver Report and the subsequent legislation, such complaints were still being voiced. The
ATCDE produced for the Select Committee examples of petty restrictions imposed on colleges of education by the local authorities (HC
182–I, 1969–70, pp. 416, 417). All were of an exceedingly trivial
nature – for instance the deputy principal of a large college being
required to have the same standard desk and chair as a deputy
headmaster. Most problems arose where LEAs tried to apply the
same regulations to a college that they applied to their schools. And
even so the ATCDE's complaints applied only to a minority of LEAs.
Even, however, if every LEA were as liberal as could be wished, the
ATCDE would still be unhappy with local authority control – not so
much for any deleterious effect as for the inferior status it symbolises
(ibid., p. 21):

'We feel that our present administrative position, whereby we have
three different masters, the DES, the local authority or the church
as the case may be, and the university, belongs to the madhouse;
that it gives us a ridiculously complex form of administration; that
we ought to be within the university ambit completely.'

Even before the Weaver reforms local authorities exercised far from
untrammelled sway over their colleges of education. Today their
control is but a remnant of what it once was.

The teaching staff themselves, often co-ordinated by an academic board, are responsible for the general work of the college, with the ATO and the university exercising supervision over curricula, course standards, examinations, teaching practice and the like. Internal organisation, management and discipline is basically the responsibility of the principal. The appointment of the principal and deputy principal is a function of the governing body, although the local authority usually has to confirm the decision or approve the shortlist. The governing body is similarly responsible for the appointment and promotion of most staff, teaching and non-teaching. For teaching staff the principal and teachers themselves are generally involved in the decision. Minor non-teaching appointments are usually delegated to the principal. The proportions of teaching staff of different grades are laid down by national regulation. There are no such regulations for non-teaching staff so the local authority, has to lay down the guidelines. The advisory committee set up on Weaver's recommendation has, however, begun to issue model complements, and local authorities are increasingly following these. Yet another area of local authority discretion is thus in practice closing.

Local authorities draw up the Instruments and Articles of Government but the secretary of state has to approve them. Perhaps the most significant remaining local authority powers are in the field of finance. For instance college budgets require the approval of their LEA. Nevertheless even here local authority discretion is hedged about – salary scales are laid down on a national basis, major capital expenditure is subject to detailed DES control.

Local authorities are free to appoint their own representative governors to the college governing bodies. Depending on the Instrument of Government, these may be in a minority or majority. In the case of the former, local authority influence is obviously less. Indeed Alderman S. M. Caffyn of Brighton asserted in evidence to the Select Committee that the town's influence over its two colleges of education was only about the same as over the University of Sussex (ibid., p. 94): 'In regard to the difference between a university council (which in our case has one third local authority members) and that of a college of education (which under the Weaver Report has the same sort of set up), I think the local authority voice is somewhat equal in both.'

The post-Weaver changes in the government of colleges of education were, therefore, very substantial. Moreover they were soon followed by pressures to introduce similar changes in other institutions of further and higher education (see the next chapter). Indeed the Weaver Report was a major influence on the demand for changes in the government of schools (discussed earlier), especially for the greater participation of teaching staff.

Financing the Colleges

The voluntary colleges are financed by a direct grant from the DES. For their current expenditure each voluntary college submits its estimates annually in a form laid down by the department. These estimates are scrutinised and may be amended by DES officials. The college must then operate within the approved estimate, although additional sums may be made available in certain circumstances (e.g. salary increases). Capital expenditure is met in a similar fashion. The DES examines proposals submitted by the voluntary colleges. Grant is then paid for approved projects.

The LEA colleges are financed by the local authorities themselves. Such expenditure is, however, included in the calculations for the Rate Support Grant. Thus through this grant the government can be taken as contributing to teacher training along with many other local authority services. Rate Support Grant payments are not, however, directly linked to any expenditure but are paid to local authorities on a formula basis.

Since some LEAs have a number of colleges and others have only one or none, it would place a disproportionate financial burden on the former if each LEA paid for its own colleges. If LEAs trained only their own students for their own schools such a burden would be unobjectionable; as students may come from anywhere in the country and may go anywhere, the burden would be unfair. Instead, therefore, there is a pooling system.

All LEAs, whether or not they have a college of their own, contribute to the pool, in proportion to their school population. LEAs meet all their current expenditure on teacher training from the pool. This includes of course all the costs of running local authority colleges. It also includes expenditure on student grants. Students receive grants from their home LEAs towards the cost of training; the size of the grants and the conditions under which they are payable are laid down in statutory regulations. Where a student attends a voluntary or local authority college of education, the LEA paying his grant can recoup it from the pool. A student who is trained at a university department of education or at an art teachers' training centre receives grant direct from the DES. Consequently neither local authority nor pool is involved.

Capital expenditure too is met by the LEAs themselves, but the DES operates programme and project controls as for schools. Thus LEAs submit their bids for every programme period and their projects cannot go ahead until included in a programme. The DES then operates detailed control over the plans and construction. Minor works are covered by block allocations, again in response to LEA bids. Throughout it is the LEAS' own money that is involved. Capital expenditure, including loan charges, is met from the pool.

Unlike the position in school building where the initiative almost always comes from the LEA, the generation of major projects of college of education building is more subtle and complex. Mr L.J.Drew of the AMC explained very clearly (ibid., p. 96):

'On one particular occasion the LEA might be well seized of the need for a college in a particular area and might well submit that proposal, perhaps in principle, to the DES. But the DES will immediately refer it to the area training organisation who will then relate it to the general overall provision of teachers because this is their responsibility. On another occasion it may well be the HMI who has advised the DES of a need for a college or, what is more important, the expansion of a college. Here again this will go to the area training organisation and rather rarely – though most unlikely – the ATO itself might come up with a proposal for a new college or for the enlargement of an existing one. It is more likely that the ATO would reach a decision about the discontinuance of a college; this can happen more commonly.'

A major effect of the pooling system is to divorce expenditure from raising the finance. No matter what a local authority spends on teacher training it will pay the same amount into the pool, dependent on its school population. From the narrow viewpoint of the LEA, therefore, parsimony is pointless; its ratepayers will bear no bigger burden if it is generous. Nevertheless tuition costs per student vary considerably between LEAS indicating different levels of expenditure on their colleges. To try to achieve some homogeneity an advisory Pooling Committee was set up in 1968. It has a membership representing the local authority associations with an independent chairman and a secretariat from the department. The colleges of education are rather suspicious of the Pooling Committee, fearing that it will be an instrument for clamping down on the overgenerous LEAS, for instance on staff–student ratios. It is a purely advisory committee, but most LEAS tend to take heed if their costs seem markedly out of line. Yet again one can see a factor tending to suppress local variation and to turn teacher training into a national service.

Nevertheless, financially the colleges are still probably in a better position than the universities, certainly no worse. Willey and Maddison (1971, p. 85) pointed out the advantage that colleges of education traditionally enjoyed over universities: 'Moreover, being linked with local government finance gives the colleges greater flexibility from year to year than that given to universities which are bound to a quinquennial grant.' While the quinquennial grant system has now been substantially amended, universities in the mid-1970s are still subject to extreme financial stringency imposed by the government. Local government colleges are no worse off.

The Supply of Teachers and the Quota System
The ratio of teachers to pupils is dependent upon the total numbers of pupils and teachers nationally and upon their respective distribution. That this ratio has in general been not only maintained but improved since the war is remarkable tribute to the success of government policies and the flexibilities and responsiveness of LEAS.

The dominant problem for at least the first three post-war decades was to increase the supply of trained teachers. Between 1946 and 1972 English and Welsh schoolteachers more than doubled their numbers from 177,135, to 366,165. Moreover this was achieved despite the lengthening of the training course. The policy was effected largely by increasing the number of places in colleges of education, a policy requiring close co-operation between the department and LEAS. The university departments of education played their part too. The encouragement of married women to return to teaching was an important subsidiary policy.

Even so, until the 1970s there was never a superabundance of teachers nationally and this exacerbated the difficulties of some LEAS, especially in industrial conurbations, in recruiting enough teachers. Distribution, as well as overall numbers, became a matter of importance. Even before the war the Board of Education under a Code of 1926 reviewed and approved the numbers of elementary schoolteachers employed by each LEA; this was, however, to control expenditure rather than teacher distribution. This was dropped when war broke out, but between 1941 and 1946 each LEA was assigned a quota of newly trained teachers who had to spend at least a year with their first employer.

In 1948 the baby boom first hit the infant schools and arrangements were introduced to control the distribution of women teachers. The NACTST urged that this scheme be replaced by one covering men as well. The teachers' unions were, however, suspicious of arrangements which appeared to reintroduce direction of labour and LEAS were hostile to more restrictions. The department had to move cautiously.

The rationing of women teachers was discontinued in 1956 and well-placed LEAs were asked to exercise voluntary restraint (see administrative memorandum 524). This did not seem to work and in October of the same year the department convened a conference of LEA and teacher representatives to discuss the distribution problem. There it was agreed that the department should introduce a comprehensive rationing scheme. This was announced in Circular 318 two months later; it came into force in January 1958 and has operated ever since.

Each year the department issues a circular prescribing for each LEA the total number of teachers which should be employed. Excluded from the quota are temporary, occasional and part-time teachers; married women returning to teaching after a break in service, or entering teaching for the first time some years after taking their degree, are not counted against the quota for the first two years. LEAs may employ as many of these as they like. Indeed even the quota itself is a voluntary control; while the department has power under the Schools Regulations 1959 to fix the maximum number of teachers which any LEA may employ, the power has never been used. Nevertheless LEAs which in the past exceeded their quotas by more than 1 or 2 per cent could expect to receive departmental representations. In fixing the quota the department takes account of the number and age distribution of pupils in each LEA, the number of small schools, the number of special classes for the handicapped, the number of immigrants, the needs of bilingual education in Wales and other considerations.

Despite slight amendments from time to time, the quota system has remained basically unchanged for fifteen years, and has achieved its fundamental purpose of a fairer distribution of staff. It seems unlikely to continue much longer. The national supply position has so improved relative to demand that it barely seems necessary. In 1972, in a much-publicised letter to a local branch secretary of the NUT, Mrs Thatcher explained that the rationale of the quota system had been totally reversed; it was no longer a maximum rationing prescription but a minimum staffing target.[4] LEAs were to be pressed not to fall below it rather than to be urged not to exceed it.

Decisions about the national supply of teachers necessarily rest partly on demographic predictions which, as is their wont, have not proved very reliable. After the high birth-rates of the 1940s there was some fall-back in the early 1950s; from the mid-1950s to the mid-1960s, however, the birth-rate rose each year. In 1965 it began to fall again and has done so ever since. After needing constantly to revise its figures upwards in the 1950s and the 1960s, the department in the 1970s had to revise them downwards and there arose concern about an oversupply of teachers. Primary pupils, the 5 to 11s, reached a peak in 1973 of about 5 million; they are forecast to be nearer 4 million by 1981. This is 600,000 less than the 1972 White Paper envisaged.

This White Paper forecast the need for 510,000 teachers by 1981 to achieve three objectives: to provide the maintained school population of 5 and over with 10 per cent more teachers than would be needed to maintain 1971 staffing standards; to supply enough teachers to staff the increased nursery education programme; to provide extra teachers to cover the absence of those on induction or training courses. Mr Reg Prentice, addressing the Council of Local Education Authorities in November 1974, claimed that 510,000 teachers would be far more than was necessary for these objectives – see DES *Reports on Education* Nos 80, 82. One feels that a rebound in the birth-rate could easily set all the DES statisticians by the ears again. Nevertheless, partly because of falling pupil numbers and partly because of economic stringency, several thousand teachers were unemployed by the end of 1975.

Local Authorities and Teacher Education and Training
Though the colleges of education are well on the way to submerging their identity completely with the rest of further and higher education, the binary system remains. Some teacher education is by universities, some by polytechnics and other colleges in the local authority sector. Nevertheless, it is difficult to find a single significant area of teacher education where local authorities wield unrestricted authority even over their own institutions. Instead their role is more subtle and complex. Local authorities participate in the decision- and policy-making process along with a number of other groups and agencies, notably teachers' unions, churches, universities, HMIS, the DES. In some decisions, e.g. finance, local authorities have a major voice; in others, e.g. curricula, their influence is slight.

Local authority influence has tended to decline since the war as their remaining areas of discretion have progressively been restricted. Nevertheless local authorities, both individually and as a group, are still a powerful force in teacher education and training. Should they be? Has the time come to remove teacher education and training from the province of local government altogether and to make it an avowedly national service on a par with university education?

The case which the colleges of education have argued before successive committees of inquiry is that teacher training and education already *is* a national service, that its location in local government is anomalous, and that the perpetuation of the binary system is exceedingly divisive for the profession.

Clearly there is much force to this line of argument. Students may come from any LEA to attend a university or local authority college and may go to any LEA to teach when they are qualified. Finance is nationally pooled, as has been described. The number and categories of teachers to be turned out is essentially a national policy decision taken by the Government in consultation with the various educational interests, including LEAs. There is unlikely to be any reversal of these nationalising features. Moreover, the binary system certainly has some undesirable aspects.

What is to be said in favour of local authority control? In the first place, whatever the theoretical arguments against it, the achievements of the binary system are impressive; just as, whatever Leigh Mallory's criticism of Dowding's tactics, the strongest argument in the latter's favour is that he did after all *win* the Battle of Britain. The massive increase in the output of qualified teachers in the last three decades, despite successive lengthening of the course, is evidence of some effectiveness. This does not disprove, of course, those who say that a different system might have done even better. Dowding might have secured an even greater victory following Leigh Mallory's big wing theory. Nevertheless the evidence of experience cannot lightly be discounted.

On a more sophisticated level the case for local authority control of some institutions of teacher education rests on two main propositions: that it is of practical benefit to such institutions and that it is appropriate given local authorities' other responsibilities. To these might be added its convenience for the government and its importance for the general status of local government.

Association with local government undoubtedly has some practical benefits for the colleges and other institutions providing teacher education. It gives them access to local authority professional staff and services – architects, estate managers, finance officers, lawyers, and so on. They would find it difficult to create all their own technical services. It is true that if all were federated with the universities they could use university technical services. This would, however, necessitate a major expansion of such services.

Another advantage enjoyed by LEA colleges is close liaison with other local authority departments. For instance a college will be able to keep the planning department informed of its requirements so that land can be reserved for its expansion rather than developed for some other purpose. Independent institutions may enjoy good relationships with local authorities but in general the channels of

F

communication are easier between different departments and agencies of the same local authority.

Liaison between a local authority college and a local authority's other *educational* activities are particularly important. Arrangements for, say, teaching practice and in-service training should be easier when both schools and colleges are controlled by the same authority. One must not exaggerate; such arrangements are not impossible otherwise. Though LEAs do not control universities, students at university departments of education are satisfactorily accommodated at local authority schools for their teaching practice. The argument is more one of degree, of greater flexibility and ease of contact. While the basic arrangements can function irrespective of control, non-routine *ad hoc* arrangements are easier to accomplish where school and colleges are similarly controlled.

In all, this constitutes a fair list of practical benefits. Nevertheless, they do not provide alone an overwhelming case for continued local authority control of colleges providing teacher education.

The second main line of argument is of the appropriateness of this control. The great majority of teachers eventually take posts in schools controlled or aided by LEAs. It is therefore entirely justified for local authorities to have a major say in the training and education process. As Lord Alexander has pointed out (HC 182–I, 1969–70, p. 120) in many other professions and occupations employers play a large part in the training of employees.

It is not only, however, on the grounds that the LEAs are *employers* that their involvement in teacher training is defended, but also because they have many other educational functions. As LEAs operate a range of educational institutions, from nursery schools to polytechnics, it is reasonable that they should also be involved with institutions providing teacher education. LEAs are the great educational co-ordinators. The CCA argued this case particularly strongly to the Robbins Committee (Cmnd 2154–VIII, 1963, p. 728):

'Talk of more co-ordination, or less separation, at all levels of education is often heard nowadays. So too are pleas for a more responsible control of public expenditure balanced, however, by equally urgent pleas for the preservation, or encouragement of academic freedom and for the avoidance of unnecessary central control. The Association are confident that an impartial study of the facts shows beyond doubt that local education authorities stand at the heart of any satisfactory synthesis of these largely conflicting aims. Within their field local education authorities constitute the most effective and sensitive system for administering public education . . . it is quite wrong to believe that the training colleges are

maintained by local education authorities, or by religious organisations, solely because the great majority of the teachers will work
in county or voluntary schools maintained by authorities. Of no
less, and perhaps even greater importance, is the fact that the training colleges, like the technical colleges, are a natural development
of the provision made or assisted by authorities. It cannot be too
strongly emphasised that both the maintained and voluntary colleges derive much of their strength and vitality from their close
association with the schools.'

Local authority control of institutions of teacher education is also
convenient for the government. If they were all incorporated into
the university sector and achieved the status and prestige of universities they would be far less amenable to government pressure.
Local authority colleges may, for instance, be asked by the department at very short notice, to change the balance of their student in-
take between aspirant primary and secondary school teachers; it is
difficult to refuse such requests (Cmnd 2154–VI, pp. 212, 213).
Voluntary colleges are similarly subject to such edicts. The local
authority colleges are rather the more resistant since they can shelter
behind the political weight of their LEA. Nevertheless, neither has the
resistant quality of a university. It is an exaggeration but not a wild
one for Willey and Maddison (1971, p. 83) to say 'While the colleges
lack autonomy the universities lack control . . .'.
Finally there is the argument that local authority control of
institutions of teacher education, no matter how attentuated, is
important for the prestige and health of local government. One
cannot remove successive powers and functions from local government without eventually killing it. This depends, however, on
whether one wants local government in the first place. This is
discussed in Chapter XIII.
The case for a major local authority voice in teacher education is,
therefore, a strong one. While the removal of this function to the
university sector would have some advantages, for instance uniting
the profession, it would have the serious practical and theoretical
drawbacks outlined. Moreover, as is discussed in the next chapter,
British universities have a tendency to conservatism and inflexi-
bility and it would be a mixed blessing from the point of view of
social policy for them to absorb all teacher education. While, however, the case for local authority involvement is strong, the actual
form it should take is more arguable.
The usual character local authority control adopts is of discretion
within a broad national framework. Local authorities have discretion to adapt and develop a service to suit local needs. Some

local variation is *desirable*. The orientation of teacher education is, however, rather different. An element of adaptation and experiment is welcome but major variation from one local authority to another would be *undesirable*. Yet the local authority influence is important. How can it be expressed?

First at a national level there should be adequate machinery to allow local authorities as a group to exercise legitimate influence. Secondly at the regional level the machinery should again reflect the proper role of local government. If there were regional local authorities there would be a strong case for making *them* responsible for teacher education (and other advanced further education). Failing this there is a clear need for effective regional co-ordinating bodies in which LEAs would have a major role. One doubts whether even the new regional committees (replacing the old ATOs) will provide this. Their responsibilities relate heavily to *educational* co-ordination – course allocation, in-service training, teaching practice – whereas the need is also for *administrative* co-ordination – building programmes, finance, supplies and the like.

What of the local authority level? Individual LEAs exercising unfettered control over individual colleges in England and Wales is not a prize worth fighting for. In reality it probably never existed and it certainly could not today. Nevertheless there is a danger today of LEAs being squeezed out altogether between an interventionist DES and increasingly autonomous colleges. Perhaps the post-Weaver changes have gone too far in eroding the responsibilities of LEAs. Institutions providing teacher education are of great local as well as national importance and the LEA is the repository of public interest and responsibility at this level.

NOTES

1 In 1974 there were 139 colleges of education, 112 provided by local authorities and 27 by voluntary bodies, primarily churches.
2 See the *Daily Telegraph*, 26 January 1972.
3 A checklist of the proposals for all colleges of education is set out in two articles in *The Times Higher Education Supplement*, 17 and 24 January 1975.
4 See *The Teacher*, Vol. 19, No. 15 (14 April 1972).

Chapter X

EDUCATING THE SCHOOL LEAVER

The term 'further education' is used today in two senses, a broad one and a narrow one. The broad sense is that set out in section 41 of the 1944 Education Act:

'(a) full-time and part-time education for persons over compulsory school age; and
(b) leisure-time occupation in such organised cultural training and recreational activities as are suited to their requirements for any persons over compulsory school age who are able and willing to profit by the facilities provided for that purpose.'

Despite the barbarous phrasing in part (b), this definition is clear. Further education is *all* education, whether full-time or part-time, vocational or recreational, subsequent to school. In particular it must include university education. (Though the definition uses the phrase 'over *compulsory* school age', the education of children who stay on *at school* beyond this age is not usually considered further education, even in its broad sense.)

The narrower sense of the term which has come into conventional use since the war and especially since the Robbins Report *excludes* university and university level education. Instead this is called 'higher education'.

The semantic confusion which can arise when further education has both an exclusive and an inclusive implication is easy to imagine. Even the Government is inconsistent. For instance the 1966 White Paper, *A Plan for Polytechnics and Other Colleges*, is subtitled *Higher Education in the Further Educational System*. This implies that the further education system is all-embracing and that higher education is but a part of it. Yet the 1972 White Paper *Education: A Framework for Expansion* uses further education in its narrow, exclusive sense. 'Strictly it comprises the whole stage beyond secondary. But it is most often used to describe the activities of the mainly – but now far from exclusively – vocation-oriented institutions, most of which are maintained by local education authorities: polytechnics and other further education colleges including colleges of art, commerce and agriculture and, in some contexts, of education.' The term 'higher education' is used in the White Paper 'to cover the full- and part-time work of universities, colleges of education and further education institutions so far as the last are concerned with "advanced" courses'. And 'advanced' courses are broadly those leading to qualifications of a higher standard than GCE advanced level.

The most striking feature of the provision of further and higher education today is the binary system. As with teacher training, some institutions of further or higher education are directly grant aided by the government and enjoy a large measure of autonomy (notably the universities), whereas other institutions of further or higher education are controlled by local authorities. The two sectors are usually distinguished as being 'autonomous' versus 'controlled' or sometimes 'autonomous' versus 'public'. Such terms only express half-truths. While the universities certainly enjoy great academic freedom it is misleading to describe them as autonomous. They are heavily dependent upon government assistance. True this is channelled through the University Grants Committee (UGC), making government control indirect. Nevertheless such control can still be real, especially on issues like university expansion and staff salaries. Moreover the inclinations of the government and the pressures from Parliament are for the controls to grow. The Report of the House of Commons Estimates Committee (Grants to Universities and Colleges, 1965) advocating university accountability for expenditure of public funds, and the subsequent opening of the books of the UGC and the universities to the scrutiny of the Comptroller and Auditor General and of the Public Accounts Committee, are only the most striking evidence of this trend. It is partly anxiety at such tendencies which led certain private interests to establish an independent university at Buckingham.

On the other hand it is also rather misleading to describe the local authorities' colleges as 'controlled'. As is explained below, while they are more directly accountable than the universities and subject to some detailed supervision by the local authorities, in academic matters they exercise a fair measure of discretion. Moreover the tendency is for this discretion to be widened.

Nevertheless the differences between the two sectors of the binary system remain significant. A university operates under a Royal Charter, can award its own degrees, is a legal entity, has senior staff with the title and salary of professor. Denied all these status symbols, a local authority college appears a decidedly lower order of creation, and one less resistant to government pressures, central and local.

Even in its narrow sense, further education is extremely heterogeneous. First there is the division between recreational and vocational or academic further education. The former, of course, covers the courses relating to leisure interests; most involve evening or weekend attendance with occasional residential courses, especially during holidays. It is rare that the excellence of this side of further education is recognised. The number and variety of courses offered, especially in the major urban centres is astonishing. Almost every conceivable interest is catered for, from the most down to earth practical (such as car maintenance) to the most esoterically aesthetic (such as Byzantine art). Most of this provision is in evening institutes which generally operate in buildings used as schools during the day, although a few have purpose-built premises.

Secondly, even when the vocational or academic side alone is considered, the range and spread of courses is still very considerable – in spread from the most applied to the purely academic, in range from CSE and below to GCE 'A' level, or even beyond in some cases (i.e. higher education). The obvious problem of accommodating such variety within the same colleges has led successive Governments to think in terms of arranging them into a hierarchy, with the top group specialising in the most advanced work, then ranging down to the bottom group providing mainly low-level courses.

Development of the System

The institutions which today provide further education have multifarious nineteenth-century origins. The first impetus was private: middle-class philanthropy, working-class self-betterment, employers' enlightened self-interest, learned societies' promotion of education in science, technology and art. These several strands, sometimes individually, more often in combination, produced the mechanics' institutes (offering instruction in the *principles* of trades or professions), the trades schools (providing *practical training* in various skills) and numbers of other institutions including Quintin Hogg's precedent-setting London Polytechnic. All such institutions catered primarily for a working-class clientele and were heavily vocational in their orientation. One can loosely term their provision 'technical education'.

The Government gradually became involved in this voluntary activity by providing financial aid and instituting national examinations. Eventually too local authorities were encouraged to provide science and art education, and after the 1889 Technical Instruction Act local authority provision expanded quickly. Much of this local authority effort in technical education was devoted to *schools* but increasingly also to post-school education. There was, however, some confusion of responsibility between the local authorities and the school boards. In the Cockerton judgement of 1900, the courts ruled that it was illegal for the school boards to provide anything other than elementary education (see Eaglesham, 1956). Responsibility for both elementary and post-elementary education was concentrated unambiguously in the local authorities when the Education Act 1902 abolished the school boards.

The twentieth century has seen a massive growth of local authority further education. Most voluntary colleges were taken over by the LEAs although the assistance and involvement of local industry and commerce often remained. The colleges often became a particular focus of LEA pride and initiative; they tended to encourage their colleges to increase the range of their courses, even to the point of offering degree-level teaching. Degrees were usually London University external degrees but in a few cases closer links were forged with a university; thus by 1945 four London technical colleges offered *internal* London University degrees and Sunderland Technical College *internal* Durham University degrees; moreover, Manchester College of Technology provided the technological faculty of Manchester University.

At this time these institutions of further education were collectively referred to as 'the technical colleges' but their actual titles were bafflingly varied. There were technical colleges (as in Sunderland Technical College), colleges of technology (as in Manchester College of Technology), polytechnics (as in Woolwich Polytechnic), colleges of commerce (as in Cardiff College of Technology and Commerce), colleges of further education, colleges of art and more individual names (such as West Ham Municipal College, Sir John Cass College, Brixton School of Building). Despite such variety all were characterised by being local authority controlled (with a few exceptions)[1] and primarily concerned with post-school education of a vocational (as opposed to academic) nature. After 1945, however, the technical colleges increasingly extended their scope to purely academic provision as the universities proved unable to cope with the rising demand for higher education.

In 1952 the Government made the first move towards establishing a hierarchy of institutions. A special 75 per cent grant was introduced, payable to colleges undertaking a high proportion of advanced work, especially teaching and research at graduate and postgraduate levels. By 1956 twenty-four English and Welsh colleges were receiving this distinctive accolade and assistance. In the same year the Government announced in a White Paper, *Technical*

Education, an even more significant step, the designation of certain of the technical colleges as Colleges of Advanced Technology (CATs). The CATs were to concentrate on advanced full-time and sandwich courses. Eight CATs were established at first; later the number was increased to ten.

A year after the White Paper, the Ministry of Education issued Circular 305 explaining a further evolution of government thinking. The technical colleges outside the CATs were ranked into three grades: regional colleges, area colleges, local colleges. Thus there was established a complete hierarchy of the institutions of further education based on the two criteria of level of work and extent of full-time attendance. At the top of the ladder there were the CATs concentrating on advanced work and primarily full-time or sandwich students; at the bottom, the local colleges had very largely part-time students attending low-level courses; the regional and area colleges occupied intermediate positions. There was a layer below the local colleges – the evening institutes. As was explained, however, these were primarily concerned with recreational provision, although some offered low-grade vocational courses.

All four levels, even the CATs (except Loughborough), remained local authority controlled. In 1962, however, the CATs were moved outside the local government sector when they were made direct grant institutions with independent governing bodies. A year later the Robbins Committee on higher education recommended that they be granted full university status. The Robbins' argument was that since the majority of their students were taking advanced courses it was anomalous that the CATs should be unable to award their own degrees. This anomaly impeded staff recruitment and deterred potential students. The Government agreed. In 1965 eight of the CATs were granted charters as independent universities; the other two, the Chelsea and Welsh CATs, became schools of the Universities of London and Wales respectively.

The Robbins Committee was happy for the other technical colleges to remain under local authority control. The Committee wanted, however, the system to be flexible so that some regional colleges might attain university status and some area colleges might become regional colleges. In fact no regional colleges were subsequently promoted. Instead the binary system was entrenched.

The implication of the Robbins Committee recommendations was the creation of a unitary (as opposed to binary) system of further education. There would have been a *single* hierarchy of institutions providing post-secondary education. At the top would have been the universities, immediately below them the regional colleges, and so on down the ladder. General caterpillar flexibility would have made promotion to the next rung possible all down the line.

This unitary concept was explicitly rejected in favour of retaining *two parallel* sets of institutions of higher education – one 'controlled', one 'autonomous'. The institutions at the top of the 'controlled' ladder would in many respects be equivalent (not subordinate) to the universities comprising the 'autonomous' sector. In 1965 at Woolwich and 1967 at Lancaster Mr Anthony Crosland, Secretary of State for Education and Science, delivered long-remembered and controversial speeches explaining his Government's decision to reject the unitary concept of further education, and to entrench the binary system by developing distinctive institutions of higher education within the 'controlled' sector to complement the universities.

Pratt and Burgess (1974, p. 34) deny that the Robbins proposals were wholly unitary in concept because not all higher education would have been in the universities; a minority of students on advanced courses, especially part-timers, would still have been left in the LEA colleges. Nevertheless the Robbins Committee envisaged future promotions to university status which would have reduced this residue; there was broad mention of ten more major colleges being so elevated by 1980, but this number was not intended to be rigid or final. In any case even if the Robbins scheme left some anomalies, such as provision for part-time students, it was totally different in orientation from a scheme which deliberately set out to create counterparts to universities in the 'controlled' sector. The new polytechnics policy did just that.

The New Polytechnics

In May 1966 the Government announced in a White Paper, *A Plan For Polytechnics and Other Colleges*, that a number of new polytechnics would be designated within the 'controlled' sector. They would form a limited number of centres where advanced work could be concentrated with the requisite staff, buildings and equipment. It was considered that, in the then wide distribution of advanced work, such resources were uneconomically used. They would be virtually 'controlled' sector universities. Unlike the universities, however, they would not discard their part-time students and sub-degree work. Instead the new polytechnics would be 'comprehensive academic communities' catering for students at all levels of higher education (i.e. advanced work) and for substantial numbers of part-timers as well as full-time and sandwich students. They *would* be expected in the long term to drop most of their *non-advanced* work.

Each new polytechnic would be formed from an existing technical college, or more usually, several adjacent colleges. To secure the advantages of scale it was envisaged that each should aim at an eventual minimum of 2,000 full-time students plus part-timers.

Technical colleges which did not become polytechnics were not to be forbidden all advanced work. In particular they would continue to provide higher education for *part-time* students, where these found it difficult to attend a polytechnic. It was envisaged, however, that the technical colleges outside the polytechnics would only provide *full-time* advanced courses in exceptional circumstances.

In an appendix to the White Paper a preliminary list of twenty-eight proposed English and Welsh polytechnics was set out. Most were based on an existing regional college with one or more other technical colleges joined to it. After consultations with local authorities and other interests, the Government added two more polytechnics to the preliminary list but resisted all pressure to increase it still further. These thirty polytechnics were designated.

The polytechnics remain within the local authority sphere. Like the other technical colleges they are LEA owned and financed. The Government has insisted, however, that as befits their status, the polytechnics be accorded a fair measure of autonomy.

Running the Colleges

As with their colleges of education, local authorities exercise far from untrammelled suzerainty over their institutions of further education, and the tendency is for institutional autonomy to be widened. The new polytechnics led the way. When the final list of thirty polytechnics was announced in 1967 the DES sent *Notes for Guidance* (administrative memorandum 8/67) to LEAs explaining how polytechnic schemes were to be submitted and suggesting principles for their instruments and articles of government. Much influenced by the Report of the Weaver Committee the year before (on the government of colleges of education), the *Notes for Guidance* insisted that polytechnics be accorded substantial autonomy. Each had to have a governing body with the main responsibility for administration delegated to it; substantial discretionary authority was also to be exercised by the director and the academic board.

A year later these requirements were given statutory force and extended from polytechincs to all technical colleges. By the Education (No. 2) Act 1968 all institutions which provide full-time further education must have both an instrument and articles of government, which respectively lay down the governing body and prescribe the conduct of each institution.

The instrument of government is made by order of the LEA and does not require governmental approval. The DES, however, issued advice about the constitution of governing bodies which is, if anything, rather more demanding of LEA self-abnegation than the *Notes for Guidance* (see Circular 7/70). It is suggested that the board of governors should not be too large, say twenty to twenty-five, and the members of the LEA should be in a minority, say between one quarter and one third. The representatives of industry and commerce should also form roughly one third, leaving the remainder a heterogeneous collection of university representatives, individual experts, the occasional head teacher, the principal of the institution and one or two representatives of the staff and perhaps students.

The articles of government (unlike the instrument of government) have to be approved by the secretary of state. The DES has urged that these articles reflect the size and status of the institution. Colleges which are large, which have a substantial number of adult students (i.e. 18 years old and over) and which provide a significant number of advanced courses should have more autonomy than colleges with the opposite characteristics. The most important factor is the amount of advanced work undertaken.

The DES has also issued model articles of government (appendix to Circular 7/70). These prescribe that responsibility for running colleges is to be split four ways: the LEA's responsibility is for the general educational character of the college and its place in the local educational system; the governor's responsibility is for the general direction of the college; the principal is responsible to the governors for internal organisation, management and discipline; the college academic board (consisting of the principal, departmental heads, representatives of other staff and perhaps students) is responsible for planning, co-ordinating, developing and overseeing the work of the college, including the admission and examination of students.

On specific matters the model articles lay down that the appointment of the principal, vice-principal and chief administrative officer (where the latter two exist) is to be made by a joint committee of the governors and LEA, subject to LEA confirmation. All other appointments to the teaching and non-teaching staff are the responsibility of the principal except that the appointment of heads of department should involve the governors and be subject to their confirmation. The governors can suspend the principal, vice-principal and chief administrative officer and can recommend their dismissal to the LEA; the principal can suspend all other staff and the governors dismiss them without reference to the LEA but subject to a right of hearing. The principal can also suspend or expel students for misbehaviour and the academic board for poor work subject again to a right of appeal to the governors or a special disciplinary committee of governors, staff and students.

The LEA has a more prominent role in finance. The college's annual estimates have to be approved by the LEA which also determines the form in which they are to appear; financial rules are laid down by the LEA in consultation with the governors. The governors have power to incur expenditure within approved estimates including virement within prescribed limits. The governors can also undertake minor repairs and maintenance (up to limit of, say, £500 per job) and order supplies and equipment (up to a limit of, say, £100 per item).

These model articles of government have not been rigidly copied. Lower-ranking colleges in particular often have less autonomy. The DES has, however, insisted on something approximating to them for colleges offering a substantial proportion of advanced work and for polytechnics. Michael Locke (Pratt and Burgess 1974, pp. 149–71) has described how, for polytechnics, the department was particularly insistent on the delegation of significant financial discretion from the LEA to the governors, and on provision for substantial participation of teachers and students in college government. Indeed in the late 1960s when most of the new polytechnics were being designated the department seemed almost obsessed with the issue of student participation. The period was marked by considerable student unrest in both universities and colleges. Successive Labour Secretaries of State for Education and their junior colleagues, especially Mrs Shirley Williams, were convinced that the heat would be taken out of student militancy if they were directly involved in college government. The DES grew progressively stricter in its demands on this issue until eventually the appointment of student governors became a *sine qua non* of the designation of a polytechnic.

While the DES has not made the same demands in respect of *all* LEA colleges, the pressure has been to weaken local authority control. For polytechnics and other major institutions the only significant direct powers still possessed by LEAs are: determining the general character of a college (whatever that may mean), appointing governors, passing the estimates and laying down financial rules. This understates the degree of influence which in practice LEAs can exercise; their power to approve estimates alone is a lever for wider intervention. 'Inconsistencies and meddling by an LEA are likely to be encouraged because decisions are the outcome of bargaining and *ad hoc* situations rather than justified or made as part of defined policy' (ibid., p. 168).

Locke argues that the net effect of the changes, especially in the polytechnics, is likely to be an enormous increase in the power of the director. The academic board is likely to be too unwieldy in size and too enmeshed in numerous committees to exercise great sway; boards of governors, composed primarily of people with heavy commitments elsewhere, are likely to be split on many issues and to be diffident about imposing their views; LEAs have been deprived of much control, formally at least; only the director is left as a single, powerful executive figure at the meeting point of all these forces.

The weakening of LEA control, although the reality is less than the formality, has occasioned some demoralisation in local authority circles. The opinion is now more frequently expressed by local authority spokesmen that the polytechnics and other advanced further education colleges should be removed from the local authority sector. What is now the point of LEA control such as it is? This question is discussed below.

The Regional Advisory Councils

The need for LEAs to co-ordinate their further education provision is obvious. Further education institutions have far larger catchment areas than schools – save for the lowest level part-time courses; often these areas extend beyond LEA boundaries. Two particular dangers arise from this: course duplication and course neglect. On the one hand the same course may be offered in several neighbouring LEAs, thus dispersing students over a number of institutions in uneconomic caseloads. On the other hand no LEA may provide a course because local interest seems small whereas on a regional basis there may be sufficient demand to warrant one institution offering it.

Such considerations led Lord Eustace Percy,[2] President of the Board of Education between 1924 and 1929, to initiate a survey into the organisation of technical and commercial education in Yorkshire in 1925. As a result a Yorkshire Committee for Further Education was created in 1928 to try to achieve a measure of coordination between LEAs and industry. In the next few years similar bodies were established for South Wales, the West Midlands, Merseyside and Greater Manchester.

The same Lord Percy was made chairman of a committee appointed in 1944 to advise the government on the needs of higher technological education in England and Wales with particular reference to the means required for maintaining appropriate co-operation between universities and technical colleges. In its report the following year the Committee stressed that technical education was not solely the concern of local education authorities but of industry

and universities too. Accordingly it proposed that these three interested parties achieve co-ordination through a system of regional
advisory councils for technological education, set up on the lines
of those existing in Yorkshire and elsewhere from before the war.
The Committee suggested that there should be eight such regional
advisory councils covering England and Wales. In addition the
Committee wanted eight regional academic boards to give advice
on academic matters both to the regional advisory councils and to
individual colleges. Thirdly the Committee wanted a central body,
a National Council of Technology, to represent the regional advisory councils and regional academic boards at the national level
and to advise the government on the national aspects of regional
policies.

The Government implemented these proposals, with some amend-
ment. In Circular 87 it was announced that both the regional and
national machinery proposed would be created – ten (as opposed to
the Percy Committee's suggested eight) regional advisory councils
and regional academic boards and a National Advisory Council on
Education for Industry and Commerce. The Circular also set out
the functions of these bodies: rationalisation of course provision;
maintenance of contact with industry; planning of new developments and the expansion of existing facilities; the review of courses
and curricula; advice on financial arrangements for dealing with
out-county students; arranging for the most effective use of specialist staff; the co-ordination of the activities of universities and
technical colleges through the regional academic board. A later
White Paper, *Technical Education* (1956), summed up these responsibilities more succinctly:

'The regional advisory councils serve two main purposes (i) to
bring education and industry together to find out the needs of young
workers and advise on the provision required and (ii) to secure
reasonable economy of provision. Associated with the councils are
regional academic boards for ensuring close co-operation between
the universities and technical colleges in the provision of advanced
courses. At the centre a National Advisory Council for Education
for Industry and Commerce, which is largely representative of the
regions, advises the Minister on national policy.'

The ten regional advisory councils (RACs) and regional academic
boards (RABs) display several unusual administrative features. First
their areas of jurisdiction are strange. There are nine RACs in England; in Wales the Welsh Joint Education Committee performs the

role. The latter, of course, has an area of jurisdiction covering the whole Principality. The nine English RACS, however, do *not* coincide with any other regional units (such as regional economic planning councils or regional divisions of HM Inspectorate). Nor do they always coincide with the boundaries of LEAs: Essex and Hertfordshire are both divided between the East Anglia RAC and the London and Home Counties RAC; Derbyshire is divided between the East Midlands and North Western RACS; Nottinghamshire is divided between the Yorkshire and East Midlands RACS. In some cases the RAC boundary is indeterminate: thus no precise boundary has been fixed in Bedfordshire but the southern part of the county is considered to fall within the jurisdiction of the London and Home Counties RAC while the rest of the county is in the East Anglia RAC; similarly West Sussex is divided by convention between the Southern and London and Home Counties RACS. Perhaps strangest of all there is overlapping jurisdiction: thus the whole of the counties of Dorset and Wiltshire fall within *both* the Southern and South Western RACS although no precise boundary has been defined; the area of Cumbria previously forming Westmorland is in both the Northern and North Western RACS; West Yorkshire is in both the North Western and Yorkshire RACS; the Middlesbrough area of Cleveland is in both the Yorkshire and Northern RACS; the Scunthorpe area of Humberside is in both the East Midlands and Yorkshire RACS.

Secondly, besides these territorial oddities the RACS and RABS are strangely heterogeneous in their functions. The Welsh Joint Education Committee has a peculiar bundle of responsibilities unlike any English RAC. The English RACS too differ among themselves. The Percy Committee had not proposed a detailed list of functions for all RACS, and the Government subsequently allowed a certain flexibility to adapt to local circumstances. Nevertheless this had its drawbacks as the Secretary of the London and Home Counties RAC pointed out (Jamieson, 1968):

'. . . it may have been a mistake to leave the regions entirely free to decide on their functions, since a slightly greater degree of uniformity might have helped in the faster development of Regional Advisory Councils. For example, the London and Home Counties Regional Advisory Council confined its function to higher technological education at that time and in retrospect, while it may have appeared reasonable, because of the number of large LEAS in that region which could cover lower level work in their own areas adequately, the lack of regional co-operation in the field of lower level courses has led to more recent problems.'

The membership and internal structures of RACs also vary considerably but there are certain common features.

RACs have between 60 and 100 members. The majority normally represent the component LEAs (both elected members and officers); another sizeable block are drawn from technical college principals and teachers; both sides of industry are represented, as are universities in the region. The remainder are somewhat miscellaneous and vary from region to region – representatives of voluntary bodies, examining institutes, sometimes district councils. Finally all RACs include some officials from the main government departments concerned with further education – the DES (invariably represented by HMIS), the Department of Employment, sometimes the Ministry of Agriculture.

The full council of each RAC meets infrequently. The work of the RAC is carried on primarily in a number of committees and sub-committees, which include co-optees as well as council members of the RAC. There is invariably an executive committee or standing committee or finance and general purposes committee as the central decision-making organ. There is a regional academic board with a substantial representation of university and technical college teaching staff which attempts to co-ordinate the provision of universities and colleges. There are always a number of subject advisory committees concerned, for instance, with assessing the needs of industry in particular fields. Sometimes there are area committees to consider the provision of courses on a smaller territorial basis than the whole region (often especially of lower-level courses).

Finally there is always a distribution of courses committee concerned with the crucial function of RACs, rationalisation of the provision of advanced courses. Since 1957 (see administrative memorandum 545) departmental approval has been required for the establishment of any new *advanced* course. Power to give or withhold approval is delegated to a senior HMI, the regional staff inspector, and his decision is made in the light of the advice of the appropriate RAC. When an LEA wishes to establish a new advanced course, application is made to the RAC. The proposal may be discussed in the appropriate subject advisory committee and area committee before it goes to the distribution of courses committee for the final RAC decision. The regional staff inspector follows the RAC advice in the great majority of cases; indeed he usually attends the distribution of courses committee meetings and the decision may be an agreed compromise between him and the LEA representatives.

The whole point of the exercise is to reduce duplication but the pressure from LEAS and from college principals and governors is to increase their colleges' range of provision. Consequently the decisions of RACs and regional staff inspectors often involve a large element of bargaining or arbitration. The clearest guiding principle as to the need for a course is the number of students attending it. In 1957, when the system was introduced, it was laid down that if a course did not attract a minimum of fifteen students, after three years the regional staff inspector should consider its closure in consultation with the RAC. Nevertheless in 1966 the Pilkington Committee (a subcommittee of the NACEIC) on Technical College Resources reported that 75 per cent of classes had between eleven and fifteen students and urged the adoption of stricter measures. The committee wanted the minimum class size to be raised to twenty-four for full-time courses, twenty for part-time and fifty when a new centre for advanced courses was involved; it also wanted an hour to be accepted as a reasonable travelling time for students. The Pilkington Committee also wanted the RACs to have a more positive role than a bargaining forum and suggested they should prepare five-year development plans. The department accepted all these recommendations (see Circular 11/66). These tighter criteria have enabled more economy of provision in advanced courses to be achieved; nevertheless both RACs and regional staff inspectors find it difficult to curb the expansionist pressures of LEAs and colleges.

More fundamentally, the RACs have never achieved a really satisfactory co-ordinative role in further education for a number of reasons. First, the universities have been only grudging participants. University teachers serve on RACs and RABs and give advice on specialist subjects but invariably resist any RAC attempt to influence university provision as being inconsistent with academic freedom. The result is a one-sided process; while universities through their involvement with RACs have some influence on the work of technical colleges, there is no vice versa. RABs do not co-ordinate unversity and college courses, but only the provision of different colleges. Indeed one RAC, the Southern, has in consequence wound up its RAB.

Secondly the Government has revealed a somewhat dismissive attitude to the RACs. They were little consulted, for instance, about the location of the post-Robbins universities and, even more significantly, the new polytechnics. Indeed so disturbed were the RACs at the apparent lack of government interest in their views that in 1968 they established a Standing Conference to try to exert some collective influence on the Government.

Thirdly the finance and staffing of RACs limit their effectiveness. They are financed by their component LEAs and could not greatly increase their demands upon them. Partly in consequence RAC staff are limited to administrative and clerical personnel. It is hard to see how RACs could become powerhouses of research and planning in further education without a considerable increase in their resources.

Their areas of jurisdiction are also a handicap to the RACs. The indeterminate boundaries, overlapping territories and lack of coincidence with any other regional units have already been mentioned. Some would argue (e.g. Nurse, 1969) that in any case the RAC areas are too large for part-time courses and for full-time courses for those under 18, yet too small for full-time courses for those over 18 where the catchment area is national. Following this line of argument the fifty-three new English and Welsh counties and metropolitan counties plus the GLC would probably be more appropriate in size to co-ordinate courses other than full-time courses for the 18-plus; the latter could be the responsibility of the NACEIC or the DES itself. On the other hand perhaps the growing use of area committees by RACs to co-ordinate localised provision answers the objection that their territories are too large. It does not deal with the point that only national co-ordination makes sense for advanced full-time courses.

It is difficult for any kind of advisory body without executive powers to find an effective role. Within the limitations discussed the RACs have achieved a certain utility. They could well do better as part of a unit of administration. If, for instance, a regional tier of government were created (as the 1973 Kilbrandon Report, especially the Peacock and Crowther-Hunt dissent, persuasively argued), RACs would be obvious candidates for absorption by it. Failing this at the very least RAC boundaries should be unambiguous and should coincide with those of HMI divisions. Also all RACs should be given a remit to co-ordinate non-advanced as well as advanced courses.

Awards and Qualifications

It was recognised early in the development of further education that there would need to be some standardisation of examinations if qualifications were to be widely acceptable. Accordingly, starting in 1839, a number of regional examining unions were formed to conduct or validate examinations in technical education. Some of these regional examining unions proved extremely durable. For instance, the City and Guilds of London Institute (founded by the City livery companies in 1878) still operates nationally recognised examinations in commercial and industrial subjects; indeed it is today the major examining body for non-advanced courses.

The government too became involved in this work, especially through the Board of Education's national certificate scheme.

Under this the board endorsed certificates issued by schools and colleges where course entry standards had been approved and the board's assessors involved in the final examination. Even more important were the national certificates and diplomas initiated by the Board of Education in association with certain professional institutes in the 1920s. These have now become firmly established as the Ordinary and Higher National Certificates (ONC, HNC) and similarly Ordinary and Higher National Diplomas (OND, HND). The certificates are for part-time and the diplomas for full-time students. Each college prepares its own syllabus and examines its own students for these certificates and diplomas but with the check of external assessment and course approval by joint committees.

This still, however, left the problem of higher level qualifications (HNC and HND are rather above 'A' level GCE and roughly the equivalent of pass degree standard). As was mentioned earlier, some colleges provided (and still provide) degree courses through association with universities, especially London University external degrees. Not being universities, the technical colleges have never been able to award their own degrees.

After the war the need to make more convenient arrangements for degree-level awards became more acute. Both the Percy Committee in 1945 and the National Advisory Council on Education for Industry and Commerce in 1949, and subsequently, urged the establishment of a national degree-awarding body for the technical colleges. The Government eventually gave way and in 1955 set up the National Council for Technological Awards (NCTA) to administer a new degree-level award for the technical colleges. The award in question, the Diploma in Technology (Dip. Tech.) was not formally entitled a degree (largely, it is thought, because of university objection) but was broadly equivalent to a degree. The NCTA was thus the first body outside a university to award a degree-level qualification in Britain.

The NCTA did not itself conduct examinations or lay down syllabuses; this was left to the individual colleges (as with the national certificates and diplomas). Instead the NCTA had an inspectorial and supervisory role. If a course content were thought unsatisfactory, or inadequately staffed or accommodated, or badly examined, the NCTA simply withheld recognition for Dip. Tech. purposes; the college itself would then have to improve matters. The standards set by the NCTA were very high. In consequence the Dip. Tech. proved a notable success and became very acceptable to industry. It was usually awarded after a four-year sandwich course.

This precedent was followed in art education when in 1961 the National Council for Diplomas in Art and Design was set up (equivalent to the NCTA) to administer a Diploma in Art and Design (equivalent to the Dip. Tech.).

The Robbins Committee recognised the success of the NCTA but wanted it transformed into an even more flexible instrument, a Council for National Academic Awards (CNAA) for Great Britain. This body would have a Royal Charter to award all levels of degrees from pass to post-graduate (not just diplomas like the NCTA), for all subjects (not just technological ones) and for full-time and part-time courses (not just sandwich courses). The Government accepted this recommendation. The CNAA replaced the NCTA in 1964.

When bowler-hatted Mr Quintin Hogg, Secretary of State for Education and Science, rode his Moulton bicycle to the Park Crescent offices of the CNAA on 30 September 1964 to inaugurate it, he started a quiet revolution in further education. The CNAA has proved even more successful than the NCTA. This success flows from two factors: first the CNAA embodies the principle of external assessment; secondly the CNAA has been particularly exacting in the standards it has demanded.

Pratt and Burgess (1974, p. 107) argue persuasively that any external evaluation is likely to stimulate creativity.

'Left to ourselves we should in designing a new course be content to reproduce what we know best. We should naturally expect to make changes here or there to suit local circumstances or particular staff, but we should probably act within the context of our own experience and be ill placed to go beyond it. The situation is quite different if we know that we are required to defend our proposals to a body of people at least as knowledgeable as we are. We cannot proceed on the basis of our assumptions: we have first to make our assumptions clear. In doing so, we may be led to question them. The need to defend our proposals forces us to make clear not only the fundamental problems but the coherence of our solutions. And it is out of this greater understanding that most of us can be persuaded to innovate.'

This thesis is substantiated by empirical evidence (Perkin, 1969) that the new post-Robbins universities, after a burst of pioneering activity, settled back into a conservative rut without the stimulus of external assessment.

The stimulant effect of the CNAA is accentuated by the rigour with which it has undertaken its responsibilities. It does not confine itself to examining the curriculum and syllabus of a proposed course, although these are subjected to detailed scrutiny, but also it assesses the qualifications and approach of the staff intending to teach it, the entry requirements, the external examiners, the library services, staff and student accommodation, facilities for private study, and so on. Moreover, CNAA approval is usually only for five years or a similar period after which the college must obtain renewed approval. Not surprisingly the high quality of CNAA degrees and other awards is becoming widely recognised.

Binary or Unitary?

The best-known exposition of the case for the binary system is that contained in Mr Crosland's Woolwich and Lancaster speeches already referred to – reproduced in Robinson (1968, pp. 193–6) and Pratt and Burgess (1974, pp. 203–13). He justified his Government's preference for the dual or binary system on a number of grounds. To begin with there was the severely practical reason that the binary system already existed and it would have required a massive upheaval (involving not just the colleges but the local authorities, the universities, voluntary bodies and boards of governors) to transform it into a complete unitary system.

Even, however, if the Government had been starting with a *tabula rasa*, there would still have been, Mr Crosland considered, a strong case for establishing a binary system. First, the demand for all advanced-level work could not be accommodated in the universities, or only by changing them radically. The universities provided overwhelmingly academic, full-time degree courses. They would have had to extend their provision massively to cater for part-time and sandwich students, to offer diplomas, certificates and other non-degree work and to teach vocational, professional and industrial courses if they were to take over all advanced further education (higher education). Such a transformation of role would have been a lengthy and difficult process, and in any case educationists were divided about its wisdom.

Secondly, Mr Crosland argued that a unitary system would depress morale and standards in the non-university sector.

'. . . the implication . . . is that we should give the universities a virtual monopoly of degree-level work either by eliminating it from FE or by transferring some FE institutions to the university sector. In other words, . . . to cream off most, if not all, full-time degree work into the universities, leaving the FE sector to sub-degree and part-time work. This would not only run counter to our whole British tradition and indeed to the Robbins Report. It would truly be 'binary' with a vengeance, converting the technical colleges into upper-level secondary modern schools and dividing the 18-year-olds into a privileged university class of full-time degree students with the remainder in FE. I can imagine nothing more socially or educationally divisive.'

Thirdly Mr Crosland argued that the participation of local government in higher education was a valuable feature of British democracy. Fourthly he claimed that heterogeneity was to be preferred to homogeneity in higher education. A monopoly of control in one kind of institution would be dangerous, given rapid expansion and constantly changing ideas. Fifthly he pointed to the need to enchance professional and technical education and the likelihood that this would be most effectively done by institutions specialising in this side of higher education.

Finally and most controversially, Mr Crosland argued that the local authority colleges were more socially responsive than the universities because they were more socially controlled. It was clearly advantageous to continue this arrangement. This last point was somewhat crudely put in the Woolwich speech and provoked much critical reaction from the universities who considered they were being accused of social irresponsibility. Indeed the whole speech received such hostile comment that, although first issued as an administrative memorandum, it was subsequently withdrawn; 'the Department of Education declared that there were no more copies available'.[3] Mr Crosland's Lancaster speech two years later was more carefully phrased. Nevertheless he reasserted the same point.

'I would not suggest for a moment that [the universities] are not responsive to any intimation of the national need that they can discern for themselves or that Governments are able to give them. They always have been responsive and never more so than today. Yet given the high degree of autonomy which they enjoy there is a sense in which the other colleges can be said to be under more direct social control. This becomes clear if we consider (to take one or two rather extreme examples) the 20 per cent productivity exercise in the colleges of education or the control over courses and class sizes in the technical colleges.'

Mr Crosland's critics have been many and virulent. Lord Robbins (1965), for instance, magisterially pronounced 'If I had known that anything so reactionary and half-baked as the binary system was going to be propounded I certainly would have suggested adding a few paragraphs to the Report, dealing with this as it deserves.'

The principal objection levelled at the binary system by its critics is that it divides higher education into superior and inferior leagues. The polytechnics have no chance of being accepted as equal to, though different from, the universities. Inevitably the system creates (Lukes, 1967), 'alphas and betas, officers and n.c.o.s., golden and silver'. The very name 'polytechnic' conjures up in British minds the image of (Robinson, 1968, p. 34) 'an educational soup kitchen for the poor'. The critics (e.g. Boris Ford, 1966) often see the unification of higher education as analogous to comprehensive reorganisation at secondary school level. Eric Robinson (1968, pp. 46–50) has pointed out, however, that the analogy is false since, unlike secondary education, higher education is not universal; thus even if polytechnics, colleges of education and universities were united into one system under the UGC this would still leave all the *non-advanced* further education under different, and in practice lower-status, arrangements. This was exactly Anthony Crosland's point.

The critics also argue that universities need not be rigid, conservative and unresponsive to social needs; American universities are held up (e.g. by Lukes, 1967) as examples of broader, more flexible institutions. In Britain, however, the tradition of what Eric Robinson (1968, p. 39) calls the 'boarding school university' shows no sign of waning. Universities pay little attention to the needs of part-time and non-degree students and tend to neglect vocational and applied courses to concentrate heavily on academic work. New universities, whether promotions from further education (like the CATs) or completely new foundations, quickly conform to this pattern. Pratt and Burgess (1971, p. 123) are damning in their indictment of this tradition.

'In coping with numbers, in extending educational opportunity to hitherto excluded social groups, in creating new structures of study and admitting an interdisciplinary approach, in institutional management, autonomy and academic freedom, in recruiting different sources of staff, in linking higher education with the outside world and in numbers of lesser ways, English technical education, through the NCTA, the CATs and the polytechnics has made and is making a profound and distinctive social revolution. In all these respects the contribution of universities in most Western European countries, including our own, has been tentative and inadequate. We feel bound to agree . . . that significant academic innovation is most likely in institutions which retain the benefits of public control.'

Pratt and Burgess also mount by far the most profound critique of the Crosland policy. Instead of complaining that the binary

policy is not unitary, they argue that the creation of the polytechnics will undermine the point of the binary policy. By selecting
thirty institutions for special treatment, by making them quasi-
universities, forces are set in motion which will turn them into full
universities. Pratt and Burgess (1974, pp. 67–88) show that the polytechnics were already growing more like universities by 1969 – the
age range of their students was narrowing, they had fewer part-
timers, fewer HNC students, more degree students, their actual student numbers were falling. They were becoming less, not more,
comprehensive academic communities. It seems inevitable that,
like the CATs before them, they will be accorded full university status
in the not too distant future.

Whatever the rights and wrongs of the binary system, government policy thus seems ill-designed to serve it. There is not room
in a book about local government and education to explore all the
alternative policies for higher and further education which might
be pursued. One alternative would certainly be Eric Robinson's
concept (1971) of a 'comprehensive university', incorporating the
whole of tertiary education in an area or region and emphasising
part-time and sub-degree studies. Whether such 'comprehensive
universities' should be in the public sector, the autonomous sector,
or some third alternative, would no doubt be hotly debated.

Local Government and Further Education

The issue of local government involvement in further and higher
education is obviously closely related to the binary versus unitary
controversy. To exclude local government from administrative
involvement in post-school education would be to create a unitary
system. Whatever such a move might gain it would involve
the loss of the greater flexibility and innovation displayed by the
'controlled' sector in further and higher education.

Apart from those who wish to establish a unitary system, the
most frequent critics of local government's role in this field are
the staff of the institutions of further and higher education. They
have often complained of petty controls and irritating restrictions
by LEAs in the past – see, for instance, Silver (1969) and Leese (1970).
It could be argued, however, that while LEAs may sometimes be
overzealous in their concern for economy they have a legitimate
duty to represent the public interest. In any case it would be a
mistake to assume that the 'autonomous' sector is immune to such
problems; every university teacher has his anecdotes about bureau-
cratic absurdities. One suspects that, as with college of education
staff, LEA control is resented more because of the lower status it
symbolises than for any real problems it causes.

A more telling criticism is that the post-Weaver reforms in college government have so reduced LEA controls that their residual powers seem barely worth having. As was mentioned, this is an opinion expressed within as well as outside local government circles. It is a difficult one to refute. LEAs must be given a clearer and more satisfactory role in respect of their colleges than paymaster or post office. Pratt and Burgess (1974, pp. 192, 193) suggest that they be made responsible for planning the development of further education in their areas and, in co-operation with others, their regions. No doubt LEAs would welcome such a positive role. On the regional level there would though be some overlap with the RACs. It also raises the question of whether advanced further education should anyway be made the responsibility of regional bodies.

NOTES

1 A small number of colleges were outside the local government sector and received grant aid direct from the government, e.g. Royal College of Art, College of Aeronautics, the six national colleges covering highly specialised technologies (National College of Agricultural Engineering, National College of Food Technology, National College for Heating, Ventilating, Refrigeration and Fan Engineering, National Foundry College, National Leathersellers' College, National College of Rubber Technology); also, from 1952, Loughborough College of Technology, because of peculiar historical circumstances.
2 Later created Lord Percy of Newcastle. His autobiography (*Some Memories*, Eyre & Spottiswoode, 1958) contains some interesting passages on inter-war educational issues.
3 See 'Poor Deal for the Polys' by Nicholas Bagnall in the *Sunday Telegraph*, 7 October 1973.

Chapter XI

FINANCING THE EDUCATION SERVICE

Education is by far the most costly of local government services. Table 11.1 reveals that over 40 per cent of the *current* expenditure of British local authorities is on education, compared to around 7 per cent for the next most expensive service, police; recently something over 18 per cent has gone on debt interest. In *capital* expenditure, education is beaten into second place by housing. Nevertheless, in aggregate, expenditure on education is still well in the lead. The burden of education is not, of course, borne solely by local government. Both directly and through grant aid to local authorities education places major demands on central government. Private educational expenditure is significant too but this chapter is only concerned with the public sector.

Comment is excited not just by the size of educational expenditure but by its growth. The proponents of other public services sometimes turn apprehensive eyes towards education, seeing it as a rampaging monster with an insatiable appetite for public funds. In money terms the increase in public expenditure on education has been staggering, especially since the war, as may be seen from Table 11.2. Naturally, though, much of this simply reflects inflation. What has happened in real terms?

There are methodological problems in assessing the exact size of educational expenditure and comparing one year with another over a long period – see the discussion by Peacock, Glennerster and Lavers (1968). Published statistics are not always adequate or consistent. Economists disagree about the most appropriate way of measuring the proportion of national income devoted to education. The very definition of education is open to dispute at the margin – school dental treatment (education or health?), youth clubs (education or recreation?), the Civil Service College (education or administration?), Sandhurst (education or defence?), and so on. Nevertheless sufficient work has been done by economists, especially after the pioneering study by John Vaizey (1958), to enable a fairly clear picture to emerge. Education now takes a much

Table 11.1 Expenditure by UK Local Authorities for Selected Years
1951 to 1973

	1951 £m.	1951 %	1960 £m.	1960 %	1965 £m.	1965 %	1970 £m.	1970 %	1972 £m.	1972 %	1973 £m.	1973 %
A Current Expenditure												
Education	320	40·5	752	43·9	1,227	42·7	2,068	41·1	2,744	43·2	3,179	41·9
Housing subsidies	15	1·9	31	1·8	66	2·3	103	2·1	43	0·7	85	1·1
Rent rebates and allowances	*	—	*	—	*	—	*	—	46	0·7	224	3·0
Police	60	7·6	116	6·8	190	6·6	356	7·1	459	7·2	524	6·9
Fire service	16	2·0	29	1·7	47	1·6	77	1·5	104	1·6	111	1·5
Roads and public lighting	81	10·3	127	7·4	194	6·8	254	5·1	322	5·1	363	4·8
Sewerage and sewage disposal	39	4·9	85	5·0	73	2·5	138	2·7	170	2·7	194	2·6
Refuse collection and disposal					65	2·3	115	2·3	147	2·3	167	2·2
Land drainage and coast protection	5	0·6	9	0·5	14	0·5	21	0·4	27	0·4	33	0·4
Parks, pleasure grounds, etc.	*	—	32	1·9	52	1·8	90	1·8	119	1·9	137	1·8
Town and country planning	22	2·8	*	—	21	0·7	51	1·0	73	1·2	87	1·1
Public health	10	1·3	19	1·1	30	1·0	52	1·0	64	1·0	70	0·9
Personal health	39	4·9	72	4·2	115	4·0	129	2·6	167	2·6	190	2·5
Personal social services	26	3·3	49	2·9	83	2·9	239	4·8	353	5·6	425	5·6
Libraries, museums, arts	10	1·3	21	1·2	36	1·3	64	1·3	88	1·4	98	1·2
Administration of justice	4	0·5	10	0·6	21	0·7	45	0·9	46	0·7	50	0·6
Rate collection	5	0·6	9	0·5	14	0·5	23	0·5	32	0·5	33	0·4
Debt interest	89	11·3	287	16·7	522	18·2	1,068	21·2	1,164	18·3	1,403	18·5
Other current expenditure	49	6·2	67	3·9	105	3·7	139	2·8	188	2·9	207	2·7
TOTAL	790	100	1,715	100	2,875	100	5,032	100	6,356	100	7,580	100

Table 11.1   Expenditure by UK Local Authorities for Selected Years 1951 to 1973

B Capital Expenditure	1951 £m.	1951 %	1960 £m.	1960 %	1965 £m.	1965 %	1970 £m.	1970 %	1972 £m.	1972 %	1973 £m.	1973 %
Education	60	12·6	114	17·3	171	12·4	295	15·1	430	17·1	521	16·1
Housing	288	60·3	255	38·7	545	39·6	742	37·9	712	28·3	956	29·5
Police	5	1·1	7	1·1	18	1·3	22	1·1	21	0·8	31	1·0
Fire Service	2	0·4	4	0·6	6	0·4	9	0·5	12	0·5	11	0·3
Roads and public lighting	11	2·3	54	8·2	106	7·7	246	12·6	309	12·3	344	10·6
Sewerage and sewage disposal}	18	3·8	44	6·7	68	5·0	138	7·1	208	8·3	261	8·1
Refuse collection and disposal}					5	0·4	20	1·0	25	1·0	23	0·7
Land drainage and coast protection	4	0·8	8	1·2	9	0·7	15	0·8	22	0·9	28	0·9
Parks, pleasure grounds, etc.	*	—	8	1·2	20	1·5	27	1·4	55	2·2	72	2·2
Town and country planning	13	2·7	*	—	41	3·0	60	3·1	84	3·3	96	3·0
Public health	1	0·2	2	0·3	2	0·2	2	0·1	3	0·1	3	0·1
Personal health	2	0·4	5	0·8	12	0·9	12	0·6	18	0·7	24	0·7
Personal social services	5	1·1	7	1·1	18	1·3	31	1·6	50	2·0	75	2·3
Libraries, museums, arts	*	—	2	0·3	5	0·4	8	0·4	14	0·6	18	0·6
Trading services	19	4·0	29	4·4	56	4·1	76	3·9	88	3·5	84	2·6
Other fixed capital formation	32	6·7	65	9·9	103	7·5	148	7·6	185	7·4	208	6·4
Loans for house purchase	17	3·6	42	6·4	168	12·2	72	3·7	173	6·9	320	9·9
Other grants and loans	1	0·2	13	2·0	22	1·6	34	1·7	107	4·3	164	5·1
TOTAL	478	100	659	100	1,375	100	1,957	100	2,516	100	3,239	100

Source: Central Statistical Office, National Income and Expenditure 1962–1973 (HMSO, annually), Section VIII 'Local Authorities'.

Notes:
1 * = Not separately listed.
2 Percentages rounded up.
3 'Education' includes expenditure on school meals and milk, and scholarships and grants to universities and colleges.

Table 11.2 *Public Authorities in England and Wales, Net Current and Capital Expenditure from Revenue on Education for Selected Financial Years 1900 to 1973*

| | £m. | | |
	LEAS	Central Government	Total
1900–1	16·2	0·7	16·9
1910–11	27·5	0·6	28·1
1920–1	70·5	5·8	76·3
1930–1	82·3	4·0	86·3
1937–8	92·4	4·3	96·7
1950–1	247·4	40·1	287·6
1960–1	706·7	87·7	794·4
1970–1	1,916·1	326·3	2,242·4
1971–2	2,232·0	361·6	2,593·6
1972–3	2,611·2	429·5	3,040·8

Source: Statistics of Education 1973, Vol. 5,
    Finance and Awards (HMSO, 1975), Table 1[1].

larger proportion of national income than it did fifty years ago but the growth has been neither steady nor constant.

Table 11.3 employs the National Income and Expenditure 'Blue Books' which provide excellent data from the 1950s onwards. The trend revealed is unmistakable. In the twenty-two-year period covered, education has more than doubled its share of national income. Prior to the 1950s the data is less accessible. Vaizey (ibid., p. 122), using a different basis of calculation, estimated that public expenditure on education was 1·2 per cent of national income in 1920 but, with some fluctuations, had reached 2·7 per cent in 1938; during the war years the proportion fell dramatically and only picked up slowly afterwards to reach 2·7 per cent again by 1948. Indeed he claimed that if expenditure on school meals, milk, the school health service and similar social expenditure were excluded from the calculations, education took annually a *smaller* proportion of national income between 1945 and 1950 than in any pre-war year, and even in 1955 was smaller than in the peak pre-war years. For Vaizey, writing in 1957 (ibid., p. 22) this was 'a striking and melancholy conclusion'. However all was changing as he wrote. As Table 11.3 indicates (and as Vaizey's own later calculations confirm), from the mid-1950s a rapid rise in real expenditure on education occurred which took a substantially larger slice of national income. By the 1970s it was at least two and a half times the best pre-war figure. Interestingly, Vaizey with hindsight attributed the turning point to Sir David Eccles' first term of office as Minister of Education (Vaizey and Sheehan, 1968, pp. vii, viii).

Table 11.3   *Public Expenditure on Education and Defence Related to UK National Income for Selected Years 1951 to 1973*

	1	2	3	4	5
				Col. 2 as	Col. 3 as
	National income £m.	Education expenditure £m.	Defence expenditure £m.	percentage of col. 1 %	percentage of col. 1 %
1951	11,857	401	1,179	3·38	9·94
1955	15,511	555	1,591	3·58	10·26
1960	20,798	916	1,630	4·40	7·84
1965	28,674	1,585	2,105	5·53	7·34
1970	39,019	2,640	2,466	6·77	6·32
1972	48,962	3,559	3,097	7·27	6·33
1973	56,259	4,134	3,403	7·35	6·05

Source: Central Statistical Office, *National Income and Expenditure 1962–1973* (HMSO, annually), Sections I and IX.

What can explain the very significant increase in real terms? Three kinds of factors, either alone or in combination, could provide an explanation. First the increase could be due to purely functional factors – growing numbers of schoolchildren, more children staying voluntarily beyond the age of compulsory attendance, higher demand for further education and like factors all creating the need for more schools, colleges, teachers, equipment. Secondly the increases could be a reflection of national economic trends and needs. Thirdly the increase could be the result of policy changes – a conscious decision to give education a higher priority in public expenditure in order to improve standards or to extend provision or both.

Functional factors must have some importance. Table 11.4 shows the number of children in maintained schools increasing by more than a third this century (partly because of policy decisions increasing the minimum period of schooling); full-time students in postschool education increased even more dramatically. Clearly these pressures must alone have substantially raised the real level of educational expenditure (unless standards had been allowed to fall). Maclure argues (1968, pp. 21, 22) that they were the dominant influence; for him the explosive growth of educational expenditure arose from more people wanting more education. Functional pressures seem, however, an incomplete explanation. Expenditure has grown even faster than response to them would appear to warrant, education having doubled its share of national income in fifty years.

Table 11.4   *Numbers of Pupils and Students in England and Wales –*
Selected Financial Years 1900 to 1973

	Full- and part-time* pupils in maintained and assisted schools (thousands)	Full- and part-time* students in grant aided further education establishments and colleges of education (thousands)
1900–1	5,772·0	—
1910–11	6,222·6	93
1920–1	6,251·7	126
1930–1	6,007·3	137
1937–8	5,599·5	173
1950–1	5,895·0	353
1960–1	7,165·0	431
1970–1	8,421·0	787
1971–2	8,661·0	806
1972–3	8,822·0	829

* Part-timers are recorded as full-time equivalents.
Source: DES, *Statistics of Education 1973*, Vol. 5, *Finance and Awards* (HMSO, 1975), Table 1[1].

In any case the existence of a demand does not guarantee that the government will meet it, as the post-war experience of nursery education demonstrates. It can be argued that it requires both massive public support and conscious government policy decisions to effect a major change in public expenditure priorities, no matter what functional factors appear to justify it. Otherwise successive governments might have attempted to gainsay the functional pressures in education instead of accommodating them.

The second group of factors seem most important to Vaizey and Sheehan. They suggest (1968, p. 129) that, apart from the growth of population, 'the rise in educational expenditure is attributable largely to the growth and changes in the rate of growth of the national income'. They argue that since economic growth leads automatically to higher tax yields, the Department of Education (along with other government departments) can bid for more – perhaps quoting numbers of children or other functional factors in justification. Moreover a growing economy demands a greater supply of skilled manpower; thus the government will feel the need to devote more resources to education. In short there is a reciprocal relationship between economic growth and real educational expenditure. This analysis has great plausibility. It does not, however, adequately explain why education's *share* of national resources should have risen. The Department of Defence, say, can bid for an increased allocation from greater tax yield. The Department of Defence can argue the need to protect a growing economy with more sophisticated weapon systems and more highly trained personnel to operate them. Yet the share of national income devoted to defence has fallen. Again, therefore, while the national economy has an enormous impact on educational expenditure, it cannot provide a complete explanation for all changes.

This leaves us with the third set of factors – policy changes. Vaizey and Sheehan (1968) largely discount these. They point out that major reforms do not always have major repercussions on expenditure levels. The Education Act 1944 did; the Education Act 1918 did not. From their data they concluded that public opinion had little direct effect on educational expenditure whether or not translated into a major reform. This seems too dismissive. One of the most interesting aspects of contemporary British culture is the enormous favour accorded education by all sections of the populace. Expenditure on education receives massive public approbation. Expenditure on other services either receives less positive support (health, social services) or is decidedly contentious (roads, defence, nationalised industries). In the term used by Sir Bruce Fraser, former Comptroller and Auditor General, education has top 'political sex appeal'.[1] Houses for old people or facilities for crippled children that one might expect to be dripping with 'political sex appeal' in practice have less. Of course if some scandal hits the headlines then considerable public attention may be attracted for a while, but there is nothing to equal the high continuous public pressure to spend more on education. True, there are signs in very recent years that the 'political sex appeal' of education may be declining. Disenchantment, especially with post-school education, is more frequently expressed; perhaps the lavishly reported antics of some students have made an impression on public opinion. On the other hand public demand for the expansion of nursery education shows no tendency to wane. In any case, even if the popularity of education has peaked, its dominant place in public affection in the last few decades must have influenced expenditure levels. Raising of the school-leaving age, expansion of further education, increased provision for nursery schools, expenditure on educational priority area schools and the like were all supported by a groundswell of public opinion.

Thus all three kinds of factor – functional, economic and political – could help to explain the real growth in public expenditure on education. Probably all three operated interrelatedly. The respective weight of each is disputable.

G

Table 11.5 England and Wales: Expenditure by LEAs and the Central Government for Selected Years 1959 to 1972

	1959/60		1964/5		1969/70		1970/1		1971/2	
	£m.	%	£m.	%	£m.	%	£m.	%	£m.	%
Nursery schools	2·4	0·3	3·1	0·2	4·8	0·2	6·2	0·3	7·0	0·2
Primary schools	204·8	25·1	297·5	21·9	482·2	22·3	555·1	22·4	656·7	22·7
Secondary schools	256·9	31·5	385·9	28·4	557·0	25·8	639·9	25·9	780·4	27·0
Special schools	16·8	2·1	26·0	1·9	45·2	2·1	53·7	2·2	73·9	2·6
Further education	76·0	9·3	139·2	10·2	246·3	11·4	286·8	11·6	332·0	11·5
Teacher training	15·0	1·8	39·0	2·9	72·4	3·3	78·6	3·2	91·1	3·2
Universities	55·9	6·8	151·3	11·1	231·4	10·7	273·1	11·0	298·5	10·3
School health	12·3	1·5	16·7	1·2	25·0	1·2	28·9	1·2	33·2	1·1
Meals and milk	54·2	6·6	77·5	5·7	102·3	4·7	110·9	4·5	119·4	4·1
Youth service	7·6	0·9	16·4	1·2	23·6	1·1	26·3	1·1	30·5	1·1
Maintenance grants	21·6	2·6	50·5	3·7	98·7	4·6	103·5	4·2	120·8	4·2
School transport	9·7	1·2	14·5	1·1	22·5	1·0	28·3	1·1	35·9	1·2
Other	28·2	3·5	43·5	3·2	73·4	3·4	85·8	3·5	100·3	3·5
Loan charges	54·8	6·7	98·4	7·2	176·7	8·2	197·4	8·0	210·3	7·3
TOTAL	816·2	100	1,359·5	100	2,161·5	100	2,474·5	100	2,890·0	100

Source: DES, Statistics of Education, Vol. 5, Finance and Awards (HMSO, annually).

Distribution of Educational Expenditure

There have been significant changes in the proportion of expenditure devoted to the various educational sectors. The most important trends have been the substantial decline in the share of resources devoted to primary education and the considerable increase for secondary education, further education, teacher training and the universities. According to Vaizey and Sheehan's calculations (1968, p. 136) the proportion of annual public education expenditure devoted to primary education halved between 1920 and 1965 while over the same period the proportion devoted to secondary education increased by a half, the proportion to further education and universities doubled and the proportion to teacher training increased eightfold. Administration and inspection, meals and milk, and school health all substantially increased their share of the total in the post-war period but then suffered a relative decline again in the 1960s; this left the percentage taken by meals and milk in 1965 still considerably above the pre-war figure, but in the case of school health, administration and inspection, the 1965 percentage was rather lower than pre-war.

Later figures in Table 11.5 reveal that total outlay on secondary schools is still well in the lead although its proportionate importance has tended to decline, whereas primary school expenditure has tended to hold its own from the mid 1960s. Expenditure on further education, teacher training and universities also seems to have maintained a roughly constant relative position from the mid-1960s after an initial leap from the early 1960s. Maintenance grants appear to have improved their relative position significantly right up until the *late* 1960s, but then settled down.

The sectoral distribution of educational expenditure may well now maintain a fairly stable pattern for some years. Small changes will of course occur; for instance the long-term decline in the importance of meals and milk expenditure will no doubt continue. Nevertheless dramatic shifts of emphasis seem unlikely in the next decade.

Table 11.6 shows expenditure *by* LEAs *alone* for 1970/1 and 1971/2. The notable difference from Table 11.5 is the far smaller expenditure on university education (although maintenance grants are still a major item). The figures emphasise the preponderance of the demands of schools. Out of the total of education and education related expenditure by LEAs, well over 60 per cent is directly attributable to schools. Moreover if expenditure on meals, milk, health and transport (from which schools are the principal beneficiaries) is taken into account, the proportion is about 70 per cent. In the words of Dr Kathleen Ollerenshaw (1969): 'In effect on

Table 11.6 *Expenditure by English and Welsh Local Education Authorities by Sector*

	£ million	
	1970/1	*1971/2*
Nursery	6·2	7·0
Primary	544·4	644·9
Secondary	626·5	762·1
Special	53·1	73·1
Total schools	1,230·2	1,487·1
Further education	280·4	325·6
Teacher training (tuition)	40·4	48·0
Universities	16·6	17·6
Other (including administration)	76·0	88·9
Total education expenditure	1,643·7	1,967·2
Teacher training (accommodation)	14·6	16·3
School health	28·9	33·2
Meals and milk	110·9	119·4
Youth service and physical training	24·1	28·0
Maintenance grants	100·7	117·5
Transport	28·3	35·9
Other	—	0·6
Total related expenditure	307·4	350·7
TOTAL ALL EXPENDITURE	1,951·1	2,317·9
Loan charges	197·4	210·3

Source: Statistics of Education, Vol. 5, *Finance and Awards* (HMSO, 1971, 1972).

local rates the expansion in further education and in the training of teachers (including awards to students) has been of great significance. But in absolute terms the advances in primary and secondary education, in buildings and equipment, and particularly in the numbers and salaries of teachers, represent by far the biggest increase'.

Salaries and wages are a massive component of local education authority expenditure – about 60 per cent of the total, with teachers' salaries alone accounting for about 45 per cent. In a service as labour-intensive as education this is not surprising. According to Vaizey and Sheehan's calculations (1968, p. 133), however, this proportion is lower than it was. Their figures are that teachers' salaries comprised 69 per cent of total expenditure in 1921, 52 per cent in 1955 and 45 per cent in 1965, while in the same period the salaries of ancillary staff rose from 7 to 12 per cent of the total. One may infer that the education service is both becoming more capital-intensive and relying more on ancillary staff; the disappearance of many rural schools with a high ratio of staff to pupils no doubt also contributed to the trend.

To sum up, the outstanding change in the distribution of educational expenditure over the last half-century has been the substantial switch in emphasis from the lower to the upper end of the educational ladder. Secondary and post-secondary education has grown far faster than primary. In broad terms this represents a diversion of resources to those with social, economic or intellectual advantage. As Vaizey and Sheehan (1968, p. 137) comment, 'In other words, what has actually happened flies in the face of the Newsom and Plowden Reports and supports the Robbins Report'.

In the last few years, however, the rapid improvement of the position of the secondary and post-secondary sectors has been halted. In any case the schools sector is still more than double the size of the post-school sector; the difference is accentuated when LEA expenditure alone is considered because of the central funding of the universities. Wages and salaries still dominate LEA expenditure but have suffered a proportionate decline of some significance over the last half-century.

Government Grants to LEAS

Government grants in aid to local authorities are of two basic types – specific or general. Specific grants are paid to subsidise one particular service or part of a service and can be used for nothing else. General (or block) grants are paid as a broad form of assistance to local government and are not earmarked for any service. Specific grants themselves may be subdivided into two categories: specific *percentage* grants in which the government meets a proportion of a local authority's expenditure on a particular service, and specific *unit* grants in which the government pays a set sum of money for every unit of a service which a local authority provides (say, every child educated or every school meal supplied). General grants are invariably paid on the basis of a formula employing factors like a local authority's population and resources; they are not thus directly related to what a local authority spends or provides. Whether the education service should be aided by general or specific government grants is an issue of great controversy which was debated particularly fiercely when the major switch from specific to general grant aid was made by the Local Government Act 1958.

In the nineteenth century government grants for education were introduced in an *ad hoc* fashion as needs and circumstances arose. Most were specific unit grants although there was the odd exotic like 'whisky money'.[2] By the twentieth century the grant system had become messy and complicated. In 1911 the Treasury set up a departmental committee under the chairmanship of Sir John Kempe[3] to examine the general relationship between central and local taxation. In its final report in 1914 the Kempe Committee included a section on grants to local education authorities. The Committee proposed that the numerous specific unit grants for elementary education be merged into one consolidated grant, partly unit and partly percentage in character; it also suggested some simplification of the grants for 'higher' (i.e. post-elementary) education.[4] The war delayed implementation of the Kempe proposals but a consolidated elementary education grant was eventually introduced in 1917. The Education (Fisher) Act of 1918 went farther along Kempe lines, merging fifty-seven separate grants into just two, for elementary and 'higher' education respectively. For 'higher' education there was a straight percentage grant of 50 per cent. For elementary education the grant was more intricate: 36 shillings per child in average attendance plus 60 per cent of the local education authorities' expenditure on teachers' salaries plus 20 per cent of their other expenditure less the product of a 7d rate This formula was designed both to relate government aid to local needs and resources and to encourage the payment of adequate salaries to teachers. Indeed to prevent parsimonious local authorities from restricting their own rates and yet gaining substantial grant aid it was also prescribed (as the Kempe Committee had suggested) that no local authority could receive *more* than two thirds of its expenditure unless its rate-financed expenditure exceeded the product of a shilling rate. A further provision that no local authority should receive *less* than 50 per cent of its recognised expenditure was clearly advantageous to richer authorities.

The essentials of the 1918 scheme remained for forty years. The formula was adjusted from time to time; occasionally special grants were added; in 1945 the elementary and 'higher' education grants were merged into one. Nevertheless the concept persisted of a specific grant system for education, adapted to local needs and resources.

All was changed in the twinkling of an eye by the Local Government Act 1958. This abolished the main education grant, together with specific grants for most other services. In their place was established a new General Grant payable to local authorities on the basis of a formula of which the main component was population.

Special percentage grants for school meals and milk which had been introduced outside the Kempe system in 1941 remained outside the new General Grant.

This change caused great concern in educational circles. It was feared that the lack thenceforth of a specific grant for education (save for school meals and milk) might lead local authorities to cut their expenditure on education. Indeed some critics asserted that this was the point of the exercise, a subtle government plot to slash educational expenditure. An AEC pamphlet (1957) announced: '. . . the Government's proposals for local government finance . . . spell disaster for the educational system of this country'; and later: 'We say that Block Grants have an inherent tendency to make authorities spend less, and that if they do spend less it will inevitably mean less on education'.

In retrospect the language of some of the critics seems extravagant, even hysterical. The growth in real resources devoted to education was not checked by the 1958 change. Why then did the Government make it, despite massive opposition from the AEC, the NUT, the WEA, the TUC and other bodies directly or indirectly associated with education? One will not be sure until government archives are opened but certain inferences are clear enough.

First the Government claimed in its 1957 White Paper, *Local Government Finance (England and Wales)*, that it was motivated by a desire to increase local authorities' financial discretion; specific grants which can only be spent on a designated service are obviously more restricting than general grants which can be spent on any local government function. The Government's claim is usually dismissed with contumely (e.g. Griffith, 1966, pp. 503–5) on the grounds that the numerous non-financial central controls, especially in the field of education (quotas for teachers, minimum and maximum class sizes, school building controls and the like), largely determine local authority expenditure; the scope for local authorities to spend grants as they wish is very small once all these controls have been obeyed. In recent years, however, the application of quantitative analysis to local authority expenditure reveals that despite the plethora of central controls there are substantial variations in local authority expenditure patterns even in education. (This is discussed more fully in the next section.) In short General Grant may have achieved a not insignificant widening of local authority financial discretion. Nevertheless it is difficult to believe that the Government would have risked such massive political obloquy just for this.

Secondly, did the Government introduce General Grant primarily to restrict the growth of educational expenditure, as many critics alleged? It is true that specific percentage grants are generally feared to have an inflationary effect. Local authorities are thought to find it easier to increase their spending on some service when they know that a certain proportion will be received back from the government. Since the amount of General Grant which a local authority receives bears no direct relationship to its expenditure, it applies no inflationary pressures. Such considerations may well have played some part in government thinking; the Government would not have been averse to eliminating unnecessary pressure on educational expenditure given that it already had more than sufficient head of steam. One doubts, however, that it was ever a serious government intention to curtail the growth of educational expenditure drastically. In any case the statistics show that this did not happen.

Thirdly, General Grant may have been introduced for a quite different reason – to facilitate government financial and economic planning. Specific grants are essentially open-ended. The amount which the government pays depends on the amount local authorities spend or provide and this cannot be predicted with certitude. The Treasury finds this most inconvenient. A general grant on the other hand is fixed in advance, usually biennially, and the Treasury knows what its commitments are. Inflation may sometimes compel the government to make supplementary general grant allocations, nevertheless the system is still more controllable than a collection of specific grants. One suspects that this was a major factor in government thinking.

One is confirmed in this view by subsequent events. In 1958 the Labour Opposition joined with the education critics to fight the introduction of General Grant by Mr Macmillan's Conservative Government. Yet when the Labour Party returned to power they did not revert to a system of specific grants for education and other local government services. On the contrary they *extended* the general grant principle. Labour's Rate Support Grant, introduced by the Local Government Act 1966 to replace General Grant, absorbed *more* specific grants including those for school meals and milk (the only specific grants left were for housing, police, major roads and some miscellaneous minor purposes). The strong suspicion must be that the Labour Government was persuaded as to the superiority of the general form of grant aid from the viewpoint of economic and financial management. Rate Support Grant, like all general grants, is paid according to a formula; this is based principally on population but with weighting factors for children, old people, density of population, declining population, children and students in education, road mileage and metropolitan costs;

Rate Support Grant also includes elements to subsidise domestic ratepayers and to aid local authorities with below-average rateable resources – see Hepworth (1971, pp. 103–12).

Thus today there are no specific education grants. Local authorities receive a lump sum of Rate Support Grant to spend as they wish, and education has to compete with other services *within* each local authority for a share of this sum.

Budgetary Discretion of LEAS

The rationale of the grant structure is apparently to internalise resource allocation decisions by LEAs. It is frequently claimed, however, that the budgetary discretion of LEAs is very small. If so the apparent internalisation would be a sham.

The argument is clear enough: legal obligations and central controls overwhelmingly determine LEA expenditure, leaving but an insignificant residue where freedom of choice can be exercised. LEAS are inescapably committed, it is claimed, to certain costs: loan charges, teaching and other salaries, student awards, pooled further education expenditure. These items together constitute the vast bulk of educational expenditure; estimates vary from 70 to 85 per cent. Moreover, loan charges are consequent upon capital expenditure which is almost entirely centrally determined in the form of capital allocations for school and college building.

The most detailed analysis yet published of resource allocation by LEAs is Dr Eileen Byrne's study (1974) of Lincoln, Nottingham and Northumberland. She strongly supports the thesis that LEA budgetary discretion is narrow; indeed she claims that it has become progressively narrower since 1945.

Nevertheless, despite all this there is much to be said on the other side. In the first place not all the constrained costs are equally inflexible. Loan charges are an unavoidable and fixed commitment, unless local authorities were to emulate Charles II and renounce their debts. Expenditure on teachers' salaries has, though, important marginal flexibilities. At first sight it would appear bereft of discretionary potential: the quota system prescribes the maximum number of teachers each LEA can employ; national salary scales lay down how much they are to be paid. Certain categories of teacher, especially part-time and temporary staff are, however, outside the quota; thus LEAs can expand or cut back employment of these according to whether their priority is to improve staffing ratios or to achieve economies. Indeed the quota itself is a *maximum* control and the LEAs may employ fewer. For most of the post-war period few LEAS would voluntarily fail to fill their quota but ·

this is becoming more common in present financial circumstances.

Moreover, though the salary ranges for different grades of teacher are settled nationally, the grade at which a teaching post is offered allows for considerable LEA discretion. Equivalent posts may be accorded different grades by neighbouring LEAs depending on whether their priority is to economise or attract high-quality applicants. (LEAs which are not very attractive to teachers – say industrial conurbations – may *need* to grade teaching posts rather high to attract satisfactory recruits.)

Student awards too leave a small area of manoeuvre for local authorities. Most grants are, it is true, mandatory. LEAs must, for instance, pay grant towards fees and maintenance at prescribed rates to any of their residents who secure a place at a university or polytechnic to read for a first degree. LEAs have discretion, however, to pay other awards, for post-graduate study for instance or perhaps for someone with a first degree who wishes to read for another.

Capital programming, like the teachers quota, is a *maximum* control. LEAs cannot invest more in educational building than their capital allocation provides but they need not spend as much (as long as their legal obligation to provide sufficient places for resident children is fulfilled). For most of the post-war period LEAs have tended to push against government restrictions, willing to spend all permitted and more. In the 1970s this is no longer necessarily the case. Not only has inflation made local authorities ever more economy minded, but the demands of competing services are receiving more sympathy. (The 'political sex appeal' of education is perhaps beginning to decline.)

Also, even those convinced of the narrowness of LEA discretion in expenditure decisions would not deny that there are *some* areas where controls are sparse or absent. In providing their schools with books, equipment, stationery and other supplies LEAs can be virtually as parsimonious or as extravagant as they choose. They have almost as much freedom in their expenditure on furniture and fittings, consonant of course with health and safety. School redecoration can be advanced or deferred, in-service training of teachers increased or reduced, school transport provided liberally or meanly, and so on.

The evidence of quantitative analyses is important too. As was mentioned earlier, these indicate that LEAs are far from identical in their allocation of resources. Boaden, for instance, in his study (1971) of English and Welsh county boroughs demonstrates not only the existence of significant variations in patterns of expenditure on education and other services, but also that these variations cannot be explained merely by differences in local authority needs or resources.

Even Eileen Byrne, with her insistence that the great mass of LEA expenditure is intractable and becoming more so, produces a wealth of evidence (op. cit., Chapter V) to qualify such a conclusion. She shows that while government control of *capital* expenditure by her three LEAs was highly effective, government exhortations or even instructions to economise in revenue expenditure were sometimes ignored or accorded only token obedience. The government found it particularly difficult to enforce its will when specific grants were replaced by General Grant.

Her researches indicate that expenditure decisions at the local level were essentially incremental in the three authorities studied (this tended, she claimed, to perpetuate cycles of deprivation). Nevertheless they also show the great importance of the personality and disposition of the chief education officer and sometimes elected members in determining expenditure patterns. Over a twenty-year period the priorities in the education services in Lincoln, Nottingham and Northumberland were largely theirs. She stresses, though, that resources in all three were inadequate to meet either implicit or explicit demand.

What can we conclude? A large proportion of LEA expenditure is undeniably difficult to vary. Central control of *capital* expenditure is particularly dominant. Nevertheless LEA impotence can be exaggerated. In the long term the predilections of individual LEAs can profoundly influence their patterns of resource allocation. Even in the short term LEAs seem increasingly willing to take the knife to previously sacred cows under the pressure of extreme economic difficulty. Moreover, Mr Reg Prentice, Labour Secretary of State for Education, committed himself to permitting more LEA discretion in *capital* expenditure. 'When the building programme for 1975/6 and subsequent years is announced there will be a much greater degree of local choice than there has ever been before'.[5] In practice, as was seen in Chapter VIII, the widening of discretion was not as substantial as this statement seemed to promise. Nevertheless the direction of change is significant.

Traditional Budgeting and Corporate Planning

Given that local authority budgeting for education contains genuine elements of choice, how are the decisions made? In the past all local authorities operated the traditional budgetary process. Towards the end of each financial year the education department of each local authority would prepare estimates for the subsequent year. These would be discussed, perhaps amended and eventually approved by the various education subcommittees (for primary, secondary, further education, the youth service and so on). After endorsement by the full education committee the estimates would go to the finance committee together with those from other spending departments. There they would be examined and discussed and perhaps certain changes insisted upon. Often where the aggregate estimates were considered too high the finance committee would impose an all round cut of, say, 5 per cent in the estimates; the education committee, together with the other spending committees, would be allowed to decide where in their own estimates the cuts should be made. Where blanket cuts were not imposed the spending departments were rivals for the favour of the finance committee. In such competition education was invariably in a strong position, rivalled only for political importance by housing in some of the larger cities. Finally, the education and other estimates would be approved by the finance committee.

This traditional style of budgeting has not entirely disappeared. Indeed in some local authorities it remains apparently unchanged. Advocacy of radical new ideas in budgeting has however become more frequent since the war. Most new concepts are more applicable to commercial or industrial organisations, or at least were usually first tried out there, but in recent years similar innovations have begun to percolate through to public authorities both central and local.

Post-war budgetary theories cannot all be described here but many have a good deal of common ground. Most stress that budgeting should not be considered a uniquely discrete operation but rather part of the general management of a public authority or firm; that budgeting should not be a limited, static, once-a-year activity but rather dynamic and continuous; that budgeting should be concerned with what programmes achieve as well as what they cost. Several approaches embrace these sort of principles but one which has gained particularly wide currency today is that termed 'corporate management' or 'corporate planning'.

The concept of corporate planning was first devised in management literature and applied to commercial and industrial organisations but subsequently to public authorities too. The starting point for corporate planning is the recognition that the firm or public authority is a corporate entity; thus the problems faced and the objectives pursued by each part of this entity must interact with the problems and objectives of every other part; consequently there should be a corresponding interaction in the use of resources – not just finance but buildings, land, staff, information and much else. Applied to local government, corporate planning produces the following kind of process – see Stewart (1971) or Eddison (1973). A local authority determines its overall goals, and then translates these into precise objectives. The objectives may be departmental (e.g. for education), subdepartmental (e.g. for primary education), or even interdepartmental (e.g. for pre-school children – involving education, health, social services). The objectives are given a priority ranking and most are related to a time-scale. Alternative ways of achieving the objectives are explicitly generated, analysed and evaluated. The alternatives which seem most likely to maximise achievement of the highest priority objectives are given preference in budgetary allocations. Indeed, budgetary decisions should ideally flow naturally from the corporate plan. When funds (or other resources) are allocated to an activity, there follows constant monitoring, feedback and review to see how far objectives are realised; where performance falls short of expectation the causes are examined, and programmes and expenditures perhaps adjusted to secure an improvement. Goals and objectives too are regularly reassessed. The corporate planning process is thus comprehensive, continuous and output-orientated.

There is some discussion today of 'community' as opposed to 'corporate' planning. The concept is even more comprehensive. It involves a local authority taking account in its planning and budgeting not only of its *own* outputs, but also those of central government and other public agencies in its area. Community planning thus attempts to incorporate the impact of all public authorities on a community – the citizens of a county or borough or whatever.

While corporate planning is a *process*, it has certain structural implications. It would clearly be more difficult to operate in the traditional, vertically fragmented local authority, with each department working to its own executive committee and with weak overall political and administrative co-ordination. Corporate planning tends thus to be associated with proposals for internal reorganisation of local authorities to achieve greater central co-ordination and control. The most contentious of such proposals were the majority recommendations of the Maud Committee on Management of Local Government (1967). They advocated reducing the number of committees in each local authority, stripping them of most executive functions and concentrating power in a small management board of five to nine councillors, serviced by a strengthened and elevated clerk. These proposals were rejected with horror by most councillors. Five years later more moderate reform proposals on the same lines put forward by the Bains Committee secured a good deal of support. They suggested that committees be allowed to retain their executive functions but that a policy and resources committee be established to provide co-ordinated advice to the council in the setting of its plans, objectives and priorities. They also wanted each authority to appoint a chief executive to act as leader of the officers and principal adviser to the council on matters of general policy.

Between the Reports of the Maud and Bains Committees a number of local authorities streamlined their committee and departmental structures, established central co-ordinating committees and appointed chief executives. In many cases management consultants were employed to produce schemes of reorganisation. The Bains Committee itself stimulated further reform – see Greenwood, Norton and Stewart (1969) and Norton and Stewart (1973).

Corporate Planning and the Education Service

How is education affected by such innovations in structure and process? All depends on the vigour with which they are implemented. A local authority which adopts an effectively centralised political and administrative structure, and which makes a determined attempt to operate corporate planning, must integrate its education service more closely with its other activities. An education department cannot easily stand out as a thing apart when it forms part of a pyramid of power, when it serves objectives which are wider than the narrowly educational and when resources are allocated to it on the basis of the part it plays in serving overall local authority purposes.

On the other hand education need not be so profoundly affected. If managerial reorganisation for a local authority merely means the establishment of a committee to operate a mild measure of co-ordination, and if corporate planning only involves some attempt at longer-term financial decisions combined with departments being asked to think about the purposes they serve, the separatism of the education service can continue virtually unbridled. Indeed an education department can engage in a limited form of corporate planning at a departmental level without involving the rest of the local authority.

Something of the varying impact of corporate planning on the education service can be seen in a report. *Management in the Education Service* (1974), produced by a group of senior education officers and DES civil servants; this recounts the experience of several LEAs in adopting managerial innovations. For instance Liverpool, Coventry and Gloucestershire all embraced corporate planning but of very diverse styles.

The views of professionals in the education service are decidedly mixed. Some are repelled by the apparent complexity of corporate planning and the jargon its *aficionados* employ. Teachers are concerned lest it be used to exclude their influence. Mr Fred Jarvis of the NUT attacked on both scores in his swingeing criticism of the report just discussed. 'Can it be that the supporters of PPB are, in fact, not so much unwilling to consult with the representatives of the teachers but unable to do so because they are talking a new form of gobbledy gook which nobody else can understand.'[6]

Undoubtedly, though, what most worries spokesmen for the education service is the tendency for corporate planning to integrate education with other local government services. Corporate planners welcome this. Mr Gordon Moore, for instance, Chief Executive Officer of Bradford Metropolitan District Council, member of the Bains Committee and one of the foremost proponents of corporate planning, has argued the wisdom of education becoming an integral part of the general provision of local government in several public speeches; he has even urged education officers to apply for chief executive posts in local government just like clerks, treasurers, and so on.[7] Such views offend those who claim that education is quite distinct in quality from any other local government service and must be treated as unique. Moreover, some fear that integration is just a cunning device to cut the resources devoted to education – witness the following diatribe by Lord Alexander.

'It may be that education looms so large in local government that those concerned with other services are naturally jealous of the resources which have to be voted to education, and this no doubt leads to a strong desire to support what is now called "corporate management" so that all those in local government who are not concerned with education may bring pressure to bear to exercise a tighter control on the education service.'[8]

On the other hand a growing body of educationalists are advocating corporate planning and allied techniques. The former deputy chief education officer for Liverpool (Birley, 1972) published a powerful plea for the transformation of educational planning on PPB lines. Others too have urged more educational interest in such innovations, e.g. Glatter (1972), Davies (1973), Stewart (1974).

Some are thinking of corporate planning applied to individual educational institutions or perhaps education departments rather than whole local authorities. Others though are prepared to favour even this, like the chief education officer for Havering. 'The new corporate management already enables us and our members to assess more effectively than hitherto the best ways of deploying capital and other resources between departments and it has made a promising start.'[9]

It is interesting too that at the national level a report in 1970, *Output Budgeting for the DES*, showed the feasibility of 'output budgeting' for all activities for which the DES is responsible. 'An output budgeting system should enable the Department both to allocate more effectively the resources made available to it, and to argue more cogently for its share of public expenditure.'

It may be that corporate planning and its relatives will be a passing fad, or perhaps that they will be a facade for the continued operation of budgeting and management in the old style. Some educationalists would be relieved at either outcome. On the other hand, it may be that there will be a genuine transformation of management and budgeting on corporate planning lines, in at least some LEAS. If so, the effect on resource allocation decisions for the education service could be profound. What seems a top priority from the viewpoint of the education service alone may appear a lower one when seen from the perspective of the needs and goals of a local community as a whole. For instance it may be that the heavy post-war emphasis on secondary and post-secondary education will be reversed; perhaps primary and nursery schools will prove more vital elements in a community plan.

The Financial Crisis in Education

Education has experienced many periods of financial stringency of varying degrees of severity. Particularly harsh retrenchments were imposed as a result of the Geddes and May Committees in the 1920s and 1930s respectively. Even in the 1950s and 1960s, halcyon days for education in retrospect, the department kept a fairly tight rein on expenditure by LEAS, and the stop–go policies of successive Chancellors of the Exchequer periodically jerked the reins back, notably in 1951, 1957 and 1963. Nevertheless in the mid-1970s the financial crisis which faces education seems its gravest yet. The problem, in a word, is inflation and of the most rampaging species. Not altogether fanciful parallels can be drawn with Germany in 1922 and 1923.

In the present crisis, education (in common with other public services) suffers doubly. Today it is widely accepted that expansion of money supply is at least a contributory factor in inflation. Recent governments, both Labour and Conservative, have attempted to restrict the growth of money supply principally by curtailing public expenditure.

Yet at the same time that retrenchments of this kind are imposed, costs continue to rise at a dramatic rate. Education, being labour intensive like most local government services, suffers particularly from soaring *wage* costs, although building costs are also a grave problem and the rising prices of furniture, equipment, books and the like would alone cause substantial difficulty.

There is an obvious contrast with the pre-war situation where costs were often stable or declining. Vaizey and Sheehan (1968, p. 132) point out: 'Thus the severe cuts of 1922 [Geddes] led only to a fall of 2 per cent in actual outlay [on education]. The even more severe cuts of 1931 and 1932 [May] led to an even smaller fall. This was because of price changes, which offset the cuts in money expenditure.'

The current crisis burst upon education with little warning. True the ratchet of inflation had been winched up remorselessly throughout the early 1970s, but there was, alas, nothing new in this. True the Chancellor of the Exchequer had announced some cuts in public expenditure in May 1973,[10] but this had seemed like 'fine tuning' of the economy. True these cuts had turned out tougher than expected. Nevertheless this still involved an increase in LEA expenditure over 1973/4.

The real crisis began when Egyptian forces crossed the Suez canal to storm Israeli positions on 6 October 1973. The economic consequences of the Yom Kippur war were shattering for Western economies as oil supplies were first curtailed and then enormously increased in price. For Britain the combination of the oil problem with major industrial disputes, especially in the coal industry, necessitated drastic action. On 17 December 1973 Mr Anthony Barber, the Chancellor of the Exchequer, announced '. . . by far the largest reduction in public expenditure for a succeeding year which has ever been made, both in absolute and relative terms';[11] £1,200 millions were cut from the estimates for the subsequent financial year. Education could not be exempted from such a holocaust. For LEAs the principal effect was a reduction in the amount of Rate Support Grant received, and economies were essential.

While LEAs were left to review their own expenditures, areas where cuts might be made were suggested in Circular 2/74. The Government felt that there had been too rapid an expansion of provision for the under-5s, and too slow a reduction (i.e. worsening) of staff–student ratios in higher education. The Government also expressed discontent at the level of non-teaching costs in schools and colleges, and urged a significant cutback in procurement expenditure (heating, lighting, maintenance, furniture, equipment, teaching materials and the like).

A minority Labour Government came to power in February 1974 and became a majority Labour Government in October 1974.

Although some modest additional expenditure was allowed in 1974, swingeing new economies were imposed in 1975 and 1976.

The prospect of the second half of the 1970s is not pleasant for LEAS. Squeezed between retrenchment and inflation, they have some very hard decisions to make. A substantial increase in expenditure is required just to maintain present standards; most LEAS find it sufficient struggle to do this, let alone effect an improvement.

Economies of all kinds have been made by LEAS: deferral of maintenance and redecoration, non-replacement of furniture and equipment, pruning of stationery and supplies, insisting that further education courses be self-supporting (at least those not leading to an examination), even substituting vegetable protein for meat and dried for fresh milk in school meals. Sheffield went so far as to extend school holidays by a week in order to reduce heating and lighting costs.[12] One feels that there is only limited scope for further economies of this kind. There is indeed talk of cutting whole parts of the education service – nursery schools, adult education, the youth service. There are also powerful voices arguing that further and higher education should bear the brunt of any new cuts. For instance, Labour spokesman Roy Hattersley, MP, proclaimed, 'I have always made plain my belief that in times of financial stringency higher education should stand further back in the resources queue than schools'.[13] Similarly Lord Alexander of Potterhill insisted, 'Spending on universities and colleges must be curbed to make more money available for schools. First priority must be the 5 to 15 year olds.'[14]

The cost of teachers' salaries must loom large in any consideration of educational economies. Some LEAS cut the numbers of extra quota teachers or even decided not to employ their full quota. By the end of 1975 at least 4,000 teachers were unemployed.

Could more funds be made available for education? The financial crisis in education is part of two larger ones – Britain's national economic problems and local government's difficulty in securing adequate sources of revenue. Despite North Sea oil the prevailing view on the first is pessimistic; on the latter the perennial problem of finding a more progressive and flexible alternative to the rates is once more under official examination with the appointment of the committee of inquiry under Mr Frank Layfield, QC. In the short run the only likely change seems to be some transference of LEA costs to the central exchequer. Professor A. R. Ilersic, for instance, has argued that salaries in the education service should be met centrally since they are negotiated nationally.[15] Lord Alexander, Mr Edward Britton (NUT General Secretary) and others, however, strongly oppose such transfers on the grounds of further loss of local authority responsibility.[16] Unless a publicly acceptable reform of the rating system is achieved in the near future, however, some shift to central funding seems inevitable.

NOTES

1 In an interview with the author in 1964.
2 The Local Taxation (Customs and Excise) Act 1890 allocated the English share of the proceeds of certain duties on beer and spirits ('whisky money') as follows: (a) £300,000 in aid of the police pension funds; (b) the residue to county and county borough councils in aid of the rates with an option to apply it to technical education.
3 An eminent retired civil servant and author of remarkably unilluminating memoirs. See *Reminiscences of an Old Civil Servant 1846–1927* by Sir John Arrow Kempe, KCB (John Murray, 1928).
4 The Kempe Committee acknowledged that in recommending consolidation of grants into one or two per service it was much influenced by the *Minority Report of the Royal Commission on Local Taxation* (Cd 638, 1901).
5 See the report of Mr Prentice's speech to the Council of Local Education Authorities in *Education*, 15 November 1974.
6 *Education*, 1 November 1974, p. 495.
7 See the report of his speech to the Society of Education Officers in *Education*, 2 February 1973, pp. 167, 168.
8 *Education*, 22 February 1974, p. 193.
9 D. H. Wilcockson, 'How Havering came to the top of the hill' in *Education Management*, p. xiv, supplement to *Education*, 8 November 1974.
10 *House of Commons Debates*, Vol. 857, No. 13, cols 38–52 (21 May 1973).
11 *House of Commons Debates*, Vol. 866, No. 35, col. 965.
12 See *The Star* (Sheffield), 26 October 1974.
13 *House of Commons Debates*, Vol. 868, No. 51, col. 33 (28 January 1974).
14 In delivering the Gwent Lecture at Caerleon College of Education. See the *Western Mail*, 10 July 1974.
15 See the report of his remarks in the *Municipal Journal*, 4 October 1974.
16 See 'State cash threat in the classroom' in the *Daily Express*, 15 October 1974 and *The Times*, 4 November 1974.

Chapter XII

REFORMING THE STRUCTURE OF LEAs

Education looms so large in the spectrum of local government services in terms of its cost, public interest and general importance, that its needs have invariably been given great weight in any scheme for local government reform. When, for instance, the structure of local government in Greater London was reformed between 1957 and 1965, the scheme eventually adopted was profoundly influenced by the claims of education. The Herbert Commission (1960) recommended a new two-tier structure in London – a Greater London Council and fifty-two new London boroughs, plus the City of London left unchanged. The Commission clearly gave a great deal of thought to the way education should be fitted into this structure. The eventual proposal was for a rather complicated division of education responsibilities between the two tiers of the new London government. Since the Commission disliked delegation, these responsibilities were to be directly assigned by statute to the two tiers. Broadly the GLC would have been responsible for policy and finance, the boroughs for running the schools and colleges; on the whole it is likely that the boroughs would have been the minor partners.

This scheme attracted vociferous opposition (Smallwood, 1965, pp. 107–16 and Rhodes, 1970, pp. 95–7, 121–4). First a large body of informed opinion opposed the division of educational functions between the two tiers, claiming that education should be administered as a unified service with all functions concentrated at one level. Secondly and more pragmatically there was much opposition to the breaking up of the LCC's education empire, in particular by the London Teachers' Association, because of its high reputation. The Government eventually decided that the boroughs should be fewer (only thirty-two plus the City) and therefore larger, so that each could be a local education authority in its own right (the Government considered there was some case for bigger boroughs, even apart from the needs of education). The GLC was assigned no education functions.

The Government's first response to the London Teachers'

Association and its allies was a half-baked proposal to retain *part* of the LCC area as a special education unit; this satisfied neither those who wanted to retain the LCC educational empire intact, nor those who wanted all London boroughs to be educational authorities. Not surprisingly the proposal attracted no support and a welter of incredulous abuse. The Government retreated abashed and yielded completely by setting up a committee of the GLC called the Inner London Educational Authority (ILEA), covering the whole of the former LCC's territory; it thus includes within its boundaries twelve of the new London boroughs and the City. The position of the ILEA was originally to be reviewed by 1970, but in 1967 the provisions for review were repealed and the ILEA left as a permanent feature of London government. Outside inner London the twenty London boroughs are each their own LEA.

It is ironic that while the size of the London boroughs was strongly influenced by the desire to make them large enough to be LEAS, twelve are not LEAS. There were some strong arguments for not breaking up the LCC's educational organisation but, approached unhistorically, it is hard to justify giving, say, Haringey all educational functions and Camden none. Moreover, the existence of ILEA poses certain problems of co-ordination in inner London between education and the other social services administered by the London boroughs. It underlines the importance of education that it alone was able to secure exemption from a structure which it had done so much to create.

The Reform of local government in England *outside* Greater London was the brief for the Royal Commission on Local Government in England, appointed in 1966 under the chairmanship of Sir John Maud (later Lord Redcliffe-Maud). At first reading of the Report (1969), education may seem to have been less influential in shaping its proposals than in the case of London. Closer study reveals, however, that education was one of the principal areas of debate within the Royal Commission and produced one of the significant differences between the Labour and Conservative schemes for local government reform published by successive Governments.

The Royal Commission majority proposed that English local government be reformed on the basis of units with a population of between 250,000 and 1 million, which embraced towns and their hinterlands rather than separating urban from rural, and which concentrated responsibility for all services at one level where possible. Applying these principles, the scheme was to divide England outside Greater London into sixty-one new local government areas. Of these fifty-eight would be unitary – a single authority responsible for all services. In the case of the three conurbations centred on Birmingham, Liverpool and Manchester it proposed a two-tier system; in each there would be one metropolitan-wide authority responsible for certain services and a lower tier of four to nine metropolitan districts responsible for the rest. Within the unitary areas and, if there was public desire, within the metropolitan areas too, the Royal Commission majority wanted 'local councils' as sounding boards of community opinion and to operate certain minor functions; the only educational one mentioned was the appointment of school managers and governors. Finally they proposed that all the English local authorities be grouped under eight indirectly-elected provincial authorities. The provinces were to have certain planning and co-ordinative functions in education especially for further education and special schools.

As the present writer has pointed out elsewhere (Regan, 1969) the unitary principle begins to wear rather thin if there are to be 'local councils' operating below and provincial councils above. Nevertheless the intention was clearly to concentrate most responsibilities including the bulk of educational functions, at the 'unitary authority' level – outside the three metropolitan areas. Why make these three exceptions? The problem was the first principle, size. While the Royal Commission majority considered that local authorities should not be much below 250,000 in population to be effective, it also felt that those with more than 1 million would suffer managerial diseconomies and problems of remoteness from the public, especially in the 'personal services' – education, social services, health, housing. In the case of Birmingham, Liverpool and Manchester, the whole built-up area, and arguably some territory beyond, formed an entity which for 'environmental services' – planning, transport, sewerage – should be treated as one. Since, however, the population embraced was 2 or 3 millions in each case, this was too big to administer the 'personal services'. Their solution was a two-tier system – a single upper-tier unit per conurbation to administer the environmental services, and several smaller lower-tier units for the personal services.

Thus, apart from the handful of marginal functions assigned to provinces and local councils, all educational responsibilities would be concentrated at one level. Inside the metropolitan areas the metropolitan districts would be the local education authorities; outside, the unitary authorities would perform this role.

Did the needs of education play much part in shaping the overall scheme of the Royal Commission majority? Clearly they did. The minimum and maximum sizes which it plumped for were heavily influenced by the evidence of education witnesses. It is true that the partisans of other services also gave evidence about the effective size of units, but there was much more from education than from any other quarter. The education witnesses did not speak with a single voice but few were willing to contemplate units with under 200,000 population. Also, most educational witnesses stressed the indivisibility of the service and this was a major factor in persuading the Royal Commission majority to allocate it in its entirety to the metropolitan districts. This decision was reinforced by the arguments of those who wanted education linked to the administration of the personal social services.

The proposals of the Royal Commission majority were challenged by a powerful *Memorandum of Dissent* written by one of the Commissioners, Mr Derek Senior. His principles for reform were radically different. He placed heavy reliance on social and economic geography to produce units that were coherent in terms of patterns of activity. He was less concerned with population size and unimpressed with the unitary priniciple. Accordingly his scheme was avowedly two-tier (he preferred the term 'two-level'). He proposed for England outside Greater London 35 regional and 148 district authorities. The regional authorities were to be responsible for planning, transport, sewerage and similar 'environmental services' plus capital investment programming, police, fire and *education*; the district authorities were to have the health service, personal social services, housing management, consumer protection and other functions involving much direct contact with the public. In four areas the same authority would exercise both regional and district functions.

Mr Senior differed from his colleagues not only in the whole shape of his scheme, but also, very interestingly, in his provision for the education service. He devoted substantial sections of his *Memorandum* to wrestling with the issues raised by education. He was dubious of the need for an undivided education service, of the advantage of the same authority administering both education and health and welfare, and even of the case for a minimum population size for education authorities. Indeed he viewed with some equanimity the removal of the whole service from local government. Nevertheless he felt that it could be fitted into his scheme. As was mentioned he allocated it to the upper of his two levels of authority – the region. This contrasted with the Royal Commission majority proposal to give education the lower tier in the three metropolitan areas. Moreover, Senior wanted the regional authorities to be obliged to take decisions relating to individual schoolchildren through district officers, each with an area of jurisdiction coterminous with a district health and welfare authority and advised by a committee drawn from that authority. He thus came perilously close to splitting the administration of education.

The Redcliffe-Maud Commission reported in 1969 with a Labour Government in office which broadly accepted the prescription of the majority. In the subsequent White Paper, *Reform of Local Government in England* (1970), however, the Government proposed extending the two-tier, metropolitan arrangements to two other areas: West Yorkshire (the conurbation centred on Leeds) and, curiously, South Hampshire (to include Southampton, Portsmouth and the Isle of Wight). Also the Government insisted that in the metropolitan areas education should be administered in its entirety by the upper-tier authority, not the lower tier as the Royal Commission majority wanted. Perhaps Senior's arguments had had some effect on government thinking.

Before the Labour Government could prepare a Local Government Reform Bill, the general election of June 1970 restored the Conservatives to power. Their White Paper, *Local Government in England* (1971) was quite different. It announced the Government's intention of introducing a universal two-tier system. This did not bring joy to the ears of Derek Senior, however, since the boundaries of the new units were not to be delineated on the basis of the socio-geographical criteria he so strongly espoused. Instead the Government preferred the Royal Commission majority's size criterion of 250,000 to 1 million population and also stressed the advantage of following existing boundaries wherever possible. Thus was produced a two-tier system of fewer, larger counties and fewer, larger county districts. The Government was also impressed by the majority Report's arguments for special treatment for the metropolitan areas and a special structure was produced for them on the lines of the Redcliffe-Maud proposals. The Government identified six such areas, the Royal Commission's three (Liverpool, Manchester, Birmingham) plus West Yorkshire (the Leeds–Bradford–Huddersfield conurbation), South Yorkshire (the Sheffield–Rotherham–Doncaster conurbation) and Tyne and Wear (Newcastle–Gateshead–Sunderland); the Labour idea of South Hampshire was not taken up. There were thus to be six metropolitan counties containing a total of thirty-six metropolitan districts. The principal difference between the metropolitan and non-metropolitan arrangements was that the upper tier was more powerful in the latter. The metropolitan counties were largely confined to 'environmental' responsibilities, while the non-metropolitan counties were assigned most of the important personal services too. Thus the metropolitan districts were made responsible for most personal services whereas the non-metropolitan districts were assigned very few, housing being the only major responsibility.

Outside the metropolitan areas education was assigned wholly to the upper tier, the new counties. Within the metropolitan areas it went entirely to the lower tier, the metropolitan districts. This scheme was enacted as the Local Government Act 1972.

Not only thus was education a major bone of contention in the reorganisation issue, but its needs played a significant part in shaping the scheme which reached the Statute Book. Educational influence on the size of local authorities has already been stressed. It is true that some of the new metropolitan districts are smaller than the local education authorities they replaced; nevertheless none is as small as some of the local education authorities in the previous system. The allocation of education to the metropolitan districts and the non-metropolitan counties largely followed from accepting the argument that the education service should be undivided and linked to the administration of the personal social services.

Of course political considerations played a part in the reorganisation too; some would argue a predominant part. Nevertheless, few would deny that functional issues were significant and amongst these education was prominent.

The story of the Herbert and Redcliffe-Maud Commissions and the fate of their recommendations not only illustrates the importance of educational considerations in local government reform, but points to the issues which provoke most debate. First, what is the most appropriate size for a local education authority? Secondly, should education be divided between two or more tiers of local government, or administered as a unity at one level? A third issue, which was rather less prominent in the arguments, is whether education should be administered by the same local authority that administers other personal social services.

The Appropriate Size for an LEA

Under the Herbert Commission's original proposals, the fifty-two London boroughs would each have had a population around the 100,000 mark. This was considered too small for effective local education authorities; hence the scheme for dividing education between the GLC and the boroughs. The Government's amendments to the Herbert Commission's proposals were intended to produce boroughs with a population of about 200,000 each (although some are smaller); this was thought big enough to sustain effective local education authorities. Despite all this, no one at the time demonstrated that a population of 100,000 was too small and one of

200,000 adequate for an effective local education authority. Nor, indeed, has anyone since.

The most determined attempts to discover the minimum size necessary for an effective local education authority were made in the research studies commissioned by the Royal Commission on Local Government in England. For instance, the Greater London Group of the London School of Economics produced a report, *Local Government in South East England* (1968). A number of services were investigated to try to throw light on the relationship between size and performance. For education only those aspects of the service most likely to reveal the influence of population size (and to some extent other quantifiable factors) were probed. No attempt was made to assess the way the *whole service* was provided by the twenty-three local authorities in question. Even so, the conclusion of the Group's research officers was (op. cit., p. 145) 'Population size was not found to be a decisive factor in performance'. Nor indeed was population density, financial resources or, with one exception, socio-economic composition. It did emerge that larger authorities tended to have greater *diversity* of provision and smaller ones greater *intensity*, but it is difficult to say which is preferable. In any case small local authorities were often able to overcome their problems of diversity by joint arrangements with neighbouring authorities.

These negative findings would have been even more apparent if the mainstream of the education service had been examined, rather than only those aspects most likely to be sensitive to population. Even the smallest local authority can provide a basic part of the service like, say, primary education, satisfactorily. Thus, so far as south-east England was concerned, there was no statistical evidence for the minimum desirable size of a local education authority.

The Group supplemented their statistical inquiry with interviews of senior officers in eight local authorities to try to test assumptions about the advantages and disadvantages of large and small authorities. Findings were decidedly unclear but there was some indication that the most desirable size for a local education authority administering education (and other functions) was in the population range 200,000 to 1 million.

The Local Government Operational Research Unit of the Royal Institute of Public Administration also produced a research study for the Royal Commission, *Performance and Size of Local Education Authorities*. Using exclusively quantitative techniques, they too sought evidence for the 'best size' for a local education authority. Again the answer was a lemon. A large part of their inquiry revealed no statistically significant results and even where it did the interpretation was dubious. Thus they found that larger authorities spent disproportionately more than smaller authorities on textbooks for primary schools. As the authors themselves pointed out, however (op. cit., p. 12); 'It could be argued from this either (i) that smaller authorities are more efficient than larger, or (ii) that larger authorities can provide a better service than smaller.' Similarly they found that larger authorities employed proportionately fewer specialist advisers and architects for educational building. This could indicate either that the larger authorities are more efficient in their deployment of such staff or that the smaller authorities provide the better service.

Perhaps the most influential piece of research commissioned by the Royal Commission was the *Enquiry into the Efficiency of Local Education Authorities* (*Research Appendices,* 1969, p. 227) conducted by HM Inspectorate. Inspectors assessed the performance of all 123 local education authorities in England outside London. The assessment covered both selected aspects of the service (like adequacy of administrative staff, willingness to experiment and relations with the public), and overall performance. The findings were that the weakest authorities were almost all below 200,000 in population and that, although good authorities occurred in all size ranges, the probability of good performance increased with size. It should be emphasised, however, that these findings were not based on quantifiable or objective evidence but were impressionistic and subjective. Not that this makes them valueless. The opinions of persons as qualified and experienced as HM Inspectors must be treated with respect – but they are just opinions.

The opinions of a number of other organisations and individuals about the appropriate size for local education authorities were presented to the Royal Commission.

The Department of Education and Science in its written evidence (1967) stated: 'There is considerable variation in the efficiency of local education authorities, but there is no means of measuring this objectively. The only way of arriving at an assessment of an authority's efficiency is by a systematic subjective appraisal of standards of provision in particular sectors of its education service.' On this basis the department's view was that the minimum population for a local education authority should be about 300,000 and the most suitable size around 500,000. It would not, however, set any maximum and envisaged even larger authorities in major urban concentrations.

The Association of Teachers in Technical Institutions (*Written Evidence of Professional Organisations,* 1968, p. 51) also plumped for a minimum population of 500,000, although it preferred a two-

tier structure of local education authorities. Other professional
bodies in the education world such as the Association of Chief
Education Officers and the National Association of Schoolmasters
(ibid., pp. 8, 236–41) were unwilling to state population limits but
they supported an increase in the average size of local education
authorities.

The Association of Education Committees insisted (*Written Evidence
of Local Government and Associated Bodies*, 1969, p. 13)
that local education authorities should be of 'substantial size' but
stated 'We do not think we can prescribe a minimum in terms of
population'. Strangely, however, they were prepared to set a maximum – $1\frac{1}{2}$ million. In oral cross-examination (*Minutes of Evidence*,
Vol. 11, 1967, p. 270), when pressed, they gave the figure of 400,000
as a minimum population figure, arguing that it required local
education authorities of this size to employ a sufficient team of
specialist advisers (fourteen to sixteen). In fact some smaller LEAS
have as many.

Thus a number of organisations (and individuals) are willing to
make assertions about the minimum, and occasionally maximum,
populations which a local education authority should embrace. At
best, however, such assertions are informed guesses. There
is some consensus of *opinion*. Few witnesses to the Royal Commission
would be happy with local education authorities containing
less than 200,000 people, although some would put the minimum
higher.

The only *objective* evidence relates to inputs into the education
service–numbers of staff, amounts of expenditure and so on. There
is no uncontentious way of measuring output. Moreover even input
evidence does not point unmistakably to any population size. An
impartial observer must be forced to the conclusion that population
size is not the most important factor determining educational performance – in so far as this can be assessed. Within broad extremes, almost any size of local authority *can* operate satisfactorily.

Larger authorities have certain potential advantages, smaller ones
certain others. Whether potential advantages are realised and potential
disadvantages overcome seems to depend on a whole complex
of factors – the personality and calibre of officers, members and
teachers, the social and economic climate of the area, the relative
status of education to the other services of the local authority and
so on.

The gravest potential problems which smaller local authorities
face are, of course, in providing the more specialist parts of the
education service. Special education is a case in point. The kinds
of handicap vary greatly in their incidence; some are rather rare.

A small local authority may contain only a handful of, say, deaf children. There may well be too few to warrant the employment of special staff or the provision of special facilities to cater for them – even if the local authority could afford to do so. In such cases the local authority will be compelled to use the facilities of a larger neighbour. Clearly a large local authority with a more convenient caseload as well as more financial flexibility is more likely to be able to cope alone. For the rarest kinds of handicapped children, however, even very large authorities find self-sufficiency impossible. No structure of local authorities can avoid the need for *some* co-operation on a regional or even national basis in special education. Nevertheless, the larger the average size of local authorities, the less need there will be.

Small local authorities face similar potential problems in providing teacher training and the more advanced sector of further education. It is somewhat illogical for a small local authority to be controlling a major institution in this field when the institution has a regional if not national catchment area. Also given the specialised needs of such institutions it is more difficult for a local education authority to administer them effectively if it has only one. A large local authority with several colleges should be able to develop greater expertise in their control. Nevertheless, all this does not mean that special education and further education *in fact* always suffer in small local education authorities.

To sum up, no one has convincingly demonstrated that local education authorities should be a certain size to be effective. Many people *believe*, however, that they should not be much below 200,000 in population. At most it can be shown that very small authorities (without defining 'very small' too precisely) suffer potential drawbacks in providing more specialist parts of the service.

The Divisibility of Indivisibility of the Education Service

One of the most firmly held beliefs of professional educational administrators today is that the education service is indivisible. Derek Senior (*Memorandum of Dissent*, 1969, para. 323) has termed this 'the doctrine of the "seamless robe"' – that responsibility for all non-university education from play school to polytechnic should be carried in each area by one unit of local government'.

The reasoning behind this doctrine seems to be partly historical. Until 1944 the service *was*, of course, divided. The two-tier system of local education authorities (outside the county boroughs) – Part III authorities for elementary education and county councils for 'higher' – is remembered with general disfavour (see *Written Evidence of Local Government and Associated Bodies*, 1969, p. 12).

The principal argument is, however, that there is no convenient or logical point at which a division could be made. There is no natural break. Consequently any split would be a damaging rupture in a continuous process.

There are two points at which a division might seriously be entertained – between primary and secondary education and between secondary and (advanced) further education. In the first case one would have lower-tier LEAs responsible for children's education up to the age of roughly 11, and upper-tier LEAs for everything thereafter; in the latter case the lower-tier LEAs would be responsible for children's education up to the age of 18, and the upper-tier LEAs subsequently.

The former is rarely advocated today. With experiments in different ages of transfer from primary to secondary school, and with the introduction of middle schools in some areas, the distinction between primary and secondary education is increasingly blurred. In any case the administrative problems of primary and secondary schools have many similarities; even their catchment areas are not vastly different. Where differences ocur they are of degree rather than kind. In short there would seem little advantage in dividing their control.

The proposal to divide responsibility for the service between secondary and further education attracts much more support today. Professional educational administrators oppose this proposal just as strongly (*Minutes of Evidence*, Vol. 11, 1967, p. 273). They point out that further and secondary education overlap. Young people who leave school at 16 may pursue the same course at institutions of further education (e.g. GCE 'A' levels) as their fellows who remain in sixth forms. Also it is difficult to separate responsibility for school-level courses in further education from more advanced work, since the same college may provide both.

These are formidable but by no means conclusive objections. NALGO has challenged them with particular cogency. In its submissions to the Royal Commission (*Written Evidence of Professional Organisations* 1968, p. 212) NALGO proposed a new structure of local government for England – 10 regional councils and 120 to 130 'most purpose authorities'. It envisaged educational responsibilities divided between these two tiers – the regions administering higher further education as well as co-ordinating *all* education, the most purpose authorities administering the rest. Under oral cross-examination (*Minutes of Evidence*, Vol. 9, 1967, p. 224) NALGO witnesses stoutly defended this proposed split in the education service. It was pointed out that the seamless robe of education is already rent in that universities are administered separately. More significantly, it was stressed

that advanced further education is *already* treated as a special case
– its finance is pooled and its course allocation and capital investment subject to special controls. The fact that some colleges offered
both advanced and non-advanced courses was not regarded as an
insuperable obstacle to rational division. The polytechnics, colleges
of education and other colleges in which a majority of courses were
advanced could be allocated to the regions, the rest of the colleges
could go to the most purpose authorities. Admittedly this would
leave *some* advanced work controlled by the lower-tier authorities
but only a minority. Any scheme short of total centralisation would
leave some ragged edges.

Why, however, go to all this trouble? What is the point of such
a split? NALGO's Mr G. H. Sylvester gave a clear and unambiguous
answer, (ibid., p. 225):

'From 18, when so much is already outside local government, my
worry is that the rest of it will go too. Colleges of education for the
training of teachers, and polytechnics when we have started them
and have taken all the care and time and trouble to get them going,
will leave local government unless there is a unit big enough,
strong enough and powerful enough and influential enough to
maintain them properly.'

These fears seem eminently well justified. The colleges of advanced technology, often a major focus of local authority pride
and initiative, were taken from them and transformed into autonomous universities following the Robbins Report. Since the colleges of education, the polytechnics and the other major institutions
have regional if not national catchment areas, and since their staffs
usually aspire to university status, it is by no means inconceivable
that they might go the way of the CATs. Their control by regional
authorities would make this less likely.

Apart from the issue of retaining local authority control over
these institutions, would they be better administered by very large,
perhaps even regional, units? Here one is back in the inconclusive
area of size and effectiveness. Institutions of advanced further
education are, however, at the specialist end of the education
spectrum where the claimed advantages of scale seem most plausible. A large administrative unit controlling a number of such
institutions *should* constitute a more efficacious arrangement than
a small unit controlling only one or two. A small area of jurisdiction can be expected to exacerbate the problem of cross-boundary
movement by students with its administrative and financial

complications. A small caseload of institutions would tend to pre-clude the employment of a wide range or large number of specialist administrative staff for further education. Similarly a meaningful policy of harmonising and rationalising provision would appear dependent on control of a number of institutions rather than just one or two. For instance in the context of Greater London there was clearly some sacrifice of co-ordinating potential in the replace-ment of Middlesex county as an education authority by several London boroughs; similarly the size of the ILEA gives it a *prima facie* advantage in administering advanced further education over the outer London boroughs (Regan and Hastings, 1972, pp. 193–5).

Nevertheless all these are again input factors and their effect on the quality of education output is arguable, especially since colleges of education, polytechnics and other advanced institutions of further education enjoy such a measure of autonomy. In any case *ad hoc* co-ordinating arrangements, like the regional advisory councils, can mitigate the drawbacks of small units of administration.

To sum up, the arguments *against* dividing responsibility for the education service are not very strong, especially if the division is broadly between the education of post-18-year-olds and 18-year-olds and under. There is some case, based on input evidence, for trans-fering advanced further education to the *upper*-tier authority in London and the six metropolitan areas, though the case is by no means overwhelming. Similarly, if regional or provincial bodies are created there would be an equivalent case for allocating advanced further education to them or at least assigning them a co-ordinating role. The Royal Commission on the Constitution, chaired by Lord Kilbrandon, recommended in 1973 that regional bodies be created throughout Great Britain. The majority of Commissioners favoured bodies with powerful devolved responsibilities for Scotland and Wales, but rather weak co-ordinating councils for the eight English regions. Lord Crowther-Hunt and Professor Alan Peacock, in a dissenting report, argued for bodies with the same considerable executive functions in Scotland, Wales and the English regions. If either type of regional body is set up it seems likely to have a role to play in advanced further education.

Linking Education with Other Local Services
Though education has some connection with almost all other local government services, the relationship is particularlly strong with three or four. Housing and planning, for instance, exert a powerful influence on educational building; most new housing developments of any size soon require a new primary school and desirably this

should be taken account of from the moment planning permission is given. The services whose relationship to education are most discussed are undoubtedly, however, the health and welfare group of functions. The health services were transferred to the new National Health Service agencies. The problems of co-ordination between them and LEAs have already been touched on. Following the Seebohm Report of 1968 and the Local Authorities Social Services Act of 1970, most of the welfare services were concentrated in the social service departments of local authorities.

The social service departments embody the Seebohm concept of a unified family service directed to the prevention, treatment and relief of social problems. Their provision embraces old people, mentally and physically handicapped people, children (especially the under-5s and those of any age deprived of a normal home life), pregnant and nursing mothers, homeless families, single-parent families, families in need of domiciliary services, and other groups with special problems and requirements. Clearly a unified, family orientation of this kind must impinge on the education service at several points. It is a commonplace that family circumstances profoundly affect a child's performance and behaviour at school. The Seebohm Committee (para. 216) stressed that teachers are often best placed to trigger off remedial action: 'It is he or she who, seeing the child daily in class, is often the first to become aware that all is not well and notes some of the familiar symptoms of disturbance or distress, such as pale face, weary eyes, under performance, neglected clothing, aggressive or sullen behaviour, withdrawal and occasional or more frequent truancy.' A ready, two-way flow of information between education and social service departments in such cases is essential.

Evidence to the Redcliffe-Maud Commission (e.g. *Minutes of Evidence*, Vol. 5, 1967, pp. 91, 92, 108) also often mentioned the importance of the links between education and the social services (and to a lesser extent other services). How, though, administratively should such links be forged? In particular is it vital that the *same local authority* administer both education and the social services?

Other things being equal one would expect co-ordination to be easier within a local authority than between local authorities. When information has to flow, and harmonisation to be achieved, across local authority boundaries the political and administrative obstacles are potentially greater. Tensions are particularly likely when the co-ordination attempted is between upper- and lower-level local authorities in a two-tier system. This has been demonstrated in London. Two of the services shared between the GLC and the London

H

boroughs, housing and planning, had the most disappointing achievements in the first five years; services allocated wholly to one or other level had a rather better record. Rhodes (1972, p. 486) concluded: 'Perhaps one of the clearest lessons to be drawn from the relationship between the GLC and the boroughs under the 1963 Act is that inherent conflicts of interest cannot be resolved by consultation and cooperation in the absence of a clear definition of where responsibility lies for the ultimate decision.' If he is correct, to allocate education to one level of local government and social services to another would be to risk just such irreconcileable conflicts. Indeed London can provide some evidence in this very field. The ILEA is unique among local education authorities in retaining its own education welfare service; this undoubtedly leads to some friction with the *family* welfare service provided by the social service departments of the inner London boroughs (ibid., pp. 190, 191).

In short there is certainly a case on both theoretical and empirical grounds for the local education authority being also the social services authority. One can, however, exaggerate the case. Internal barriers to co-ordination – for instance arising from personality conflicts or the unwieldiness of very large organisations – can be as serious as inter-authority problems. Similarly, co-operation between officials of different local authorities *can* be successful. Senior asserted this most forcibly in his dissenting memorandum to the Redcliffe-Maud Report. He argued (para. 334) that day-to-day co-operation between heads of schools, medical officers and social workers was in no way dependent on their being employed by the same local authority. He adduced no evidence, though, of successful working arrangements of this kind. On the other hand, since the school medical service is now out of the hands of local government and administered by the area health authorities, some such working arrangement between medical staff and LEA officials is essential.

On the whole a fair conclusion would be that a conjunction of responsibility for education and the social services is desirable though not essential. Given the structure of local government that emerged from the Local Government Act 1972, there was everything to be said for making the non-metropolitan counties responsible for both education and the social services. Within the metropolitan areas, too, the balance of advantage lay in making the metropolitan districts responsible for both. The Labour Government's scheme to give education to the top tier and social services to the lower tier would have risked significant problems of co-ordination. Instead the large-scale administration desirable for more specialist parts of the education service could have been achieved

by allocating advanced further education *only* to the upper tier.
Splitting the education service would be to risk less.

Implications for Education of the 1972 Reforms
Though some commentators would have liked a more radical reorganisation, the Local Government Act 1972 effected a massive
enough change in the structure of local government in England
and Wales. Its repercussions on the administration of education,
as on other services, were substantial.

First, though, one must distinguish between the effects of this
particular reorganisation, and those resulting from almost any. Most
reorganisations produce a shake-up of staff. New men achieve
positions of responsibility and naturally wish to prove themselves
by raising standards of provision and implementing new policy
ideas. Moreover, changes on the official side are often comple-
mented by changes on the political, and new chairmen of committees are more likely than long-standing occupants of such posts to
back innovations. Thus, in the short run at least, improvements in
provision and changes in policy are likely to ensue from most
structural reorganisations.

What, however, are the consequences peculiar to this reorganisation? The net effect was to produce fewer and larger LEAs in England and Wales. True there were local exceptions, notably around
the metropolitan areas where parts of large county administrations
were broken off to form smaller, independent metropolitan districts
as full local education authorities; but these are exceptions to prove
the rule. In England the number of LEAs was reduced by the 1972
Act from 145 (79 county boroughs, 45 counties, 20 London
boroughs and the ILEA) to 96 (39 counties, 36 metropolitan districts,
20 London boroughs and the ILEA). In Wales the corresponding
reduction was from 17 (13 counties and 4 county boroughs) to 8
(counties). Over England and Wales together, therefore the number of LEAs fell by more than a third – 162 to 104. Moreover this
under-represents the degree of rationalisation achieved, since it
takes no account of the abolition of the divisional executives and
excepted districts by the same legislation. While not full local
education authorities, they had a substantial administrative role.
Their demise represents a major concentration of power at local
education authority level.

Immediately before reorganisation, two of the old English
counties and thirty county boroughs had less than 100,000 population. All the present English LEAs exceed this figure – though admittedly some not very greatly. The smallest is a county, the Isle of
Wight, with 109,680, followed by Kingston London borough with

H*

138,620, Barking with 157,800 and South Tyneside metropolitan district with 172,990. Similarly in Wales seven of the old, unreformed counties and one of the county boroughs (Merthyr Tydfil) had populations lower than 100,000. The smallest reformed Welsh county, Powys, is just under with 99,310 and all the others exceed 200,000.

There are some interesting changes at the upper end of the scale. The ILEA remains the biggest LEA in the country with a population of 2,649,540. It used to be followed by Lancashire with 2,428,000 and Yorkshire West Riding with 1,774,000. With the truncation of the former county and the disappearance of the latter, second place is now filled by Kent with (since its absorption of Canterbury county borough) 1,434,960; third comes Hampshire with 1,422,060 (after some loss to Dorset but the absorption of Portsmouth and Southampton county boroughs). With the biggest LEAS about the same size, but the smallest much larger, the range of size has been compressed.

In the same way the reorganisation has tended to reduce the extremes of wealth, if one takes rateable value per capita as a broad indication of wealth.

The reduction in the number of LEAS and the increase in their average size lessens the need for inter-authority co-operation (sometimes satisfactory but always a risk). For instance, cross-boundary movement by pupils and students should be cut. Similarly LEAS should need to rely less on their neighbours for special school places since on average each has a greater number and range of institutions for the handicapped. With the elimination of their weakest brethren administratively and financially, LEAS are on average stronger. Each has a more satisfactory rateable base, a wider range of administrative staff, a more substantial caseload of minority educational needs than the smallest and weakest had before. Of course some LEAS may still be regarded as rather weak (certain metropolitan districts perhaps); nevertheless far weaker ones could be found before 1974.

The implications of the reorganisation for central–local relations are subtle and ambivalent. The promotionalism of the DES has already been discussed. Is it likely to be accentuated or moderated by the reorganisation? The answer is, both. The reduction in the *number* of LEAS should facilitate central control; the increase in their *average size and strength* should make it more difficult. Fewer LEAS means fewer chief education officers for Elizabeth House staff to get to know, fewer chairmen of education committees to deal with, fewer separate administrations for HMIs to liaise with, fewer sets of policies to monitor, fewer building programmes to vet. Harmonisation on a country-wide basis should be easier.

On the other hand bigger and stronger LEAS means more independent-minded local education authorities. Those with a sounder financial base are more confident of their role than those all too conscious of their financial weakness. Large local authorities are administratively and professionally more powerful than small ones. Their staff are more numerous and cover a wider range of skills and specialisms. They are thus better able to resist central intervention. Moreover their very size enables them to develop greater expertise through more practice. A major county building a score of schools each year knows as much about building schools as the department, if not more, and would resent and resist more departmental supervision than it thinks necessary. A very small local authority building only one school every two or three years must necessarily accept heavy departmental supervision for this relatively unfamiliar task.

Large LEAS are also more powerful *political* entities than their smaller brethren. A large local authority represents a sizeable section of the population, can usually enlist the support of a considerable group of MPs and can therefore mount a formidable campaign to oppose some government decision. Of course, in the last resort the central government is the stronger, but politically damaging conflicts will be avoided where possible. Even small local authorities, if determined in their opposition, can be formidable foes; one thinks for instance of the problems caused to the Government when Clay Cross Urban District Council remained implacably resistant to implementing government housing policy, or, even more significantly, tiny Rutland able for so long to repulse all attempts to merge it with neighbouring Leicestershire. If such pygmies can be so difficult to overcome, how much greater would be the impact of a Kent or a Lancashire determinedly employing its political muscle. Government departments tread as delicately as Agag in their dealings with such giants to reduce the chances of a confrontation.

Which trend will predominate – more control because of fewer numbers or less because of larger size? At the time of writing it is far too early to tell, but unless the financial crisis totally undermines local government autonomy the chances are that the latter will. The department is likely to find it difficult to maintain the level of control it presently exercises over LEAS, especially in the area of capital expenditure.

Chapter XIII

SUMMING UP

Before drawing together the principal themes of the previous chapters, it is necessary to clear two fundamental issues. First, should education be a locally administered service at all, or should it be provided directly by the central government? Secondly, if it is to be locally administered should this be by multi-functional local authorities as at present or by special *ad hoc* education authorities?

Both questions are in turn related to an even more basic one, namely, what is the case for having local government in the first place? To provide a thorough, reasoned answer would go beyond the compass of this book. Nevertheless, since it is so crucial to an understanding of British educational administration, it is important to set out at least the bare bones of the case.[1]

Why Local Government?
The two essential features of British local authorities are, first, that they are elected and, secondly, that they have a measure of discretion in the exercise of their functions. They have, of course, other features also, but these two determine their fundamental character. If they were appointed not elected their political status would be very weak; they would be largely the creatures of the body (presumably the central government) which appointed them; certainly they could not powerfully challenge it. As elected bodies (whatever the turnout) they are significant political entities. Secondly if, irrespective of their status, they had no discretion, if in other words they were simply agents of the central government, then again their character would be entirely different. Central–local relations would constitute the relationships between the centre and its decentralised agents, akin, say, to that between local post offices and the national Post Office Corporation.

What is the point of these local political entities with discretionary powers? Could we do without them in Britain? The answer must be, yes. Local government in the sense defined is not an *indispensable* feature of the modern administrative state, nor even of the modern democratic state. Public administration in Britain would not necessarily collapse if local authorities were abolished, nor would our liberal democracy go by the board. Nevertheless, having admitted this, the case for local government is that it is an extremely *valuable* institution. Without it both administration and democracy would be damaged, even if not mortally.

To begin with, how would public administration be adversely affected by the demise of local government? First, if all services were centrally operated this would involve enormous, cumbrous administrative machines. The Redcliffe-Maud Commission considered it likely that serious difficulties would arise in the administration of many services in units much larger than 1 million population. The evidence for the figure it chose is not strong; nevertheless increasing size must eventually produce administrative elephantiasis. Certainly the mind boggles at the prospect of the administration of such services on the basis of 55 million people. A national refuse collection service, say, would as surely as one can predict anything in public administration, suffer massive dis-economies and dysfunctions of scale. Secondly, in nationally run services any mistakes made can have serious, perhaps catastrophic, consequences for the whole country. If for instance a national refuse collection service were to introduce a new, disposable dustbin liner, only to find a year later that it reacted very adversely to wet tea leaves, the cost and dislocation involved in recalling those distributed and in destroying stocks would be enormous. A county or borough which commits an error in the administration of some service affects primarily only its own citizens.

Thirdly national services would be more conservatively run, partly, indeed, because of the need to avoid costly mistakes and partly because there would be only one centre of initiative rather than many. Where services are run by local authorities, even though the central department may have a powerful supervisory role, decision-making power is polycentric. Every chief officer and every committee chairman regards his county or district service as to some extent a separate empire for him to mould. Since there is some discretion in all services at the local level there is great scope for innovation and pioneering work of both a technical and policy kind. The history of most local government services from housing to the social services, from planning to the police, and not forgetting education, reveals that new developments more often than not started out with an idea tried first by a local authority. The results would be published, or explained at some conference, or reported to the appropriate central department; other local authorities would emulate the pioneer and the new development would gradually spread to become widely, sometimes universally, adopted. Not all local authorities are throbbing centres of experiment and innovation; nor, indeed, is every new idea successful. Nevertheless, given the number of local authorities, there is a constant flow of useful innovations. If all services were centralised much of this would be lost.

On the democratic side, if local authorities were abolished this would entail the disappearance of 26,000 elective posts. The significance to democracy of the people who fill these posts at present is not just in the work which they do but in the knowledge and experience they gain. They learn what it is like to be on the *elected* end of the democratic process – subject to public pressures, compelled to make difficult choices in the allocation of scarce resources. The diffusion of this kind of experience must make for a healthier democracy. Without local government only the 635 MPs at Westminster would have the opportunity to gain it.

Also local government permits a measure of community self-government. A torrent of books and articles have been addressed to the slippery concept of community and it would be impossible to do justice to the debate here. If, though, there is any substance to the concept, it must involve an identity of interest and feeling as assessed objectively (say by socio-economic factors) or subjectively (say by public opinion surveys), or possibly both. Not all local authorities are necessarily communities on either count, but few would deny that some are; the parishes especially are widely accepted to be genuine communities. In any case, if all local authorities were swept away, all possibility of local community self-government would go with them. Again this would be a loss to liberal democratic values. Local as well as national communities should desirably have a voice in their own affairs.

Finally, local government is a check on the dangers of excessive centralism. Even in a liberal democracy a central government unchallenged by other powerful political entities can become sloppy in its policy decisions. Local authorities are not, of course, the only potential challengers. In a pluralist society like Britain there are a good many powerful interest groups able to take on the Government with reasonable prospect of extracting some concessions. Nevertheless local authorities are particularly important since they constitute in some respects that rare phenomenon, a powerful *consumer* interest group – consumers of schools, roads, libraries, and so on. The value of local government in this role can best be illustrated by contrasting the experience of local government and non-local government services. If for instance one looks at the health service since the war it is now clear that there was a gross under-investment in hospitals at least until the mid-1960s; indeed many would complain that the health service generally has been starved of funds. Why should this be? One undoubted reason is that the policy of under-investment by successive governments could not be effectively challenged by the bodies running it. The hospitals and general practitioners were made the responsibility, not of local authorities but of appointed *ad hoc* bodies, when the health service was set up. Appointed *ad hoc* bodies by their very nature are not powerful political entities. A regional hospital board, for instance, as a creature of the central government, was a virtual political eunuch. It could protest at being deprived of investment capital but its protests would sound like mere squeaks in the general cacophony of the body politic; the Government could safely ignore them. If by contrast major local authorities were to be deprived of investment for schools, housing, roads, the political uproar would be deafening. No Government would lightly risk such a reaction. Investment in local government services has been very substantial since the war; they may not have secured all they wanted but in contrast to, say, the hospitals they have obtained a reasonable share of the national cake. The recent reorganisation of the health service deprived local authorities even of their rump of local health services and established a new and complex *ad hoc* structure. It seems reasonable to fear that the new *ad hoc* bodies will be just as unsuccessful in their dealings with the central government. The health service sorely needs the political muscle of the local authorities behind it.

To sum up, therefore, elected local authorities with some discretionary power are an extremely valuable, even if not utterly indispensable, feature of the British political scene. The centralised alternative to them would have significant administrative drawbacks and unfortunate repercussions on democratic values; the quality of public policy-making would be lowered. How do these conclusions affect one's view of the administration of education?

Should Education Be a Locally Administered Service?
There is no doubt that education *could* be administered as a national service but the arguments marshalled in the previous section against centralised administration apply particularly forcefully to education. A national education service would be a huge and unwieldy structure. It would be deprived of the innovative pressure supplied in the past by many LEAS. The new ideas in both technical and policy fields attributable to LEAS have already been described in Chapter II. A centralised service would lose this major source of inspiration.

The kind of democratic drawbacks outlined previously would

also apply to a centralised education service. Democratic control would be weakened. The unfortunate minister nominally in charge of the monster would certainly have a rough ride. There would be much less lay influence generally; it would be a heavily professionally-orientated service. The policies which the minster was able to effect (say in the sphere of capital expenditure) or which the professional machine imposed on him might be ill-conceived, but without LEAs to challenge them might well be implemented.

Much would be risked and little advantage gained by substituting a centrally run education service (either in the form of a public corporation or of an ordinary departmental arrangement) for the present polycentric structure. There are those, however, who would claim that it is not polycentric but *de facto* already centralised.

Mr Derek Senior, (*Memorandum of Dissent,* 1969, para. 320), following the words of the AEC evidence to the Redcliffe-Maud Commission, described education as a 'national service locally administered' rather than (as is the case with most other local authority services) a 'local service nationally supervised'. The distinction is highly dubious.

If all that is meant is that there are presently more central controls over education than over most other local authority services, then it would be simpler to say just that rather than to employ grandiose, theoretical aphorisms. Moreover, the message of previous chapters in this book is that central controls are very patchy in education. They are substantial for instance in capital expenditure but thin in curriculum affairs. There is still very considerable scope for initiative and discretion at the local level.

If on the other hand Senior and the AEC imply something more profound, that there is something in the nature of education which inherently separates it out in national interest from other services, then one would disagree. It is difficult to think of any local government service which does not have *some* national implications and therefore legitimate central interest. Even street cleaning, if incompetently done, could lead to traffic hazards or health risks affecting a very wide area. All local government services have a mix of local and national implications and characteristics; the particular mix at any time depends on a complex of factors – political, social, technological. All services including education lie on a continuum from the lightly controlled to the heavily controlled. Education is not on some different plane altogether. At present education is certainly found more towards the central control end of the spectrum and street cleaning towards the local discretion end, but this need not always be so. The discovery of a virulent germ, for instance, in street refuse could lead to stringent national controls overnight. As to education the present degree of central control results partly from the promotional attitude of the DES, partly from the enormous public interest in the service and partly from the belief of many economists that it is a major factor in economic growth. The attitudes of all three – department, public and economists – could change.

In short there is nothing which marks out education for all time as a service peculiarly in need of central control. Moreover to deny the existence of substantial areas of local discretion in the service today is to disregard the evidence. There may indeed be some widening of local discretion consequent upon local government reorganisation. To create a completely centralised service would be a radical change and, as has been argued, one fraught with danger and disadvantage.

The powerful case for continued local responsibility and discretion still leaves open, however, the issue of what kind of bodies should exercise it. This must be considered next.

School Boards or Local Authorities?

The British decision to abandon the initial system of *ad hoc* authorities, the school boards, in favour of giving educational responsibilities to local authorities is almost unique in international experience. In most parts of the world where there is any local responsibility for education it is placed on special *ad hoc* authorities. This even applies to most parts of the English speaking world; in, for instance, Canada, the USA and New Zealand the normal system is of separate school boards.

What are the advantages of the two systems? The advocates of *ad hoc* boards sometimes claim that specialist authorities will develop greater expertise than authorities with multitudinous functions. This is rather specious. Local authorities have separate education staff and separate education committees and it is hard to see what greater expertise they could have. It would be more valid to argue that single-purpose authorities often have greater *expedition* or what Professor Peter Self (1972, p. 264) calls 'effectiveness', the ability to accomplish limited, clearly-defined objectives. Thus in war-time a desperate need for an increased supply of Spitfires could be successfully tackled by the creation of a Ministry of Aircraft Production. Single-purpose units are generally most 'effective', however, when competing with more traditional, multi-purpose organisations; in other words the 'effectiveness' is achieved at the expense of other services or objectives. It would be difficult to substantiate a case for giving education such a privileged position by making it *alone* the responsibility of a system of single-purpose authorities. If on the other hand there is a host of *ad hoc* agencies then their 'effectiveness' is less marked since they are in competition like with like. In any case the purposes of an education service are too diffuse and contentious to be reduced to a set of simple, clear, agreed objectives.

Secondly it is often asserted that education is more likely to become a political issue when it is run by local authorities rather than *ad hoc* boards. This again seems a spurious argument. Education is a highly contentious topic in Britain. There is enormous and continuing public interest in it compared to the more sporadic interest shown in other services. It has often provoked bitter party political and religious dissension, even when run by *ad hoc* authorities. There is no reason whatsoever for thinking that public and party political interest would fade if education was taken from local authorities. Even if it did, why should one assume that this is a desirable result? This is not the place to discuss again that old academic chestnut, the benefits and drawbacks of party political involvement in the running of local services. Suffice it to say that there is certainly a case for regarding such involvement as entirely legitimate and on balance beneficial.

Thirdly, it could be argued that a system of specialist education boards could be tailored to the size and population requirements of the education service. In contrast the boundaries of cities and counties are not drawn exclusively to serve the needs of education. As has been shown above, however, the area and population which would suit an education unit best is a matter of inconclusive debate; there is no cast-iron evidence. If there were it would probably indicate different needs for different parts of the service. Moreover, as was again shown above, the requirements of education have been a major consideration in recent local government reforms.

Finally, since education has to compete for funds with other services when administered by local authorities, its proponents fear that it may not get a fair share, or what they would consider to be one. There is some truth in this. Not every local authority will regard education as top priority. Certainly many do not spend all that their education committee would like. It could, though, be argued that this is entirely desirable. Local authorities running a number of different services are more likely to take a reasoned view as to what should be education's share of expenditure. An independent education board is likely just to want as much as possible – not necessarily an intelligent use of resources. The finance of education could be used, too, in a different way to justify the removal of the service from local government, namely that the cost is so great that it is weakening local government. Freed from this incubus, local government could be independent of central government grant aid, and thus a healthier, more autonomous institution. The counter to this line of reasoning would be to argue that the creation of an effective system of local government finance would be a more satisfactory way of tackling financial difficulties in local government than removing services. In any case the allocation of education to special purpose local agencies does not *ipso facto* make the central government financially responsible. In North America, for instance, the school boards generally raise taxes locally, often precepting on the multi-purpose local authorities. Such an arrangement in Britain would do nothing to strengthen local government.

When one turns to the advantages of continued local government control of education it is clear that they are often the obverse of the arguments just examined for special-purpose authorities. The first and perhaps most important group are variations on the theme of co-ordination – the obverse of expedition and 'effectiveness'. The desirability of close links between education and other local services, especially planning and housing, has already been stressed in the section on corporate planning. On the whole such links are more easily forged when the same agency is responsible. Similarly the allocation of resources in a local authority between the various services can be based on an appraisal of the whole range of provision, and marginal decisions can employ reasoned trade-offs (sacrifice x less education to achieve y more housing, or whatever). In theory at least, education should receive its just deserts in the context of local needs, circumstances and wishes. A special-purpose agency, by its very nature, could not operate on such a basis. Indeed the employment of planning, programming and budgeting systems (PPBS), corporate planning and related decision-making methodologies at the local level is predicated on the existence of multi-purpose agencies. The case for special authorities for education is in any case no stronger than that for many other services – certainly housing, roads, social services, police. If there were *ad hoc* authorities for all these, the administrative jungle would be thick and public confusion considerable.

The last four words lead to consideration of the second group of advantages of local government control of education, the democratic ones. Multi-purpose agencies simplify public accountability and facilitate public understanding. A litter of *ad hoc* agencies can lead to voter fatigue if they all have to be elected, massive problems of patronage if they are instead appointed, and public uncertainty about who is responsible for what. All drawbacks are far less apparent when local authorities control all or most local services.

I

True if *ad hoc* agencies were the rule the education board would probably be better known than most. Nevertheless accountability could still be obfuscated. An education board could explain away its failures by alleging lack of information from a housing agency about new developments, lack of co-operation from a police agency to control school vandalism, competition for land from a hospital agency, short-sighted widening of a highway by a road agency outside examination halls, and so on. The great democratic strength of multi-purpose local government is that responsibility is clearly concentrated and citizens can apportion blame and credit accordingly. Without *ad hoc* agencies, local authorities can only attempt to slough off responsibility for failures on to the central government (which admittedly they sometimes try to do). In general, though, it is reasonable for a citizen to judge the council of a local authority by its record in office and to vote in municipal elections accordingly. Most local electors in Britain may not vote on such a basis; nevertheless this would hardly be a reason for weakening democratic control further by dispersing local government responsibilities among *ad hoc* agencies.

Finally, the prestige value of education to local government is enormous. Arguments about the cost burden of education to local government usually underestimate this factor. For many people the service which they are most aware of their county or borough providing is education. Deprived of this, one suspects that local authorities would recede into very shadowy institutions for the man in the street (save for the irritation stimulated by the rate demand). The level of public knowledge is low enough as it is. Of course this argument will leave unmoved those who regard local government as a dispensable institution. Here one must refer the reader back to the discussion of the value of local government.

The advantages of continued local government responsibility for education to public services in general and to democratic values seem very considerable. Where, however, does the balance of advantage lie for education itself? On the one hand, education could perhaps be given an unfair edge over other services if it *alone* were permitted a system of special-purpose authorities. Much would depend on how such authorities were financed, but they might be able to secure a larger share of public funds (though education cannot claim to be badly treated at present). On the other hand, education would be handicapped by the administrative boundary created between it and other local services. Also, if the new *ad hoc* education authorities were appointed not elected, then the service would certainly suffer from the deprivation of political muscle provided now by the local authorities.

Trends in the Education Service

The previous chapters, in presenting a comprehensive view of the education service in England and Wales, have covered a large number of changes and developments. In the midst of these certain substantial trends can be discerned. Four in particular stand out: integration, institutional autonomy, experimentation and, more faintly, lessening central control.

First there is an integrationist trend. This comprises two elements: the integration of education with other local government services, and the integration *within education* of the different parts of the service. Through the increasing adoption of corporate planning and similar comprehensive approaches to decision taking by local authorities, education is becoming ever more firmly combined with the provision of other services. While managerial developments have provided the main impetus to this trend, the abolition of a separate education grant in 1958 was also a considerable factor. It is difficult to treat a service as a special case when its finance is so inextricably mixed with that of other services. Certainly the re-introduction of a specific education grant would be an anti-integrationist move. Perhaps the integration of education with other local services has also been marginally assisted by changing public attitudes. The growing public criticism of, and the disenchantment with, education has already been mentioned. It is no longer the undisputed queen of local government services, to be treated with unique, regal deference.

Such integration is far from welcome in all quarters. Educational administrators in particular traditionally regard their service as *sui generis*. The Society of Education Officers, in its evidence to the Layfield Committee, proclaimed: 'We are local government men but not at any price.'[2] Of course this assertion contains an implication which is fallacious – that education would necessarily obtain more funds outside local government than inside. It is, moreover, revealing of an attitude of mind – that education in the last resort is apart from, and perhaps superior to, all other local government services. Whatever the feelings of education officers, however, it seems likely that the integrationist trend will continue.

Integration within the service is even more marked. Teacher training and education has all but disappeared as a separate category of education provision. It is now closely bound up with other further and higher education. There is some movement, too, to greater integration of the upper reaches of school education with the lower reaches of further education. (This adds force, incidentally, to the case for separating the administration of advanced and non-advanced further education, the latter being ever more bound up with schools and school-level work, the former looking more like university provision with every year that passes.) Integration is also a feature of special education. The whole emphasis now is upon trying to provide for handicapped children, so far as is possible, in ordinary schools. Some, for instance, teachers of the blind are arguing that such integration can go too far.

Secondly, somewhat in contrast to the integrationist trends, there is a distinct trend to institutional autonomy. It is most marked in the post-school sector; previous chapters have described the increased power and authority of the staff and governors of colleges of education, polytechnics and other institutions of further and higher education. There is even some indication of similar trends in schools. The discretionary power of the head teacher in many matters has been emphasised. The abolition of divisional administration, however, and the consequent increased emphasis on governing bodies could lead to rather more authority being delegated to them. At the time of writing the result of the inquiry into school management and government is still awaited.

Thirdly, there is the post-war trend, which shows little sign of abating, to experiment and pioneer. Education has perhaps always been a forum for innovation. Nevertheless the ferment since the war has been extraordinary; not only have the new ideas come in a torrent but a good many of them have actually been tried out. Novelty has been particularly marked in teaching methods and curriculum issues, but far from restricted to these areas. School structure and organisation have also felt the impact of change – mixed age grouping in some primary schools, non-streaming in some secondary schools, many different varieties of the comprehensive schools, increasing adoption of middle schools, and so on. Examinations and qualifications, too, at both school and post-school level, have been a frequent area for experiment. Indeed the post-school sector generally has as much if not more experience of change – the rise and transmogrification of the CATs, the establishment of the polytechnics, the changes in teacher training and the lively controversy about it which continues. Some would argue that the neophilia has been overdone. There is, for instance, growing pressure for a reversion to more traditional methods in teaching reading.[3] Nevertheless it seems unlikely that there will be a period of stability in the near future in all aspects of education, even if there is some slowing of the rate of experimentation in teaching methods. So many issues are still a subject of impassioned debate; so many problems are still unresolved; experimentation will undoubtedly continue.

Yet curiously this scene of change has taken place within the confines of a relatively stable administrative setting. The broad outlines of the Butler Act still apply – successive rather than overlapping stages of education, the denominational schools settlement, the role of LEAs, and so on. The LEAs themselves have undergone one major shake-up, first in London and then in the rest of England and Wales. In many parts of the country, however, there was more continuity than change.

Finally there is the trend to less central control. This is less marked, and in some respects contradictory. The abolition of cost-per-place limits may have been due to *force majeure*; nevertheless it represents a significant slackening of central control. The other lesser relaxations in the area of capital expenditure which have been mentioned are also important, simply because capital expenditure is traditionally an area of such heavy control. On the other hand an area of traditionally light control, the curriculum, shows some signs of being tightened. LEAs are encouraged to experiment with middle schools but compelled to follow departmental ukase on comprehensive schools. An oversupply of teachers, a strong possibility in the next few years, could well lead to a dropping of the quota system; yet as far ahead as one can see, teachers' pay is likely to be settled between the Government and the teachers' unions, with the LEAs nominally responsible but exerting only a weak influence. Following local government reorganisation, the increased average size of LEAs should make them more resistant to central control, their reduced number perhaps more susceptible. The balance of these trends appears to come down in favour of more local discretion. It would of course be naive to expect a massive relaxation of central controls over LEAs. Education is too costly and too politically sensitive a service. Nevertheless it is not unreasonable to foresee *some* continued removal of restrictions.

The Future of the Education Service

The greatest threat to the future health of education is undoubtedly the economic one. In this education is no worse off than other public services, indeed is better off than many: in 1976 the health service, for instance, seemed in graver economic peril. If Britain's descent into the economic abyss continues at the accelerating rate maintained over the last decade, it is not only education that will suffer; a social and economic upheaval of substantial proportions would appear the inevitable eventual outcome. Moreover, even if the national economy is re-established on a sound footing, local government finance still has unsatisfactory features which affect education along with the other services. Again, though, education would

probably lose more if it left local government altogether. Nevertheless in an ideal world local government would be given an independent, stable, yet flexible source of income sufficient to cover its
responsibilities. No source of income is likely to permit unlimited
expansion of educational provision but it is reasonable to hope for a
financial base which would make possible the general effectiveness
and progress of the service, in the context of other public services.
This is not an ideal world. One suspects that some mix of central
grants and local income will continue to finance the service. Not that
this would necessarily be disastrous. From the late 1940s to the mid-
1960s such a financial base was able to finance the biggest expansion
of educational provision in the country's history.

Apart from finance some would argue that policy disputes,
especially those based on party political ideology, threaten the
development of education. Professor Dror, for instance, argues that
educational planning is hindered by the switches of policy on comprehensive schools following changes of government in London.
It would of course have been pleasant for a national consensus
to have been achieved, say in the 1940s, on comprehensive schools.
Nevertheless one can exaggerate the degree of damage and uncertainty caused even in this field. Overall the effect of the controversy
has been only to slow the rate of change to comprehensive schools;
there has been little unscrambling of them. On most other educational issues, moreover, the party stances are not so implacably opposed. (The argument about direct grant schools is really an
extension of the comprehensive one.) The great expansion of
educational provision in the 1950s and 1960s reflected broad agreement between the parties.

Finally, where is power likely to lie in education in the future?
It is unprofitable to debate whether education is a national service
locally administered or a local service nationally supervised. These
are merely catch phrases, which can be given as much or little
meaning as one chooses. Education, like all services, has, and will
continue to have, national and local importance. The relationship
between DES and LEAs which one would like to see would be akin
to that between the chairman of a meeting or a seminar and its
members. The chairman should give a strong lead on occasions
and should certainly have a casting vote; nevertheless he should
not attempt to prescribe all that is to be said and done. The DES
certainly must always be able to bring influence to bear on LEAs
when there are national considerations and, equally important,
should give strong advice when the evidence of accumulated experience suggests that a certain course is wisest. Circular 2/75 on
the ascertainment of handicapped children is an excellent example

of such advice. Indeed, perhaps the DES has been somewhat laggard in this role.

In any case power in the education service has never been a simple two-way split between central department and local authorities and is likely to become even less so. The trend towards institutional autonomy, especially the pressure by teaching staff for greater control of their own schools and colleges, and the tendency to more parental involvement, are likely to produce very subtle relationships between all the parties concerned.

All those involved in education can look back upon the achievements of the service in post-war Britain with pride. The administrators and teachers in education are of very high calibre; the service seems to inspire the utmost commitment and dedication, not only amongst staff but among politicians, local and central, who became involved in it. Given this, one must be optimistic about the future.

NOTES

1 In recent years few British commentators have attempted a reasoned case for having local government. Perhaps the two most useful sources are: L. J. Sharpe, 'Theories and Values of Local Government' in *Political Studies*, Vol. 18, No. 2 (June 1970); and Dilys M. Hill, *Democratic Theory and Local Government* (George Allen & Unwin, 1974), especially Chapter II. Neither, however, in my view adequately combines the administrative and democratic side of the case.
2 See *Education*, 27 November 1974.
3 The Bullock Committee, though, is inconclusive about whether new teaching methods have led to poorer standards of literacy. See *A Language for Life*, Report of the Committee of Inquiry, chairman Sir Alan, later Lord, Bullock.

BIBLIOGRAPHY

(Reports of Royal Commissions, Committees of Inquiry, Working Partie
and the like are listed under the names of their chairmen)

Albemarle, Lady (1960), *The Youth Service in England and Wales*, Report of the Committee, Cmnd 929.

Allsopp, Elizabeth and Grugeon, David (1966), *Direct Grant Grammar Schools*, London, Fabian Research Series, 256.

Armytage, W. H. G. (1970), *Four Hundred Years of English Education*, 2nd edn, London, CUP.

Association of Education Committees (1957), *The Threat to Education: The Case against Block Grants*, London, Councils and Education Press.

Bagnall, N. (ed.) (1974), *Parent Power: A Dictionary Guide to Your Child's Education and Schooling*, London, Routledge & Kegan Paul.

Bains, M. A. (1972), *The New Local Authorities: Management and Structure*, Report of a Study Group, London, HMSO.

Barker, Rodney (1972), *Education and Politics 1900–1951: A Study Of The Labour Party*, London, OUP.

Barker, Rodney (1975), 'Politics and the Reform of Education' in *Municipal Review*, No. 541.

Baron, G. and Howell, D. A. (1968), *School Management and Government*, Research Studies 6 of the Royal Commission on Local Government in England, London, HMSO.

Baron, G. and Howell, D. A. (1974), *The Government and Management of Schools*, London, The Athlone Press.

Batley, R., O'Brien, O. and Parris, H. (1970), *Going Comprehensive: Education Policy Making in Two County Boroughs*, London, Routledge & Kegan Paul.

Bavin, A. R. W. (1973), *A Report from the Working Party on Collaboration between the NHS and Local Government*, London, Department of Health and Social Security and Welsh Office.

Benn, Caroline and Simon, Brian (1972), *Half Way There: Report on the British Comprehensive School Reform*, 2nd edn, Harmondsworth, Penguin Books.

Birley, Derek (1972), *Planning and Education*, London, Routledge & Kegan Paul.

Blackie, John (1970), *Inspecting and the Inspectorate*, London, Routledge & Kegan Paul.

Boaden, Noel (1971), *Urban Policy-Making: Influences on County Boroughs in England and Wales*, London, CUP.

Board of Education (1943), *Educational Reconstruction*, Cmd 6458.

Boyson, R. (1972), *The Voucher In Schooling: An Exercise In Genuine Participation*, London, National Education Association.

Briault, Eric (1973), *16–19 Growth and Response*, Vol. II, 'Examinations', Second Sixth Form Working Party, Schools Council Working Paper No. 46, London, Evans/Methuen.

Bullock, Sir Alan (later Lord) (1975), *A Language for Life*, Report of the Committee of Inquiry, London, DES.

Butler, Clifford (1973), *Preparation for Degree Courses*, Report of a Joint Working Party, Schools Council Working Paper No. 47, London, Evans/Methuen.

Butler, Lord (1965), *The Education Act of 1944 and After*, University of Essex Noel Buxton Lecture, London, Longmans.

Butler, Lord (1971), *The Art of the Possible*, London, Hamish Hamilton.

Byrne, Eileen (1974), *Planning and Educational Inequality: A Study of the Rationale of Resource Allocation*, London, National Foundation for Educational Research.

Carnegie UK Trust (1964), *Handicapped Children and Their Families*, Reports on the Problems of 600 Handicapped Children and their Families, London.

Caston, Geoffrey (1971), 'The Schools Council in Context' in *Journal of Curriculum Studies*, Vol. 3, No. 1.

Confederation for the Advancement of State Education (1967), *Educating Our Handicapped Children*, London.

Conservative Party (1974), *Putting Britain First: A National Policy from the Conservatives*, London, Conservative Central Office.

Cortis, Gerald A. (1972), 'The James Report: attitudes of senior staffs in the colleges' in *Higher Education Review*, Vol. 4, No. 3.

Crowther, Sir Geoffrey (1959), *15 to 18*, Report of the Central Advisory Council.

Crozier, Margaret (1960), 'Ineducable?' in *Times Educational Supplement*, 8 July.

Davies, J. L. (1973), 'Management by Objectives in Local Education Authorities and Educational Institutions' in *Educational Administration Bulletin*, Vol. 1, No. 1, and Vol. 2, No. 1.

Dent, H. C. (1971), *The Educational System of England and Wales*, 5th edn, London, University Press.

Department of Education and Science (1964), *Slow Learners at School*, Education Pamphlet No. 46.

Department of Education and Science (1965), *The Education of Maladjusted Children*, Education Pamphlet No. 47.

Department of Education and Science (1966), *A Plan for Polytechnics and Other Colleges: Higher Education in the Further Educational System*, Cmnd 3006.

Department of Education and Science (1966), *Harris College, Preston*, Building Bulletin No. 29.

Department of Education and Science (1967), *Designing for Science*, Oxford School Development Project, Building Bulletin No. 39.

Department of Education and Science (1967), *Sixth Form Centre*, Rosebery County School for Girls, Epsom, Surrey, Building Bulletin No. 41.

Department of Education and Science (1967), *Units for Partially Hearing Children*, Education Survey No. 1.

Department of Education and Science (1968), *Observations by the Department of Education and Science on the Recommendations in Part I of the*

Report from the Select Committee on Education and Science, Session 1967–68, Cmnd 3860.

Department of Education and Science (1970), *HMI Today and Tomorrow*.

Department of Education and Science (1970), *Output Budgeting for the Department of Education and Science*, Education Planning Paper No. 1.

Department of Education and Science (1972), *Education: A Framework for Expansion*, Cmnd 5174.

Department of the Environment (1971), *Local Government in England: Government Proposals for Reorganisation*, Cmnd 4584.

Department of Health and Social Security (1971), *Better Services for the Mentally Handicapped*, Cmnd 4683.

Donnison, D. V. (1970), *Second Report*, Public Schools Commission.

Durham, Bishop of (1970), *The Fourth R*, Report on Religious Education, London, SPCK.

Eaglesham, E. J. R. (1956), *From School Board to Local Authority*, London, Routledge & Kegan Paul.

Eddison, Tony (1973), *Local Government: Management and Corporate Planning*, Aylesbury, Leonard Hill Books.

Edmonds, E. L. (1962), *The School Inspector*, London, Routledge & Kegan Paul.

Fleming, Lord (1944), *The Public Schools and the General Educational System*, Report of the Committee on Public Schools.

Foley, Winifred (1974), *A Child in the Forest*, London, BBC Publications.

Ford, Boris (1966), 'Crisis in Higher Education' in *New Statesman*, 21 January.

Fulton, Lord (1968), *The Civil Service*, Report of the Committee 1966–8, 5 vols.

Glatter, Ron (1972), *Management Development for the Education Profession*, London, George Harrap for the Institute of Education.

Godber, Sir George (1967, 1972 and 1974), *The Health of the School Child 1964–65, 1969–70* and *1971–72*, Reports of the Chief Medical Officer of the Department of Education and Science.

Gould, Sir Ronald (1969), *Struggle for Education*, London, NUT.

Greater London Group (1968), *Local Government in South East England*, Research Studies 1 of the Royal Commission on Local Government in England, London, HMSO.

Greenwood, R., Norton, A. L. and Stewart, J. D. (1969), *Recent Reforms in the Management Arrangements of County Boroughs in England and Wales, Recent Reforms in the Management Structure of Local Authorities – the London Boroughs* and *Recent Reforms in the Management Structure of Local Authorities – the County Councils*, Occasional Papers Nos 1, 2 and 3, INLOGOV, University of Birmingham.

Griffith, J. A. G. (1966), *Central Departments and Local Authorities*, London, George Allen & Unwin.

Hadow, Sir W. H. (1927), *The Education of the Adolescent*, Report of the Consultative Committee.

Halsall, Elizabeth (1973), *The Comprehensive School: Guidelines for the Reorganisation of Secondary Education*, London, Pergamon.

Harris, J. S. (1955), *British Government Inspection as a Dynamic Process: The Local Services and the Central Departments*, London, Stevens.

Heclo, Hugh and Wildavsky, Aaron (1974), *The Private Government of Public Money*, London, Macmillan.

Hepworth, N. G. (1971), *The Finance of Local Government*, 2nd edn, London, George Allen & Unwin.

Herbert, Sir Edwin (1960), *Report of the Royal Commission on Local Government in Greater London, 1957–60*, Cmnd 1164.

Hill, Dilys M. (1974), *Democratic Theory and Local Government*, London, George Allen & Unwin.

Hill, M. (1968), *R.I. and Surveys*, London, National Secular Society.

Howell, D. A. (1967), 'The Management of Primary Schools', Appendix 13 of *Children and their Primary Schools*, Vol. II (Plowden Report).

Inner London Education Authority (1968), *Learning For Life*.

Institute of Christian Education (1964), *Survey of Parents of Sixth Formers*, London.

Izbicki, John (1975), 'Examining the Inspectorate' in the *Daily Telegraph*.

James of Rusholme, Lord (1972), *Teacher Education and Training*, Report of the Committee, London, DES.

Jamieson, R. D. (1968), *The Present and Future Role of RACs in the Field of Further Education*, London, Association of Technical Institutions.

Jennings, A. (1974), 'The Role of the Schools Council in the Reform of the Sixth Form Examinations' in *Secondary Education*, Vol. 4, No. 2.

Johnson, E. M. (1963), *A Report on a Survey of Deaf Children Who Have Been Transferred from Special Schools or Units to Ordinary Schools*, London, DES.

Kempe, Sir John Arrow (1914), *Final Report of the Departmental Committee on Local Taxation*, Cd 7315.

Kempe, Sir John Arrow (1928), *Reminiscences of an Old Civil Servant 1846–1927*, London, John Murray.

Kilbrandon, Lord (1973), *Report of the Royal Commission on the Constitution 1969–73*, Vol. I, Cmnd. 5460 also *Memorandum of Dissent* by Lord Crowther-Hunt and Prof. A. T. Peacock, Vol. II, Cmnd 5460–I.

King, R. (1970), 'The Head Teacher and His Authority' in Bryan Allen (ed.), *Headship in the 1970s*, Oxford, Blackwell.

Kogan, Maurice (1971), *The Politics of Education: Edward Boyle and Anthony Crosland in Conversation with Maurice Kogan*, Harmondsworth, Penguin Books.

Labour Party (1951), *A Policy For Secondary Education*, London.

Labour Party (1973), *Labour's Programme for Britain*, London.

Leese, J. (1967), 'Tertiary Education' in *Technical Education and Industrial Training*, Vol. 9, No. 2.

Leff, S. and Leff, Vera (1959), *The School Health Service*, London, H. K. Lewis.

Local Government Training Board (1974), *Training of Education Welfare Officers*, London.

Locke, Michael (1974), 'Government' in Pratt and Burgess (1974).

Lockwood, Sir John (1964), *Report of the Working Party on the Schools' Curricula and Examinations*, London, Ministry of Education.

Lukes, J. R. (1967), 'The Binary Policy: A Critical Study' in *Universities Quarterly*, Vol. 22, No. 1.

MacLure, Stuart (1968), *Learning Beyond Our Means?*, London, Councils and Education Press.

McNair, Sir Arnold (1944), *Teachers and Youth Leaders*, Report of the Committee, London, Board of Education.

Maud, Sir John (later Lord Redcliffe-Maud) (1967), *Management of Local Government*, Report of the Committee, 5 vols, London, Ministry of Housing and Local Government.

May, P. R. (1967), *Attitudes to Religion in Schools*, Durham, University Press.

Ministry of Education (1944), *Principles of Government in Maintained Secondary Schools*, Cmd 6523.

Ministry of Education (1945), *The Nation's Schools: Their Plan and Purpose*, Pamphlet No. 1.

Ministry of Education (1946), *Special Educational Treatment*, Pamphlet No. 5.

Ministry of Education (1956), *Education of the Handicapped Pupil 1945-55*, Pamphlet No. 30.

Ministry of Education (1956), *Technical Education*, Cmd 9703.

Ministry of Education (1957), *The Story of Post-War School Building*, Pamphlet No. 33.

Ministry of Education (1958), *Secondary Education for All – a New Drive*, Cmnd 604.

Ministry of Education (1961), *Educational Building in England and Wales*, Memorandum submitted to Sub-Committee F of the Estimates Committee, 8th Report, Session 1960–61, HC 284.

Ministry of Housing and Local Government (1957), *Local Government Finance (England and Wales)*, Cmnd 209.

Ministry of Housing and Local Government (1961), *London Government: Government Proposals for Reorganisation*, Cmnd 1562.

Ministry of Housing and Local Government (1970), *Reform of Local Government in England*, Cmnd 4276.

Morrell, D. H. and Pott, A. (1960), *Britain's New Schools*, London, Longmans, Green & Co. for the British Council.

Musgrave, P. W. (1968), *The School as an Organisation*, London, Macmillan.

National Advisory Council on the Training and Supply of Teachers (1965), *The Demand for and Supply of Teachers 1963–86*, 9th Report, London, HMSO.

National Union of Teachers (1969), *Into the '70s: A Policy for a New Education Act*, London.

National Union of Teachers (1971), *The Reform of Teacher Education*, a policy statement presented by the Executive to the Annual Conference at Scarborough, London.

National Union of Teachers (1972), *James: A Critical Appraisal*, London.

Newsom, Sir John (1963), *Half Our Future*, Report of the Central Advisory Council for Education, London, HMSO.

Newsom, Sir John (1968), *First Report*, Public Schools Commission, London, HMSO.

Norton, A. L. and Stewart J. D. (1973), 'Recommendations to the New Local Authorities' in *Local Government Studies*, No. 6.

Norwood, Sir Cyril (1943), *Curriculum and Examinations in Secondary Schools*, Report of the Committee of the Secondary Schools Examinations Council, London, Board of Education.

Nurse, P. (1969), *The Regional Advisory Councils*, unpublished M.Sc. thesis, London School of Economics.

Oakes, Sir Cecil (1957), *Report of the Royal Commission on the Law Relating to Mental Illness and Mental Deficiency 1954–1957*, Cmnd 169.

Odhams Press Research Department (1962), *Survey of Young People 16–25*, London.

Ollerenshaw, Dame Kathleen (1969), *Education and Finance*, London, Institute of Municipal Treasurers and Accountants.

Owen, Roger J. (1975), 'Religion in Our Schools' in *Life of Faith*, Nos. 4455–60.

Parry, J. P. (1972), *The Lord James Tricycle*, London, George Allen & Unwin.

Pateman, C. (1970), *Participation and Democratic Theory*, London, CUP.

Peacock, Alan, Glennerster, Howard and Lavers, Robert (1968), *Educational Finance: Its Sources and Uses in the UK*, Edinburgh, Oliver & Boyd.

Percy of Newcastle, Lord (1945), *Higher Technological Education*, Report of the Committee, London, Ministry of Education.

Percy of Newcastle, Lord (1958), *Some Memories*, London, Eyre & Spottiswoode.

Perkin, H. (1969), *Innovation in Higher Education: New Universities in the UK*, Paris, OECD.

Perry, Valerie (1974), 'Consultation in Large Secondary Schools' in *Secondary Education*, Vol. 4, No. 3.

Peschek, D. and Brand, J. (1966), *Policies and Politics in Secondary Education*, Greater London Paper No. 11, London School of Economics.

Plowden, Lady (1967), *Children and their Primary Schools*, A Report of the Central Advisory Council for Education (England), 2 vols, London, DES.

Pratt, J. and Burgess, T. (1970), *Policy and Practice: The Colleges of Advanced Technology*, London, Allen Lane The Penguin Press.

Pratt, J. and Burgess, T. (1974), *Polytechnics: A Report*, London, Pitmans.

Ralphs, Sir F. Lincoln (1973), *The Role and Training of Education Welfare Officers*, Summary of the Report of the Working Party, London, Local Government Training Board.

Redcliffe-Maud, Lord (1969), *Report of the Royal Commission on Local Government in England 1966–1969*, Vol. I, Cmnd 4040; also *Memorandum of Dissent*, by D. Senior, Vol. II, Cmnd 4040–I, and *Research Appendices*, Vol. III, Cmnd 4040–II.

Regan, D. E. (1969), 'Start not end of a debate' in *Socialist Commentary*, August 1969.

Regan, D. E. (1970), 'Mr Crossman and the Purblind Doctors' in *Justice of the Peace and Local Government Review*, Vol. 134, No. 23.

Regan, D. E. and Hastings, S. (1972), 'Education' in G. Rhodes (ed.), *The New Government of London: the First Five Years*, London, Weidenfeld & Nicolson.

Richards, P. G. (1956), *Delegation in Local Government*, London, George Allen & Unwin.

Robbins, Lord (1963), *Higher Education*, Report of the Committee on Higher Education, Cmnd 2154; also *Appendices*, 6 vols, Cmnd 2154–I to 2154–V, *Evidence* Part One, vols A to F, Cmnd 2154–VI to 2154–XI, and Part Two *Documentary Evidence*, Cmnd 2154–XII.

Robinson, E. E. (1968), *The New Polytechnics*, London, Cornmarket.

Robinson, E. E. (1971), 'A Comprehensive Reform of Higher Education' in *Higher Education Review*, Vol. 3, No. 3.

Royal Institute of Public Administration (1959), *Budgeting by Public Authorities*, London, George Allen & Unwin.

Royal Institute of Public Administration Operational Research Unit (1968), *Performance and Size of Local Education Authorities*, Research Studies 4 of the Royal Commission on Local Government in England, London, HMSO.

Royal Medico-Psychological Association (1960), *Memorandum on the Recruitment and Training of the Child Psychiatrist*, London.

Russell, Sir Lionel (1973), *Adult Education: A Plan for Development*, Report of a Committee of Inquiry, London, DES.

Saran, R. (1967), 'Decision Making by a Local Education Authority' in *Public Administration*, Vol. 45,

Saran, R. (1973), *Policy-Making in Secondary Education: A Case Study*, London, OUP.

Schon, Donald A. (1971), *Beyond the Stable State: Public and Private Learning in a Changing Society*, London, BBC.

Seebohm, Lord (1968), *Report of the Committee on Local Authority and Allied Personal Social Services*, Cmnd 3703.

Segal, S. S. (1967), *No Child is Ineducable: Special Education Provision and Trends*, London, Pergamon.

Schools Council (1965), *Change and Response: The First Year's Work*, London, HMSO.

Select Committee on Education and Science (1968), *Her Majesty's Inspectorate (England and Wales)*, Report, Part I, Session 1967–68, HC 400–I.

Select Committee on Education and Science (1970), *Teacher Training*, Session 1969–70, HC 182–I.

Select Committee on the Estimates (1965), *Grants to Universities and Colleges*, 5th Report, Session 1964–5, HC 283.

Select Committee on Expenditure, Sub-Committee on Education (1974), *Educational Maintenance Allowances*, 3rd Report, Session 1974, HC 306.

Self, P. J. O. (1972), *Administrative Theories and Politics: An Inquiry into The Structure and Processes of Modern Government*, London, George Allen & Unwin.

Senior, Derek (1969), see Redcliffe-Maud.

Sharpe, L. J. (1970), 'Theories and Values of Local Government' in *Political Studies*, Vol. 18, No. 2.

Sheldon, Sir W. (1967), *Child Welfare Centres*, Report of the Sub-Committee of the Standing Medical Advisory Committee, Central Health Services Council, London, DHSS.

Silver, Harold (1966), 'Education and the Working of Democracy' in *Technical Education and Industrial Training*, Vol. 8, Nos 5, 6.

Smallwood, F. (1965), *Greater London: The Politics of Metropolitan Reform*, New York, Bobbs-Merrill.

Society of Education Officers (undated, 1974?), *Management in the Education Service: Challenge and Response*, London.

Spens, Will (1938), *Report of the Consultative Committee on Secondary Education with Special Reference to Grammar Schools and Technical High Schools*, London, HMSO.

Stewart, J. D. (1971), *Management in Local Government: A Viewpoint*, London, Charles Knight.

Stewart, J. D. (1974), 'Corporate Management and the Education Service' in *Educational Administration Bulletin*, Vol. 3, No. 1.

Summerfield, Arthur (1968), *Psychologists in Education Services*, Report of a Working Party, London, DES.

Tizard, J. (1960), 'Brooklands Experimental Unit' in *The Times Educational Supplement*, 8 July.

Thomas, Elfed (1964), *The Handicapped School Leaver*, Report of a Working Party commissioned by the British Council for the Rehabilitation of the Disabled, London.

Underwood, J. E. A. (1955), *Report of the Committee on Maladjusted Children*, London, Ministry of Education.

Vaizey, J. (1958), *The Costs of Education*, London, George Allen & Unwin.

Vaizey, J. and Sheehan, J. (1968), *Resources for Education*, London, George Allen & Unwin.

Weaver, T. R. (1966), *Report of the Study Group on the Government of the Colleges of Education*, London, DES.

Wilcockson, D. H. (1974), 'How Havering Came to the Top of the Hill' in *Education Management*, supplement to *Education*, 8 November.

Willey, F. T. and Maddison, R. E. (1971), *An Enquiry into Teacher Training*, London, University Press.

Younghusband, Dame Eileen (1970), *Living With Handicap*, report of a working party on children with special needs, National Bureau for Co-operation in Child Care, London.

INDEX

Administrative Memoranda (from the Ministry or Department of Education: no. 524 159; no. 545 177; no. 8/67 171

adult training centres 74

advanced further education 166–72, 177–9, 182, 186, 221–4, 227, 239; *see also* higher education

Advisory Centre for Education 58

Advisory Committee on the Supply and Training of Teachers 141–2, 151

age of compulsory attendance at school 10–11, 37, 73, 191; *see also* raising of the school leaving age

age of transfer between schools 38, 222

age ranges of schools 38–9, 73

agreed syllabus for religious education 43–5, 66, 68

Albemarle Committee (and Report) 11, 123, 244*n*

aldermen 36*n*

Alexander, Sir William (later Lord Alexander of Potterhill) 29–31, 114–15, 119, 162, 207, 210

all-age schools 38, 47, 121–2, 124, 126

Allsopp, Elizabeth 41, 244

Andrew, Sir Herbert 106, 110, 113

Anglican schools 44, 103–4

aphasic pupils 85, 90

appointment and dismissal of staff: teachers 19, 43–6, 55, 62–3, 114, 155, 172; non-teaching staff 19, 43–4, 63, 155, 172

area health authorities 82–3, 96, 226

area training organisations (ATOS) 141–4, 147, 151, 155, 157, 164

Armytage, W. H. G. 100, 244

articles of government for schools and colleges 55, 60, 62, 68, 153, 155, 171–3

ascertainment of handicapped children 78, 79–85, 87, 96, 242

Association of Chief Education Officers 220

Association of County Councils 30

Association of District Councils 30

Association of Educational Psychologists 91

Association of Education Committees (AEC) 29–30, 36*n*, 114, 149, 199, 220, 234, 244

Association of Governing Bodies of Girls' Public Schools 39

Association of Governing Bodies of Public Schools 39

Association of Metropolitan Authorities 30

Association of Municipal Corporations (AMC) 28, 30, 157

Association of Teachers in Colleges and Departments of Education 152, 154

Association of Teachers in Technical Institutions (ATTI) 219

Association of University Teachers (AUT) 149

asthmatic pupils 89

at risk registers 82

Attlee, Clement (later Lord Attlee) 49

audiometricians 95

autistic children 77, 79, 90

Avon county 21 *table*

Bachelor of Arts in Education – BA (Ed.) 146, 148, 150

Bachelor of Education – B.Ed 137–8, 143–4, 150–2

Bagnall, N. 58, 186*n*, 244

Bains Committee 205–7, 244

Barber, Anthony 209

Barker, Rodney 12*n*, 48–9, 244

Barking 23 *table*, 228

Barnardo's Homes 91

Barnet 23 *table*, 50

Barnsley 22 *table*

Baron, G. 58, 60, 62–4, 244

Batley, R. 50, 244

Bavin working party 96, 244

Bedfordshire 21 *table*, 176

Benn, Caroline 38, 51, 244

Bentham, Jeremy 103

Berkshire 21 *table*, 61

Bexley 23 *table*, 51–2

binary system 139, 143, 145, 150, 160–1, 166, 169, 182–5

Birley, D. 207, 244
Birmingham 22 *table*, 66, 75, 214, 216
Blackie, John 110, 115, 117, 244
blind and partially-sighted pupils 74, 85, 88, 92–3, 240
Boaden, Noel 202, 244
boarding education and boarding schools 39–41, 85, 87–8, 90, 93, 122, 125, 129, 184
Board of Education 10, 13, 35, 36*n*, 45, 59, 140, 158, 179–80, 244
Board of Education Act 1899 36*n*
Bolton 22 *table*
Bourne, Richard 12*n*, 72*n*
Boyle, Sir Edward (later Lord Boyle) 15 *table*, 37, 70, 139, 247
Boyson, Rhodes 58, 244
Bradford 22 *table*, 207, 216
Bradford Independent Labour Party 48
Brand, J. 64, 249
Brent 23 *table*, 26
Briault Report 71, 244
Brighton 62, 155
British and Foreign Schools Society 103
Britton, Sir Edward 210
Brixton School of Building 168
Bromley 23 *table*
Brown, Colonel Douglas Clifton 9
Buckinghamshire 21 *table*, 52
budgetary discretion of LEAS 201–3
Building Bulletins 135
Building Research Station 134
Bullock, Sir Alan C. L. (later Lord Bullock) 141, 243*n*
Bullock Committee 243*n*, 245
Burgess, T. 170, 181–2, 184–6, 249
Burnham Committees 30, 36*n*
Bury 22 *table*
Butler, Richard A. (later Lord Butler) 9–12, 15 *table*, 39, 46, 72*n*, 245
Butler Act, *see* Education Act 1944
Butler (Clifford) Report 71, 245
Byrne, Eileen 201, 203, 245

Cabinet Office 16 *table*
Caffyn, Alderman S. M. 155
Calderdale 22 *table*
Cambridgeshire 21 *table*
Camden 213
Campaign for Moral Education 67
Canterbury 24, 228
capitation allowances 56, 63

Cardiff College of Technology and Commerce 168
Carnegie UK Trust 81, 245
Cass, Sir John, College 168
Caston, Geoffrey 71, 245
categories of handicapped children 74–9
Central Advisory Committee (on teacher training) 140
Central Council of Local Education Authorities 30, 160, 211*n*
central – local relations in education 31–5, 53, 135, 228–9, 234, 241–3
central schools 47
central statistical office 189*n*
Central Youth Employment Executive 108
Centre for Curriculum Renewal and Educational Development Overseas 108
certificate of education 137; *see also* teachers' certificate
Certificate of Extended Education 71
Certificate of Secondary Education (CSE) 24, 71, 167
Chancellor of the Exchequer 14, 208, 209
Chataway, Christopher 27, 36*n*
Chelsea College of Advanced Technology 169
Cheltenham Ladies College 39
Cheshire 21 *table*, 87
chief education officer 28, 63–4, 116, 128, 133, 203, 207, 228
child guidance 97–8, 125
child psychiatrists 83, 97–8
Churchill, Sir Winston 9, 12*n*
Church of England Board of Education 91
church schools 53; *see also* denominational and voluntary schools 10
Circulars (from the Ministry or Department of Education): 87 175; 264 127; 276 86; 300 86, 90; 305 169; 347 97; 348 87; 3/60 123; 11/61 86; 14/61 80; 24/61 89; 12/63 122; 10/65 49–51; 7/66 80; 10/66 50–1, 122; 11/66 178; 10/67 86, 122; 11/67 123; 13/68 130; 19/68 124; 11/69 79; 7/70 172; 10/70 51; 6/71 79; 4/73 77, 86, 90; 7/73 151; 8/73 24; 12/73 131; 2/74 209; 3/74 97; 4/74 51; 8/74 122, 126–7; 13/74 132;

2/75 80–4, 242; 5/75 151
City and Guilds of London Institute 179
City of London   20, 30, 212
Civil Service Department   16 *table*
Clay Cross UDC   229
Cleveland   21 *table*, 176
Clwyd   21 *table*, 26
Cockerton judgement   168
college government   152–6, 160–4
College of Aeronautics   186*n*
College of Teachers of the Blind   91–2
colleges of advanced technology (CATS) 169, 184–5
colleges of art   46, 139, 166, 168
colleges of commerce   166, 168
colleges of education (formerly teacher training colleges): control of 62, 139–40, 152–6, 160–4, 166, 171, 183–5, 223–4, 240; courses provided by 92, 136–9; finance of 156–8; regional coordination of and integration with other higher education 140–52, 183–5; students attending 136–7, 192 *table*
colleges of further education   166, 168, 174
colleges of higher education   136, 152
Committee of the Privy Council on Education   103–4, 106
comprehensive education (including the reorganisation controversy)   32, 41, 46–53, 106, 125, 134, 184, 240–2
comprehensive schools: types of   46, 48, 52–3, 240; inspection of 109, 119
Comptroller and Auditor General 166, 193
Confederation for the Advancement of State Education (CASE)   58, 76, 83–4, 245
Confederation of British Industry (CBI) 70
Conservative Party education policy 49–52, 58, 152, 242, 245
co-option to education committees 24–7
corporate planning and education 203–8, 237, 239
Cornwall   21 *table*
Cortis, Gerald A.   149, 245
cost limits for educational building 127–8, 241
Council for National Academic

Awards (CNAA)   70, 111, 147, 150–1, 181–2
County Councils Association (CCA) 29, 30, 162
county schools   42–3, 163
Coventry   22 *table*, 49, 206
Coxon, Alderman J. R.   154
Crosland, C. Anthony   15 *table*, 49, 170, 182–4, 247
Crowther-Hunt, Lord   179, 224
Crowther Report   11, 245
Croydon   20, 23 *table*, 25, 35
Crozier, Margaret   75, 245
Cumbria   21 *table*, 176
curriculum of schools   63, 68–71, 240–1
Curriculum Study Group   69

Darlington   50
Davies, J. L.   207, 245
deaf and partially hearing pupils   74, 85, 88–9, 92–3, 94*n*, 221
delegation of educational functions 17–20, 212
delicate pupils   74, 80, 85, 89
denominational schools   41, 43, 67; *see also* church and voluntary schools
Dent, H. C.   73, 245
Department of Customs and Excise 16 *table*
Department of Education and Science (DES): aid to direct grant schools 41; allocation of further education courses 177; building programmes 125–35, 156–7; classification of handicapped children 77–9; competition for government expenditure 192; creation, organisation, location 13–17; evidence to Redcliffe–Maud Commission 219; output budgeting 208; place of HMIS 105–15, 118–20; policy on educational building 121–5; policy on education welfare 99; policy on reform of teacher training and education 149–52; policy on special education 86–91; publications 245–6; relations with, and controls over, LEAS 27, 32–5, 51, 53, 228–9, 234–5, 242–3; relations with Schools Council 70; role in ascertainment of handicapped children 80–5; role in conduct of schools 60–3; role in

government of colleges of education 153–6; role in government of institutions of further education 171–4; role in supply and distribution of teachers 136, 141–3, 158–60

Department of Employment 16 *table*, 177

Department of Energy 16 *table*

Department of Health and Social Security 16 *table*, 84, 246

Department of Industry 16 *table*

Department of Inland Revenue 16 *table*

Department of the Environment 16 *table*, 246

Department of Trade 16 *table*

Department of Trade and Industry 15

Derbyshire 21 *table*, 176

Development Group (of the DES) 134–5

Devon 21 *table*, 100

diabetic pupils 89

Diploma in Art and Design 181

Diploma in Higher Education (Dip. HE) 145, 148–51

Diploma in Technology (Dip. Tech.) 180

direct grant schools 39–42, 51–2, 54, 59, 242

distribution of educational expenditure 195–7

divisibility or indivisibility of the education service 213, 215, 217, 221–4, 239–40

divisional executives 17–20, 65, 227

Doncaster 22 *table*, 216

Donnison Commission 42 246; *see also* Public Schools Commission

Dorset 21 *table*, 176, 228

Dowding, Air Chief Marshal Lord 161

Drew, L. J. 157

Dror, Y. 242

Dudley 22 *table*

Durham, Bishop of 68, 246

Durham County 21 *table*, 82, 154

Durham University 168

Dyfed 21 *table*

Eaglesham, E. J. R. 168, 246

Ealing 23 *table*

East Anglia Regional Advisory Council 176

East Ham 20

East Midlands Regional Advisory Council 176

East Sussex 21 *table*

Eccles, Sir David (later Viscount Eccles) 15 *table*, 190

Eddison, Tony 205, 246

Edmonds, E. L. 104, 246

educational expenditure, growth of 187–93

educationally subnormal (ESN) pupils 74–8, 80, 85, 87–8, 92, 97, 122, 124–5

educational psychologists 80, 83–4, 97–8

Education Act 1902 11, 17, 29, 59, 105, 137, 140, 168

Education Act 1907 95

Education Act 1918 (Fisher Act) 12n, 193, 198

Education Act 1921 47, 73

Education Act 1936 45

Education Act 1944 (Butler Act): central–local relationship 31; definition of further education 105; education committees 23–4; impact on public expenditure 193; local responsibility for education 17–18, 54; major provisions 9–12, 241; parents' rights 57; passage of the Act 9; power to appoint HMIs 110; provisions for special education 73, 94; religious worship and instruction 65, 68; school health and welfare 95; school managers and governors 59; standards of school building 129; teachers' pay 36n; types of school recognised 37–8, 40, 44–5, 48

Education Act 1946 12n

Education Act 1959 12n

Education Act 1962 12n

Education Act 1964 12n

Education Act 1967 12n

Education Act 1968 12n

Education (No. 2) Act 1968 12n, 153, 171

Education Act 1973 12n

Education Bill 1906 11

Education Bill 1944 9, 10, 72n

Education Bill 1970 11, 32, 51

education committees 23–7, 116, 153, 204, 228, 235–6

Education (Handicapped children) Act 1970 12n, 76

Education (Milk) Act 1971 12n

Education (Miscellaneous Provisions)

Acts 1948, 1953   12*n*

education officers   27–8, 207

education priority areas   94, 123, 193

Education (Provision of Meals) Act 1906   95, 100

Education (School Milk) Act 1970 12*n*

education welfare officers   99, 100

education welfare service   98–100, 226

Education (Work Experience) Act 1973   12*n*

elementary education   17, 168, 198, 221

Elementary Education Act 1870 (Forster Act)   12*n*, 105

elementary schools   37–8, 47, 59, 121, 129

elementary school teachers   158

Elementary School Teachers' Certificate   140

eleven-plus examination   47, 50

Elliott, W. R.   118

Enfield   23 *table*, 50

English, Cyril   110

epileptic pupils   74, 85, 89, 91

Epsom   134

Essex   20, 21 *table*, 52, 176

Eton   39

excepted districts   17–20, 227

expenditure on education   187–94

Factory Act 1833   103

Fettes   40

finance and the future of education 241–2

finance of teacher training and education   156–8, 160

finance of voluntary schools   43–6

financial crisis in education   208–11

financial decisions in conduct of schools   54–6, 62–3

financial decisions in conduct of institutions of further education 173

first schools   38

Fisher Act, *see* Education Act 1918

Fleming Committee   39, 41, 246

Foley, Winifred   100, 246

Ford, Boris   184, 246

Foreign and Commonwealth Office 16 *table*

Forster Act, *see* Elementary Education Act 1870

Fraser, Sir Bruce   193

Fulton Committee   28, 246

further education: awards and qualifications   179–82; binary system 182–5; building programmes 123–5, 132–4; concept of   17, 37, 165–7; development of present system 167–71; expenditure   191, 193, 194 *table*, 195, 196 *table*, 210; government of institutions   155, 171–4, 186, 240, 243; HM Inspectors and further education   108, 110, 114, 117–20; integration with sixth form work   35, 239; integration with teacher training and education 136, 139, 146, 160, 164; regional co-ordination   174–9; responsibility for   17, 19; separate control of 221–4

Gateshead   21 *table*, 216

Geddes Committee   208–9

General Certificate of Education (GCE) 41, 71, 166–7, 180, 222

General Grant   198–200, 203

Glatter, R.   207, 246

Glennerster, H.   187, 249

Gloucester City   75

Gloucestershire   21 *table*, 206

Godber, Sir George   87, 96–8, 246

Gordon Walker, Patrick C.   15 *table*

Gould, Sir Ronald   10, 246

government grants to LEAS   197–201, 239, 242

grammar schools   40–2, 46–53, 109

Greater London Council (GLC)   20, 30, 212–13, 217, 225–6

Greater London Group (LSE)   218, 246

Greater Manchester   174

Green Book on Education 1941   10

Greenwood, R.   206, 246

Griffith, J. A. G.   31, 33–4, 126, 199, 246

Grugeon, David   41, 244

Gwent   21 *table*

Gwynedd   21 *table*

Hadow Committee (and Report)   11, 47, 246

Hailsham, Lord, *see* Quintin Hogg

Halsall, Elizabeth   48, 246

Hampshire   21 *table*, 228

handicapped children's schools   40, 139; *see also* special schools

Haringey   23 *table*, 53, 61, 213

Harris, J. S. 103, 113, 247
Harrow Borough 23 *table*
Harrow School 39
Hastings, S. 224, 250
Hattersley, Roy 210
Havering 23 *table*, 207
Headmasters' Conference 39
headteachers: appointment 63; rela-
  tions with governors and managers
  61, 64–5; relations with HM Inspectors 105, 112–13, 116–17; role in
  ascertainment 80; role in running
  schools 68–9, 71–2, 240; role in
  special schools 85–6
Heath, Edward 14, 37, 101
Heclo, H. 125, 247
Hepworth, N. G. 201, 247
Herbert Commission 212, 217, 247
Hereford and Worcester 21 *table*
Hertfordshire 20, 21 *table*, 35, 176
higher education (post-elementary)
  17, 37, 198, 221
higher education (post secondary):
  awards and qualifications 179–82;
  binary versus unitary 143, 182–5;
  definition 165–7; development of
  the system 167–71; economies in
  provision 209–10; government of
  institutions (including polytechnics)
  155, 171–4, 186, 240, 243; integration with teacher training and education 136, 145, 149, 151–2, 160,
  239; regional co-ordination 151–2,
  174–9
Higher National Certificate and
  Diploma (HNC and HND) 180, 185
Hill, Dilys 243n, 247
Hill, M. 72n, 247
Hillingdon 23 *table*, 25
Hogg, Quintin M. (later Lord Hail-
  sham) 13, 15 *table*, 181
Home and School Council 57
Home Office 16 *table*, 33, 124
Horsbrugh, Florence (later Baroness
  Horsbrugh) 15 *table*
hospital schools 76, 85, 125
Hounslow 23 *table*
House of Commons Select Committee
  Reports: Educational Maintenance
  Allowances 57, 250; Grants to
  Universities and Colleges 166, 250;
  HM Inspectorate 104–7, 113–20,
  250; Teacher Training 144–5, 154–
  5, 250

Howell, D. A. 58, 60, 62–4, 244, 247
Huddersfield 216
Humberside 21 *table*, 176

Ilersic, A. R. 210
independent schools 39–40, 42, 54,
  58, 92, 111–12
indivisibility of the education service,
  see divisibility or indivisibility
infant schools 38
Inner London Education Authority
  (ILEA) 20, 23 *table*, 27, 43, 51, 66,
  95, 99, 102n, 213, 224, 226–8, 247
Inspectors, HM: activities 85, 110–14;
  development 103–5; evidence to
  Redcliffe–Maud Commission 219;
  organisation 15, 108–10, 119–20;
  relations with LEAs 116–17; relations with local inspectors 114–15;
  role in further education 117–19,
  176–9; role in teacher training and
  education 140, 157, 160; status
  105–8
Institute of Christian Education 72n,
  247
instruments of management and
  government 59, 62, 72n, 153, 155,
  171–2
integration of independent and maintained schools 39–42
intelligence quotient (IQ) 77–8
interchange of pupils between schools
  48–9
Interim Committees for Teachers
  140–1
Isle of Wight 21 *table*, 216, 227
Izbicki, John 117, 247

James Committee (and Report) 11,
  137, 139, 144–51, 247
Jamieson, R. D. 176, 247
Jarvis, Fred 207
Jeger, Lena 53n
Jennings, A. 247
Johnson, E. M. 94n, 247
joint education committees 24
joint examination boards 140, 142–3
junior art departments 46
junior commercial colleges 46
junior schools 38
junior technical colleges 46
junior training centres 74–6

Kay-Shuttleworth, Sir James 104,
  137–9

Kempe Committee 198–9, 211n, 247
Kent 20, 21 table, 24, 27, 228–9
Kilbrandon Committee (and Report) 179, 224, 247
King, Ronald 55, 247
Kingston upon Thames 23 table, 52, 227
Kirklees 22 table
Knowsley 22 table
Kogan, M. 247

Labour Party education policy 48–52, 58, 152, 200, 210, 242, 247
Lancashire 21 table, 228–9
Lavers, R 187, 249
Law, Richard K. (later Lord Coleraine) 15 table
Layfield Committee 210, 239
Leeds 22 table, 25, 216
Leese, J. 185, 247
Leff, S. and V. 247
Leicestershire 21 table, 35, 229
Leigh-Mallory, Air Chief Marshal Sir Trafford 161
licensed teachers 146, 149–50
Lincoln City 201, 203
Lincolnshire 21 table
Liverpool 22 table, 51, 59, 206–7, 214, 216
Lloyd, Geoffrey W. 15 table
Local Authorities Social Services Act 1970 225
Local Authority Associations 28–31, 36n
Local Education Authorities (LEAs): advantage over central control 233–5; advantage over school boards 235–8; budgetary discretion 201–3; creation 17; education committees 23–7; local inspectors 105, 114–16; numbers 20–3, 227–9; reform of structure 212–17; relations with department 31–5, 53, 135, 228–9, 234, 241–3; relations with HM Inspectors 116–17; role in further education 185–6; role in running schools 54–5, 59–66, 69, 71–2; role in teacher training and education 160–4; size of population 21–3, 217–21, 227–9; staffing 27–8; wealth 21–3, 228–9
Local Government Act 1958 18, 197–8
Local Government Act 1966 200

Local Government Act 1972 20, 30, 36n, 60, 217, 226–7
Local Government Operational Research Unit (RIPA) 218
Local Government Training Board 99, 100, 247
Local Taxation (Customs and Excise) Act 1890 211n
Locke, Michael 173, 247
Lockwood, Sir John 70, 247
London and Home Counties Regional Advisory Council 176
London Boroughs 20, 23 table, 212–13, 217–18, 224–7
London County Council (LCC) 20, 35, 49, 89, 97, 99, 212–13
London Government Act 1963 20, 226
London Teachers' Association 212
London University 168–9, 180
Lord Chancellor's Department 16 table
Lord Mayor Treloar Trust 92
Lord President of the Council 13–14
Loughborough College 169, 186n
Lukes, J. R. 184, 248

MacLure, Stuart 191, 248
Macmillan, Harold 200
McNair Committee 137, 140–2, 144, 284
Maddison, R. E. 141, 144, 157, 163, 251
maintained schools and colleges 43, 54–5, 58, 60, 124, 136, 163, 191, 192 table
maintenance allowances and grants 57, 156, 194 table, 195, 196 table, 202
maintenance of schools 19, 43–5, 210
major works programmes in school building 124, 129–31
maladjusted pupils 78, 85–8, 92–3, 97, 122, 124
Mander, Sir Frederick 10
Manchester City 22 table, 214, 216
Manchester College of Technology 168
Manchester University 168
Marlborough 39
Maud Committee 205–6, 248
May, P. R. 72n, 248
May Committee 208–9
Mental Health Act 1959 94n
Merseyside 174

Merthyr Tydfil 101, 228
Merton 23 *table*
Methodist schools 44, 104
Middlesbrough 176
middle schools 38, 51, 53, 222, 240–1
Middlesex 20, 42, 49, 224
Mid Glamorgan 21 *table*
Midland Society for the Study of Mental Subnormality 91
Milk Act 1934 100
Minister for Arts and Science 13
Minister for Science 13–14
Minister for the Arts 14
Minister for the Disabled 94
Minister of Education (and Ministry): and Burnham Committees 36*n*; attitude to direct grant schools 42; change to DES 13–14; creation 9; curriculum initiative 69–70; establishment of excepted districts 18; names of ministers 15 *table*; policy on CATS 169; publications 248; religious education syllabus 66; special education policies 75, 80, 85; standards for school building 129; supervisory powers 31; *see also* DES
Ministry of Agriculture, Fisheries and Food 16 *table*, 25, 177
Ministry of Aircraft Production 235
Ministry of Defence 16 *table*, 192
Ministry of Health 33, 75, 124
Ministry of Housing and Local Government 248
Ministry of Overseas Development 16 *table*
Ministry of Technology 14
minor works programmes for school building 121, 124–5, 129, 131–3
modern schools, *see* secondary modern schools
Moore, Gordon 207
Morrell, D. H. 121, 248
Morris, Alfred 94
Mulley, Frederick W. 15 *table*, 42
multi-lateral schools 48, 52
Musgrave, P. W. 72*n*, 248

National Advisory Council on Education for Industry and Commerce (NACEIC) 175, 178–180
National Advisory Council on the Training and Supply of Teachers (NACTST) 93, 141, 143, 148, 158, 248
National Association of Governors and Managers 65
National Association of Head Teachers 62
National Association of Labour Teachers 48
National Association of Local Councils 30
National Association of Local Government Officers (NALGO) 222–3
National Association of Parent–Teacher Associations 58, 70
National Association of Parish Councils 29–30
National Association of Schoolmasters 62, 220
National Bureau for Co-operation in Child Care 78
National Children's Home 91
National College for Heating 186*n*
National College of Agricultural Engineering 186*n*
National College of Food Technology 186*n*
National College of Rubber Technology 186*n*
National College of Teachers of the Deaf 92
National Council for Diplomas in Art and Design 180
National Council for Teacher Education and Training 147–9
National Council for Technological Awards 180–1, 184
National Council of Technology 175
National Foundation for Educational Research 70, 91
National Foundry College 186*n*
national health service and education 82–3, 95–7, 225–6, 241
National Health Service Reorganisation Act 1973 95
national income and education 187, 190–3
National Leathersellers' College 186*n*
National Milk Publicity Council 100
National Savings Department 16 *table*
National Society for Autistic Children 90
National Society for Mentally Handicapped Children 75, 91
National Society for the Education of

the Poor in the Principles of the Established Church 103

National Society for the Prevention of Cruelty to Children 91

National Union of School Students 57

National Union of Teachers (NUT) 52, 56–7, 62, 70, 93, 137–8, 148–9, 159, 199, 207, 210, 248

nautical training schools 46

Newcastle Commission 104

Newcastle upon Tyne 22 table, 71, 216

Newham 23 table

Newsom Report (1963) 11, 197, 248

Newsom Report (1968) 40, 249; see also Public Schools Commission

non-advanced further education 179, 184, 223, 239

Norfolk 21 table, 99

Northampton City 143

Northamptonshire 21 table

Northern Ireland Office 16 table

Northern Regional Advisory Council 176

Northumberland 21 table, 201, 203

North Tyneside 22 table

North Western Regional Advisory Council 176

North Yorkshire 21 table

Norton, A. L. 206, 246, 249

Norwood Committee (and Report) 48–9, 249

Nottingham City 201, 203

Nottinghamshire 21 table, 35, 176

numbers of schoolchildren 121, 159–60, 191–3

Nurse, P. 179, 249

nursery education and nursery schools: building nursery schools 122–5, 129, 132, 160; definition of nursery schools 37, 42; direct grant nursery schools 40; independent nursery schools 39; placement 99; resources for nursery education 38, 192–4, 196 table, 208–10

Oakes Report 74, 249

O'Brien, O. 50, 244

occupational therapists 95

occupation centres 75

Odhams Press Research Department 72n, 249

Oldham 22 table

Ollerenshaw, Kathleen 195, 249

Open University 147

Ordinary National Certificate and Diploma (ONC and OND) 180

orthoptists 95

output budgeting 208

Owen, Roger J. 72n, 249

Oxford City 134

Oxfordshire 21 table

parents and schools 43–4, 50, 54, 56–8, 61–2, 66, 69, 72, 74, 79–81, 83

parent–teacher associations (PTAS) 57

Parris, H. 50, 244

Parry, A. J. P. 148, 249

Part III authorities 17, 19, 29, 221

Pateman, Carole 26, 249

Paymaster General (in DES) 14

payment by results 104–5, 117

Peacock, A. T. 179, 187, 224, 249

Pease, J. A. 12n

Percy, Lord Eustace (later Lord Percy of Newcastle) 174, 186n, 249

Percy Committee 174–6, 180

Perkin, H. 181, 249

Perry, Valerie 56, 249

Peschek, D. 64, 249

physically handicapped children 74, 77, 79–80, 85–6, 89–90, 92

physiotherapists 95

Pilkington Committee 178

Plowden Committee (and Report) 11, 38, 76, 82, 94, 123, 197, 249

policy, programming, budgeting systems (PPBS) 207, 237

polytechnics: development of 168–71, 240; flexibility of provision 184–5; government of 62, 171–4; LEA responsibility for 139, 165–6, 221–4; regional co-ordination of 143, 147, 151, 178; role in teacher training and education 92, 136–7, 145, 148, 150–2, 160, 162

Pooling Committee on teacher training finance 157

Poplars Special School 92

Portsmouth 216, 228

Pott, A. 121, 248

Poulson, John 17

Powys 21 table, 228

Pratt, J. 170, 181–2, 184–6, 249

Prentice, Reg E. 15 table, 42, 51–2, 65, 160, 203, 211n

preparatory schools 39

President of the Board of Education 9, 12*n*, 13, 140, 174

Preston 134

primary education and primary schools: age of transfer from primary education 37–9, 47, 222; building primary schools 121–2, 125–9, 132; definition of 17, 37; direction and management of primary schools 54–65, 72*n*; expenditure on primary education 194–7, 208; handicapped children in primary schools 86; milk for primary children 101; religion in 66; responsibility for primary schools 17–19, 42–6; teacher training for primary schools 138

psychiatric social workers 83, 97–8

Public Accounts Committee 166

Public Bodies (Access to Meetings) Act 1960 27

Public Expenditure Survey Committee (PESC) 125

public schools 39, 59, 109

Public Schools Commission 1861–4 59

Public Schools Commission 1966–1970 39

pupil involvement in school government 54, 56–8, 61

pupil teachers 137–9

qualified status of teachers 136, 149–50

quinquennial school building programmes 130–3

quota system for teachers 158–60, 199, 201–2, 210, 241

raising of the school leaving age 11, 37, 73, 121–4, 130, 191, 193

Ralphs Committee 99–100, 249

Rate Support Grant (RSG) 28, 125, 156, 200–1, 209

Ravenswood Foundation 92

Reading Borough 61, 64

recognition of independent schools as efficient 39, 92

Redbridge 23 *table*, 52

Redcliffe-Maude Commission (and Report) 213–17, 225–6, 231, 234, 249

Regional Academic Boards (RABS) 175–8

Regional Advisory Councils for Technological Education (RACS) 111, 174–9, 186, 224

Regional Co-ordinating Committees for the Education and Training of Teachers 151–2, 164

Regional Councils for Colleges and Departments of Education 147–8, 151

Regional Economic Planning Councils 176

regional staff inspector 117–18, 177–8

religious education in schools 10, 43–5, 54, 65–8

remedial gymnasts 95

Remuneration of Teachers Acts 1963, 1965 12*n*, 36*n*

reorganisation of LEAS 20, 23, 66, 212–29

reserved places 41

reserved teachers 43

residuary places 41

Rhodes, Gerald 212, 226, 249–50

Richards, Peter G. 19, 250

Richmond upon Thames 23 *table*

Robbins, Lord 183

Robbins Committee (and Report) 11, 13, 137, 143, 152, 162, 165, 169–70, 178, 181–2, 197, 223, 250

Robinson, Eric E. 182, 184–5, 250

Rochdale 22 *table*

Roedean 39–40

rolling programme of educational building 130–3

Roman Catholic Education Society 91

Roman Catholic schools 42–4, 57, 91, 104

Rotherham 22 *table*, 216

Rousden 100

Royal College of Art 186*n*

Royal Commission on the Constitution 179, 224

Royal Commission on the Law Relating to Mental Illness and Mental Deficiency (Oakes Commission) 74, 249

Royal Institute of Public Administration 250

Royal Medico-Psychological Association 98, 250

Royal National Institute for the Blind 91

Royal National Institute for the Deaf 91
Rugby 40
rules of management for primary schools 55, 60, 62, 68
Rural District Councils Association 29–30
Russell Report 11, 250
Rutland 229

St Helens 22 *table*
St John Stevas, Norman 52, 101
Salford 22 *table*, 89
Salop 21 *table*
Sandwell 22 *table*
sandwich courses and students 169–70, 180, 182
Saran, R. 42, 250
Schon, Donald A. 118, 250
school attendance officers 99
School Boards Association 29
school boards 29, 59, 98, 105, 114, 168, 235–8
school building 27, 87, 107, 112, 121–35, 199, 201, 203, 228–9
school care service 99
school governors 43–4, 51, 54–5, 57–65, 69, 72, 113, 116, 214, 240
school health and welfare 95–102, 187, 190, 194 *table*, 195, 196 *table*, 225–6
school inquiry service 99
school managers 43–4, 51, 54–5, 58–65, 69, 72, 113, 116, 214, 240
school meals 19, 26, 95, 99–100, 189*n*, 190, 194 *table*, 195, 196 *table*, 199–200, 210
school medical staff 95–101
school milk 19, 96, 100–01, 189*n*, 190, 194 *table*, 195, 196 *table*, 199–200
school psychological service 97–8
Schools Action Union 57
Schools Council for the Curriculum and Examinations 70–2, 108, 111, 115, 149, 250
Schools Inquiry Commission 59
science facilities in schools 121–2, 124
Science Museum 14, 16 *table*
Scottish Departments 16 *table*
Scunthorpe 176
secondary education and secondary schools: age of children in secondary education 10, 37, 38–9, 222; building secondary schools 121–2, 125–35; comprehensive secondary education 43–53; direction and government of secondary schools 68–72, 54–65; expenditure on secondary education 194–7, 208; handicapped children in 86; inspection of 108, 114–17; non-maintained secondary schools 39–42, 44–5; religion in secondary schools 66; responsibility for secondary education 17, 19, 222
secondary modern schools 46–8, 109, 119, 182
Secretary of State for Education and Science: appeals to 57, 74; approval of, and making, articles of government 60; appointments to Burnham Committees 36*n*; classification of handicaps 77–9; creation of the office 13–14; names of office holders 15 *table*; powers 31–2; role in curriculum matters 69–71
Seebohm Report 225, 250
Sefton 22 *table*
Segal, S. S. 75, 78, 250
Self, Peter J. O. 235, 250
Senior, Derek 215–16, 221, 226, 234, 249–50
senior pupils 38, 47, 51, 121
senior schools 47
severely subnormal (SSN) children 74–7, 87
Sharpe, L. J. 243, 251
Shearman, H. C. 13
Sheehan, J. 190, 192–3, 195–7, 209, 251
Sheffield 22 *table*, 210, 216
Sheldon Working Party 84, 251
Silver, Harold 185, 251
Short, Edward W. 15 *table*, 68, 144
Simon, Brian 38, 51, 244
sixth-form colleges and centres 38, 51, 134
size of LEAS, *see* LEAS
Smallwood, F. 212, 251
Society for Autistic Children 91
Society for Education Officers 211*n*, 239, 251
Solihull 22 *table*
Somerset 21 *table*
Southampton 216, 228

South Eastern Architects' Collaboration 134

Southern Regional Advisory Council 176, 178

South Glamorgan 21 *table*

South Hampshire 216

South Tyneside 22 *table*, 228

South Wales Committee for Further Education 174

South Western Regional Advisory Council 176

South Yorkshire 216

spastic pupils 90

Spastics Society 91

special education and special schools: ascertainment 79–85; building special schools 122–5, 129, 131; categories of handicap 74–9; definition of special school excludes county school 42; expenditure on 194–7; general character 73; inquiry into 93–4; integration with primary and secondary education 240; milk for special schools 101; provision 85–92; size of LEAS for special education 220–1; staffing 92–3

speech defective children 74, 85, 90

speech therapists 90, 95

Spens Report 48, 251

spina bifida children 77, 79, 90

staff councils 56

Staffordshire 21 *table*, 57

standards of school construction 128–9

Standing Conference of RACS 178

HM Stationery Office 16 *table*

Stewart, J. D. 205–7, 246, 249, 251

Stewart, Michael 15 *table*

Stockport 22 *table*

student participation in college government 172–3

student awards 202

student teachers 136–7

Study Group on the Government of Colleges of Education, *see* Weaver Report

Suffolk 22 *table*

Summerfield Committee 98, 251

Sunderland 22 *table*, 216

Sunderland Technical College 168

Surrey 20, 22 *table*, 134

Sutton 23 *table*, 52

Sylvester, G. H. 223

Tameside 22 *table*

teacher supply 93, 158–60, 241

teacher training colleges, *see* colleges of education

teachers' centres 70, 146–7

teachers' certificate 137–9, 150–1

teachers' grades 72n, 202

teachers' involvement in running schools 54, 56, 61–2, 72, 243

teachers' salaries 36n, 72n, 196–8, 201, 210, 241

teacher training and education: administrative responsibility for 139–40, 160–4, 221; building programmes for 123–5, 132–3; content 136–9, 149–52; expenditure on 194–7; finance of 156–8; government of institutions 152–6; integration with other further and higher education 151–2, 239; James Report on 144–9; McNair Report on 140–4

teaching practice 138–9, 142, 151, 153, 162, 164

technical colleges: awards by 180; binary system and 182–5; direct grant colleges 186n; evolution of 167–71; regional co-ordination of 174–9; representation on Schools Council 70; similarity in status to colleges of education 162–3; teacher training and 92, 136, 139

technical education: origin of 167–8; Lord Percy and 174; whisky money for 211n

Technical Instruction Act 1889 46, 167

technical schools 40, 46–9

textbook provision in schools 19, 202, 219

Thatcher, Margaret H. 14, 15 *table*, 51, 93, 101, 122–3, 141, 144, 159

Thomas Committee 82, 251

Tizard, J. 251

Tomlinson, George 15 *table*, 49

trade schools 46

Trades Union Congress (TUC) 70, 199

Trafford 22 *table*, 52

Treasury, HM 13, 16 *table*, 125–6, 128, 198, 200

two-tier local government 212, 214–16, 219–22, 225

Tyne and Wear 216

ultra vires 32

264 LOCAL GOVERNMENT AND EDUCATION

Underwood Committee (and Report) 78, 87, 97–8, 251
UNESCO Report on Education and Mental Health 83
unitary local authorities 213–16
unitary system of further and higher education 169–70, 182–5
universities: expenditure on 194–7, 210; finance of 158, 166; lack of external assessment in 181; CATS changed into 169; relationship to other institutions of higher and further education 170, 174–80, 182–5, 222–3, 240; representation on Schools Council 70; role in teacher training 136–40, 142–3, 147–52, 160–2; student grants 202
university departments of education 92, 136–7, 142–3, 145, 156, 158, 162
University Grants Committee (UGC) 13–14, 16 table, 166, 184
University of Birmingham 92
University of Buckingham 166
University of Dublin 92
University of Manchester 92
University of Sussex 155
University of Wales 169
Urban District Councils Association 29–30
urban programme 123–4
use of school premises 43–4, 62

Vaizey, John 187, 190–3, 195–7, 209, 251
Victoria and Albert Museum 14, 16 table
voluntary aided schools 42–6, 51–2, 54, 65, 69, 124
voluntary colleges 139, 156, 164n, 168, 186n
voluntary controlled schools 43–6, 59, 65
voluntary schools 42–6, 55, 59–60, 65, 69, 91–2, 103–5, 132, 135, 163, 164n
voluntary special agreement schools 43, 45–6, 65, 124
voucher system for schools 58

Wakefield 22 table
Walsall 22 table, 51
Waltham Forest 23 table, 61
Warnock Committee 93–4

Warwickshire 22 table
Weaver, T. R. (later Sir Toby) 118
Weaver Report 153–5, 164, 171, 186, 251
Welsh College of Advanced Technology 169
Welsh Educational Office 14
Welsh Inspectorate 14, 108, 109 table
Welsh Joint Education Committee 24, 175–6
Welsh Office 14, 16 table, 125, 132
West Glamorgan 22 table
West Ham 20
West Ham Municipal College 168
West Midlands 174
Westmorland 176
West Riding of Yorkshire 35, 176, 216, 228
West Sussex 22 table, 176
whisky money 198, 211n
White Papers (in datal order): 1943 Educational Reconstruction Cmd 6458 48, 244; 1956 Technical Education Cmd 9703 168–9, 175, 248; 1957 Local Government Finance (England and Wales) Cmnd 209 199, 248; 1958 Secondary Education for All – a New Drive Cmnd 604 121, 130, 248; 1961 London Government: Government Proposals for Reorganisation Cmnd 1562 248; 1966 A Plan for Polytechnics and Other Colleges: Higher Education in the Further Educational System Cmnd 3006 165, 170–1, 245; 1970 Reform of Local Government in England Cmnd 4276 216, 248; 1971 Local Government in England: Government Proposals for Reorganisation Cmnd 4584 216, 246; 1971 Better Services for the Mentally Handicapped Cmnd 4683 246; 1972 Education: A Framework for Expansion Cmnd 5174 123, 149–52, 160, 165, 246
Wigan 22 table
Wilcockson, D. H. 211n, 251
Wildavsky, A. 125, 247
Wilkinson, Ellen C. 15 table, 49
Willey, F. T. 141, 144, 157, 163, 251
Williams, Shirley 173
Wilson, Sir Harold 51, 101
Wiltshire 22 table, 176
Winchester 39
Wirral 22 table

Wolverhampton   22 *table*, 62
Woolwich Polytechnic   168

Yom Kippur War   209
Yorkshire   174–5, 228
Yorkshire Committee for Further
   Education   174

Yorkshire Regional Advisory Council
   176
Yorkshire (West Riding)   228
Younghusband Report   78, 251
Youth Service   27, 34, 123–4, 128,
   187, 194 *table*, 196 *table*, 204, 210